Dare to Do

Also by Sarah Outen

A Dip in the Ocean

Dare to Do

Taking on the planet by bike and boat

SARAH OUTEN

NICHOLAS BREALEY
PUBLISHING

London • Boston

First published in Great Britain in 2016 by Nicholas Brealey Publishing
An imprint of John Murray Press
An Hachette UK Company

1

Maps drawn by Jim Shannon

A CIP catalogue record for this title is available from the British Library

Hardback ISBN 978-1-85788-641-2
Trade paperback ISBN 978-1-85788-647-4
Ebook ISBN (UK) 978-1-85788-919-2
Ebook ISBN (US) 978-1-47364-461-8

Typeset in Bembo MT by Palimpsest Book Production Limited,
Falkirk, Stirlingshire

Printed and bound by Clays Ltd, St Ives plc

Nicholas Brealey policy is to use papers that are natural, renewable and recyclable products and
made from wood grown in sustainable forests. The logging and manufacturing processes are
expected to conform to the environmental regulations of the country of origin.

Nicholas Brealey Publishing
John Murray Press
Carmelite House
50 Victoria Embankment
London EC4Y 0DZ, UK
Tel: 020 3122 6000

Nicholas Brealey Publishing
Hachette Book Group
Market Place Center, 53 State Street
Boston, MA 02109, USA
Tel: (617) 523 3801

www.nicholasbrealey.com
www.sarahouten.com

For Roo
And for everyone in my invisible peloton

Contents

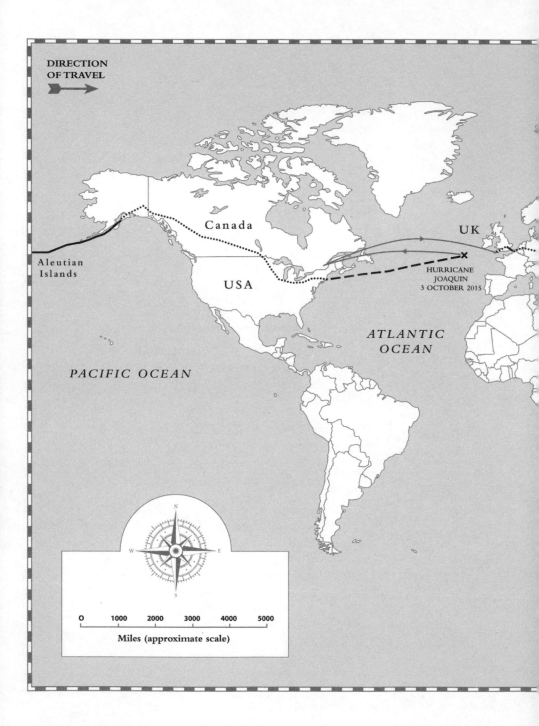

DIRECTION
OF TRAVEL

Aleutian
Islands

Canada

UK

USA

HURRICANE
JOAQUIN
3 OCTOBER 2015

ATLANTIC
OCEAN

PACIFIC OCEAN

N

W E

S

0   1000   2000   3000   4000   5000

Miles (approximate scale)

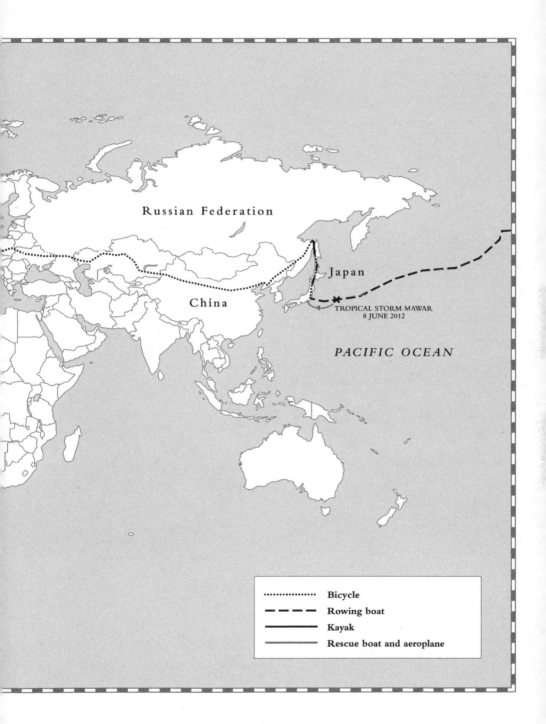

···············	Bicycle
− − − −	Rowing boat
——	Kayak
——	Rescue boat and aeroplane

Russian Federation

China

Japan

TROPICAL STORM MAWAR
8 JUNE 2012

PACIFIC OCEAN

'Come to the edge,' he said. 'We can't, we're afraid!' they responded. 'Come to the edge,' he said.

'We can't, we will fall!' they responded. 'Come to the edge,' he said.

And so they came. And he pushed them. And they flew.

Apollinaire

Prologue: What Next?

Mauritius: 3 August 2009

The warm dry air tasted of land. I reached to climb up the ladder, aware that I was about to cross a threshold. I was leaving my tiny rowing boat, *Dippers*, where I had just spent four months alone rowing between Australia and Mauritius, to step ashore. A tangle of coffee-coloured arms reached down through the dark to pull me up to the quayside. My worn-out lycra shorts were rotten to see-through in places, my skin was tanned and freckled and my hair was scruffy and bleached by the sun. I couldn't stop grinning, which made up for the fact that I couldn't do more than stutter my hellos.

'Pizza! You want some pizza, Sarah?' Of course I did; I hadn't had cheese in months. I stepped towards the open box but toppled backwards, caught by the curious crowd who laughed at my wobbly land legs. Pizza — so familiar, and yet it felt so surreal to actually be here, eating it. Life ashore was the same; I remembered what it had been like before, but what about now, after four months of solitude, on seas wilder than I'd been able to imagine? Of being watched by whales as long as swimming pools. Of running out of water and going thirsty. Of being saved by a tether no wider than a belt. I already knew, without knowing it all, that my journey across the Indian Ocean had changed my perspective on many things.

For someone who had just emerged from solitary, the questions of the gathered crowd felt like something of a well-meaning bombardment. How do you go to the toilet? What happens in storms? Did you capsize? Were you all alone? Did you get scared? Could you get Facebook? What are you looking forward to? What's next? The last question was both easy and not to answer.

I had ideas but no fixed plans. I'd see what happened. See how I felt and what felt right. Those two words had been on repeat ever since the quayside in Mauritius and I found myself playing with replies, depended on who was asking. To those who knew me, 'I'm training to be an accountant' made us both laugh at the absurdity of it. (The ocean had only enhanced my distaste of spreadsheets.) 'I'm thinking about swimming to the moon' was a jesting nod to my conviction that crazy things can be very possible and others' assumptions that big should lead to bigger. I wanted another journey but, nudged by comments about when I was going to get a 'proper job' and settle down, at first I thought I ought not to just yet. 'I am going to be a teacher' was believable to both the listener and to me, at least as a holding statement. I had coached and taught youngsters in various guises before and, following the row, I had presented at lots of schools; weaving adventure stories with some science and geography, and a call to be curious and brave in forging your own path and to embrace failure. I already felt a bit like a teacher of sorts. Yet, having deferred a teacher-training place at university before I went away, maybe I already knew that I wasn't destined to a life inside the classroom full time just yet.

At sea, I had spent many days imagining new journeys. I wanted more exploration and immersion for so many reasons and yet I could wrap it up with one: I loved it. I was connected, aware and open in a way that I had never been before. At sea, my focus was (in this order) to stay alive, row as much as possible and stay as happy as possible; the simplicity was refreshing and wholesome. I had felt my most alive, even if sometimes I glimpsed my mortality a little too closely. The waves reminded me that nothing lasts forever, that even the most unpleasant things change and generally settle to something more comfortable and manageable. The ocean had shown me how to accept unchangeables, to chart progress amid stasis, and it had shown me the importance of letting go, of literally pushing puddles away from the oars to move on to clear water. It hadn't just been one of the most useful and interesting lessons in how to live, but also in life. Finite supplies and limited communications taught me frugality and rationing. Bagging my rubbish,

I saw just how much we produce in four months, whereas at home it gets zipped away weekly. Drifting plastic linked me to strangers in far-off lands. As I rowed through inky seas glowing with bioluminescence under skies rioting with stars, I felt present. I appreciated tiny moments and I loved how those linked up to trace my constellation of efforts across the map. The juxtaposition of space stretching around me in all dimensions was humbling, exciting.

Three months after landing I had dinner at Windsor Castle. After my short address for the hosting charity, in front of the tuxedoed hundreds, Prince Edward popped the same question: 'What's next?' Knights in armour and chainmail stared through slit-eyed helmets, poised for my answer.

'I might teach . . .'

'No no, what about another journey? You must have another journey planned?' Not one to deny royalty, I announced my tentative idea to make a global journey. 'Using a rowing boat, a bike and a kayak.' Pressing me for a date, I felt a bit under pressure and said: '2011, 2012?'

I scrunched my toes in excitement. I had had a rough idea of looping the planet using human power: rowing across the Pacific and Atlantic oceans, cycling across the continents in between and kayaking to join up the dots. But now I had said it out aloud. Suddenly it was clear to me: I was single and with no commitments, healthy and keen – making now the perfect time.

The story ahead is of having a go, failing, having another go and of ultimately letting go. The years ahead became some of the most vivid, most treasured and, at times, the most difficult of my life. But setting out, all I knew is all we ever know – that I knew nothing about how the story would unfold.

PART I

Having a Go

Eurasia and the Pacific

**London to Japan | April 2011 – June 2012 |
Kayak, bike, row | Total miles from London: 11,800**

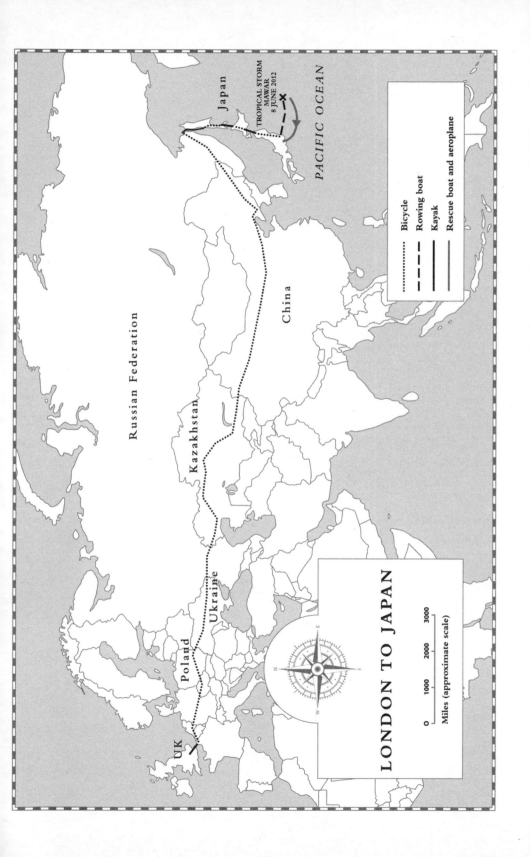

LONDON TO JAPAN

PACIFIC OCEAN

TROPICAL STORM
MAWAR
8 JUNE 2012

Japan

China

Russian Federation

Kazakhstan

Ukraine

Poland

UK

Bicycle
Rowing boat
Kayak
Rescue boat and aeroplane

Miles (approximate scale)

0   1000   2000   3000

I

'Just come home safe': Europe

London to Belgium | Kayak and bike |
April 2011 | 200 miles

Tower Bridge, London, 1 April 2011. I pulled on my delivered-just-in-time new paddling gear and peered downstream across London's familiar skyline. 'Let's just see what happens, Outen. It'll be fine. It has to be,' I told myself, wiggling my toes inside their new boots.

'I just wanted to say goodbye before it gets mad,' said Sara Davies, my project manager, as she slipped through the door and wrapped me in a hug.

'Thank you, my friend. We wouldn't be here if it wasn't for everything you've done. I'm so grateful,' I said, batting away tears.

'It's exciting, isn't it?' she beamed, wiping away her own. 'Just come home safely – that's all we want. Now, you've got one more interview outside and then it's speeches,' she said, reading off her clipboard. I had already visited the schoolchildren who had come down to watch the send-off, been interviewed by streams of press and hugged as many of my guests as possible. I had also been to the loo more times than I could count.

My kayak and bike sat across the front of the stage where I stood next to Fiona O'Hara, my lead sponsor at Accenture.

'How are you feeling?' she said in her broad Northern Irish accent, smiling as I gripped her arm.

'I'm nervous!'

'You've got nothing to be nervous of. You've done all the hard work. Enjoy it. They're all here for you.'

We listened as the commander of the base welcomed us officially to HMS *President*. I looked around at all the faces who had helped me get there and who were already willing me home safely. A part of me couldn't quite believe we had got this far.

As I walked across the deck and towards the gangway down to our kayaks I gripped the arms and eyes of friends and family, wondering when I would see them again. Or if. It had only just hit me that two and a half years felt like quite a long time to be away; before, it had just been another number amongst the nuts and bolts of planning. My only focus had been getting ready to go by April 1st, to set out on my journey around the Northern Hemisphere. Aiming not to use sails or engines (although my gear would go by those means), I planned to row, cycle and kayak eastwards from London back to London, across land and sea, starting from the place I last finished from leg to leg. Lying on the floor in my tiny bedroom at my mum's house, my pencil had wandered in all sorts of loops and diversions, before I chiselled it into something that I thought looked realistic based on other journeys by fellow wanderers and would fit in roughly that time-line. I would kayak and cycle from London to Japan, row the North Pacific to Canada, cycle across North America and row home across the North Atlantic, with a final triathlon from Falmouth to London. Each leg on its own was ambitious, so to join them up successfully and return home approximately on time would be down to a good dose of luck, too. I aimed not to come home at all between legs, spending time in location planning and preparing for the onwards leg where there was time for it. But if I needed to leave my route for any reason, or there was a delay between legs, then I would go back to the same place to restart.

Routes and logistics revolved around unmovable seasons and weather windows for ocean crossings, planning when and where I needed to be and with what kit ahead of or following me. Training and fitness centred around building a core base of strength and stability and maintaining endurance across a range of disciplines.

My team and I identified trigger points for mental issues and remembered ways to deal with them or thought up new ones. Custom vehicles were built and readied: a rowing boat called *Gulliver*, a kayak called *Nelson* and a bike called *Hercules*. I collected gear and clothing for land and sea and summer and winter. Some of it had to be logoed with the insignia of my major sponsors.

Visas and spare passport. Medical training and jabs. Maps and trackers. Crisis plans and a hefty insurance policy from an insurer willing to join us. Most of them were not willing to go anywhere near it.

Which left us with the trickiest and most fickle task of all: reconciling large bills and budgets with my bank accounts and overdrafts. It was going to be an extremely expensive project due to the scale, remoteness and length of the journey. By the time I left it had absorbed all of my earnings and savings and the slush of my overdraft, and the remainder was (mostly) met by nearly seventy sponsors who partnered with the project because it (or I) aligned with their brand, values or goals. The final piece fell into place with just three weeks to go before April 1st. I had been speaking for Accenture at their International Women's Day event in London. As I walked out to the drinks reception, Fiona grabbed my arm: 'We need to talk about money.' I thought I had filed my expenses claim incorrectly; actually they wanted to be the main sponsor. Up to that point I was determined to set off and figure out the deficit as I journeyed, though in hindsight, having had to do that, I now know that it is a mission and a half to fill in such a big gap while underway and under time pressure.

My team became a diverse mix of people who had been a part of my Indian Ocean row and newcomers, a mix of volunteers and professionals. I had a project manager, a PR manager, a couple of doctors, a psychotherapist, a logistics manager, a support kayaker, an accountant and a weather router, mostly working from the UK. Some found me, I found others or they were recommended to me and some I had worked with on the Indian Ocean. For fifteen months we all slogged away together in preparation.

There was another key element to this adventure, and that was the idea of sharing the journey and the benefits. We scoped an education project for linking up with students around the world via live links or school visits and with online resources. I chose charities to work with based on close links and causes: the breast cancer awareness charity CoppaFeel!, the accessible sailing charity Jubilee Sailing Trust, the MND (motor neurone disease) Association and WaterAid for their championing of safe hygiene and water supplies around the world.

'THREE CHEERS FOR SARAAAAAAAH!' shouted my mum from the gangway above us. And everyone hollered in response. 'Just come home safely,' she had said at our final hug moments before we got on the water. 'We' in this instance was me and Justine Curgenven, in our separate kayaks – mine blue, hers red. From the earliest planning stages I knew that I needed to team up with someone for the kayaking as my experience was limited and the leg between Russia and Japan especially would be remote and technical. 'Justine! You need Justine!' said some paddlers when I asked if they had any ideas about how and where I find this person. I was suitably awed that someone was known in the sea kayaking world by only their first name and, upon Googling her, saw that a string of kickass kayak journeys and films had made her world renowned. Justine helped train me at first and then I popped the question. Happily, she had said yes. After kayaking from London to France, Justine would then rejoin me in far eastern Russia, six months hence, to kayak with me to Japan, with a trip out to China to film me for a week.

I paddled away from the pontoon nervously, having been too busy with finding sponsorship to kayak for months, afraid that the choppy tidal Thames would pull me over. Elephants, not just butterflies, paraded about inside. I was nervous. I was excited. I felt a bit sick with the adrenaline. A helicopter buzzed somewhere above, the VHF radio in my buoyancy aid crackled with traffic while the two Royal Navy escort boats carrying my family, press and sponsors hummed into position. River traffic frothed past, kicking up wake. On all sides London plodded on with its midday routine.

The claxon blared. Waving upwards to supporters holding flags and signs of encouragement, I laughed and whooped as I paddled underneath Tower Bridge, officially on my way. It felt good to be moving, although it also felt like there was a very fine line between upright paddling Sarah and upside-down Sarah. I talked gently to *Nelson*, my kayak, about how I would really prefer to stay on top of the water if he would oblige and do the wet bit.

When the boats turned to go, taking my family and sponsors back upstream with them, I watched as long as I could until the river curved them away. 'Bye . . .' I said flatly, for only me and Justine to hear. Landmarks of London slid by as the Thames doodled her way eastwards, passing through the Thames Barrier and sweeping towards the sea through the flatlands of Essex and Kent. I appreciated the silent spaces amongst the chat as Justine left me alone with my thoughts.

The Thames is tidal from Richmond, some 20 miles or so upstream of Tower Bridge. Hence we planned to kayak in bursts with the twice daily ebb, making the most of the six-hour flow to gain miles towards the coast, resting ashore during the flood. We had our tents in our kayaks and enough food to be self-sufficient for the two to three days it would take us, so we could literally sleep anywhere dry enough. Rest would be token and swift: I had already promised my protesting brain and body that it could happen in France or beyond, but for now I just wanted to get across the water and put some miles on the log. The need to reach Russia's far eastern coast before winter set in and the sea froze was already pressing, even without unplanned mishaps. Had I set myself up for a ridiculous failure? The only answer would come in doing.

As the sun set we hauled out at Gravesend Rowing Club for food and a few hours' sleep amongst the racked boats. We launched again in the wee hours onto a black sea, disturbing sleeping swans from their slipway roost. Picking out the blinking colours of navigation markers, we threaded our way through safe channels, skirting no-go zones. As I paddled I wrestled with the urge to scratch at my neck, which was already being irritated by crusty salt, seawater and friction from the rubber seal on my drysuit that niggled at my sensitive skin. But dawn threw pinks and oranges across vast skies and I noticed the fatigue and irritation drift off like a cloud for a while. I wallowed in its space, grateful for the new energy. Left side, right side, left side, right side, pulling and pushing, pulling and pushing. I just needed to be the hamster on the wheel and keep things turning until France: repeat, repeat, repeat.

My digestive system also seemed to be stuck in repeat: food wasn't staying put for long. On our second night we camped near a ruined castle on a steeply shingled beach, waking in the early hours to a throng of stars. Diarrhoea forced me running to the waterline and I hoped that it would sort itself out by the Channel crossing, which could possibly happen the next day. By the time we reached Kingsdown beach in Kent – by most people's definition of an early Sunday morning – I was ready for bed. My forearms creaked like violin strings and my hands were hotspotted with the beginnings of blisters. A lady got chatting to us and, on hearing that I was feeling poorly, went home and reappeared with a plate of scrambled eggs and toast. I hoped that we wouldn't be paddling tomorrow and lay down on the pebbles to sleep. Logistics manager Tim and my friend Claire arrived with the car and whisked us away to Ramsgate Sailing Club to sleep and sort. Still feeling ill, I fell asleep quickly and woke up to hushed voices. 'I know Sarah, she'll want to go tonight,' said Claire. She was right: if we didn't go now, the next clear window might be days away. Low-pressure systems waltzed in off the Atlantic regularly at this time of the year.

We got on the water at 10.30 p.m., neon glow sticks on our buoyancy aids and little white lights at either end of our kayaks. I had hired a compulsory escort boat – given that the Channel is the busiest shipping lane in the world and authorities on both sides are cautious about people getting squashed. Tim and a photographer rode on the escort boat, while Claire drove to Dover to catch the ferry, ready to shadow me for a few days on the other side. Unbeknownst to me, on Tower Bridge day Claire had disappeared off to get an emergency passport, having only discovered the day before that hers had expired. Perennially late, but always getting the job done, we have been adventure buddies since our teens. I was glad that she was there.

'If I had known it was this rough, we wouldn't have come,' said Justine, disappearing behind the wave that had just rolled under my own kayak. I was very glad that we *hadn't* known it was this rough earlier because I was glad we were on our way. This was only the second time I had ever kayaked in the dark and I was concentrating 112 per cent, determined not to go over. I couldn't yet roll my kayak reliably, so a capsize would almost certainly involve a swim. Deep water scares me, so I thought it was better just to stay upright.

Around midnight, I shouted to Justine that it was time for our hourly break and that I really had to have a wee. We rafted up and Justine leaned across my boat to hold them together. I released my spray deck and stood up in my boat, putting one foot across the back of Justine's. I reached around to undo the stiff and awkward zip, moved all the layers out of the way and aimed between the boats (if you can't get it between the boats, you always aim for the other person's). Just as I was getting ready to rezip, my foot slipped off Justine's deck and I fell between the two boats, scrambling back into my own cockpit before the English Channel poured into my unzipped drysuit. Feeling lucky to have avoided disaster, I shimmied back into my cockpit quickly and we paddled on. I had cinched the hood of my drysuit tightly over my hat, not having yet learned the need for a waterproof one like Justine was wearing, and I made a note with every drip of water which sploshed onto my head to bring mine along for the next leg.

A few hours later Justine began hallucinating and I found I was reasoning with myself as to which way was up, distorted by reflections. Stars wavered as I struggled to stay outside of my eyelids and the lights of passing ships crawled jerkily across the horizon. I sang songs, making them up when I forgot the words, always returning to the comforting, unthinking familiarity of school hymns. I recited poems. I counted strokes. I sang some more. I allowed myself the count of ten with closed eyes before making myself wake up again. I bit my cheek to keep myself awake. France kept moving further away from us or sat annoyingly at the same distance as we waltzed north and south with the tides. Justine navigated and I followed, keeping check on our course with the compass mounted on my front deck. I was very chuffed to have her on board for her experience, knowledge and sense of fun. I was also glad to be a duo of women, given the sometimes chauvinistic attitudes towards our sex that we might somehow need a bloke to get the job done. Those who don't have watery experience have sometimes questioned why I needed her at all, given that I had rowed across the Indian Ocean. The answer is in the contrast of the two disciplines and the boundary of sea and shore. To kayak remotely safely in tidal, exposed waters, you need coastal skills and insights. To row across an ocean, the balance is heavily weighted in favour of the open, relatively safe middle and the technical skills are different. I would need to learn by doing. I am also glad that Justine took a punt on my lesser kayaking skills. 'Put it this way. I would rather have someone with the right attitude and a good survival instinct than someone who has pretty skills and some certificates,' she said.

As dawn switched the light on, the horizon beyond us grew cranes, buildings and ports. Calais lay before us. I scoured westwards for a slither of England, but just saw the giant metallic commuters slugging along. The last lights of home had disappeared many hours ago. My first ever tide race in a kayak bounced and snatched at us a mile from shore and I gritted my teeth and the paddle equally against the unknown movements, concentrating, bracing and reacting. Cold wee now sloshed up and down my legs after I had been unable to hold on any longer nor stop in the chop to raft up as normal. I gave the suit an ironic ten out of ten for waterproofness. Small surf nuzzled us ashore onto cool sand, the morning sun low. Staleness wafted into the freshness as I pulled back my spray deck and lumbered out to wobble a little circle on the spot. We had left Tower Bridge sixty-five hours and 110 miles ago. It had taken eight hours of paddling through the night to make it from Kent to Calais.

No one seemed bothered about looking at our passports and so we sorted the kayaks for a return journey on the escort boat. I gave *Nelson* a little pat and told him that I would see him on the other side of the continent in six months' time; I was already very fond of my little blue-and-white boat. I had named him thus in the hope that the endurance and bravery of the great Mandela and the British naval lord of centuries gone would help us home. Holed up in a *pension*, all of us shattered, we slept. Then we got to sorting and drying kit before focusing on bike stuff. *Hercules*, smart and black and steady, sat patiently on his two kickstands while we each tinkered with this and that and loaded the set of matching panniers. Having thrown an array of 'Things I Might Possibly Need On The Bike' into the car at home amid the departure madness, I now had to sort out what I actually wanted to take with me. In turn that was trimmed into a collective version of what we thought I needed as the team vetoed much of my stuff into ever-growing 'Piles of Shame' to return home. Frustratingly, due to mixed communication amid the busyness of leaving, a bag with my spare daily medication for my hypothyroidism had not made it out of London and so Accenture stepped in and couriered it over. Doubly frustratingly – and with a dollop of embarrassment, too – in another communication mishap my tent poles hadn't made it out of my kayak, and so plans were made to get them out to me down the road in Germany, where I would be meeting one of my sponsors. I looked forward to soloing and knowing where all my stuff was day to day. That said, we were all alive and here, and I was grateful for that.

For those first few days the team tracked me to capture film and photos and generally check I was all set up. The satellite communication unit which I had spent thousands on to allow me to send film remotely was proving to be a pain to configure and Tim spent many an hour frowning at his computer or the phone trying to get it on side. My goal was to be blogging and tweeting from the road and connecting with schools too, using an iridium satellite phone in remote areas or wi-fi in others. Sometimes one of the team rode with me and we chattered along the quiet lanes and bike paths into Belgium, stopping to watch horse and plough trudge peacefully or contemplate the stark monocultures of white crosses in war cemeteries. One night Tim waved us in to the roadside camp he had sorted at a lush dairy farm and we fed from the purring gas stove, a herd of cows muttering and mooing in the byre. Machines clunked and buzzed and pumped, while they chomped great mouthfuls of beet; the herdswoman gave us fresh milk and smiles.

The next day in a dew-sparkled field as the sun climbed steadily we packed up together for one last time. 'Do you need this?'

'Have you got that?' 'What should I tell so and so?' 'Where's the whatchamacallit – has anyone seen it?' Extra treats were lashed on top of *Hercules*' already bulging panniers. All the rush and busyness of recent months had built to this quiet crescendo, the chat and decisions now my own, unknown names on the map lay ahead ready to be connected by my wheels. Ferry times dictated swift goodbyes, so I hugged each in their turn, holding on especially tightly to Claire. 'See you when I see you, my friend' and she planted a kiss on my cheek in reply. I swung a leg over *Hercules*' frame, kicked both stands and pushed off with the unsteady gait of a carthorse just risen. I stood up on the pedals, wiggled the leather handlebars for momentum and clipped in my cleated shoes with a clunk.

'Goodbyeeeeeeeeeee!' I hollered as they stood quietly, Tim and Justine behind lenses and Claire just standing, watching, a flat smile belying the emotion. Birds chattered in busy hedgerows and distant cows called from a far-off field as tarmac and wheels rolled onwards together. I heard them shout back. The road curved, and we were gone.

2

Kindness of Strangers: Europe

Belgium, Netherlands, Germany, Czech Republic,
Poland, Ukraine, Russia | Bike | April – May 2011 |
3,000 miles

From France, Belgium and into Holland, I had threaded eastwards along well-designed, well-signed and neatly maintained cycle lanes bursting with a user population which bisected and represented the entire population. Wiry lycra-clad racers in training. Shoppers on sit-up-and-beg bikes with loads or passengers. It was not uncommon to see one tiny person on the back, one on the crossbar and one on the handlebars, a real family vehicle.

I love that there is a version of bike for everyone, whoever and wherever you are in the world and your life: it is the ultimate democratic vehicle. I love how you are open to the world in a way which you cannot be when you are boxed in a car. You are humble in a way which a motorcycle is not. It is unimposing. I also love how being a biker means that other bikers stop to chat, just for the fact you are riding a bike, like Claus the seventy-year-old German in neon 1980s lycra, who was so excited about my bike gadgetry. There were also joggers and walkers along the bike paths, some with more or less enthusiastic dogs. They ranged from varying levels of strolling to earnest Nordic walking or full-on marathon walking with hip wiggles. Rollerbladers sashayed and waltzing skiers pushed themselves along on wheeled skis with poles and talked about winter.

'Can I help you?' said a voice in good English and I tried not to look surprised that I had been called out as a Brit. Mieke had seen me straddling *Hercules* with one leg on the curbside in Venlo one night, snaffling a snack while I looked between map and signposts. A fellow tourer, she told me I was daft to pedal over to Germany tonight and should come home with her instead. If the road hadn't run out at a river that afternoon I would have been there already. But there had only been a ferry and no bridge, which would mean voiding my human-powered aims. While I had thought briefly about chancing a swim, I reasoned against it: there would be other bridges.

Our bikes parked outside amid crowded rows of others, we grabbed tall beers and Mieke told me of tours past and planned through Europe, solo and in groups. I felt like I was speaking to a future version of myself and, as we rode home through the dusky forest along roads I had already pedalled that afternoon, I looked forward to curb-jacking and hosting my own riders and rovers one day. 'To bicycles!' we toasted, and sipped the smooth blackberry whiskey that Claire had given me for sharing with new friends, its warmth and sweetness echoing Mieke's hospitality.

As dawn broke and the forest came to life with birdsong, Mieke escorted me through avenues of tall trees and quaint villages. Velvet mists hung low over dykes like floating blankets and I was glad to be out, muscles and moods awakening, grateful to be sharing the specialness of this one, extraordinary ordinary morning that would stick with us both for years to come.

'So, this is it, dear Sarah. It's time for you to go on alone now. Here is the border,' said Meike in the middle of a small non-descript road. There wasn't even a sign. She pressed a tiny Saint Christopher into my hand – I wasn't really going on alone. Many people were already stuffed into or clinging on to *Hercules* in the same way. An hour later I rolled to a silent stop to watch a hefty bird of prey launching itself from a field side. A shining otter caught my eye as she tore at her fresh-caught fish on a riverbank before slinking back into the water.

I made it to Essen after punching hard along increasingly busy roads, once finding myself on an autobahn by mistake, cars honking at me as they shot past. I was using a low-resolution map, which amused my sponsor Peter, who, like many others, imagined I must be using GPS. Maps were fine for now and I liked not having to rely on a GPS. I waited a day for the errant tent poles before pushing on, and Peter drove them out to me a day later. The irony was not lost on us: I had embarked on a complex expedition, for which Peter's company EY had sponsored me a lot of money, and two weeks in my tent poles hadn't even made it out of Calais.

Along the rivers Ruhr and Rhine, twiddling up and up into the thick forests of mountainous Bavaria, I wound my way past roadside asparagus sellers, black-and-white timber-framed houses and elaborately painted giant eggs and ribbons in village wells ready for Easter Sunday. I settled into my routines, using sunrise and sunset to beckon me to the pedals and tell me when to stop. And so it was that I diverted off the main road into Finkenau in search of some water one evening. I chose a bright red house on the assumption that you must be a warm soul to live there (my House-choosing Science was rudimentary) and the fact that I had seen a lady watering the garden with a hose. I pictured a swift filling process and final miles to an as yet unchosen camp spot. Water bag, stop, wince a little at changing positions from sitting to standing, straighten up, creak a bit, kick out the stands. I walked over in the least waddling way that I could (saddle rawness – let's leave it at that). By now I was quite proud of my, '*Entschuldigen Sie, bitte . . . Haben Sie Wasser, bitte?*' So I was slightly disheartened, although also relieved, when Jennifer answered me in perfect English. Of course I could have water, but no, she wasn't going to give it to me from the hose. In fact, would I like to stay the night? I gratefully accepted. Had I not chosen the red house, I would have been out in my tent, some-where in the forest, likely wondering what I would do if a wild boar charged me. I had asked for a bag of water and got a bath. A wide sea of bubbles complete with a G&T on the side and a spin in the washer for my clothes, now so grim they were quite antisocial.

The next morning, Family Engelhardt rode me on my way, a mini peloton of smiles; the boys peppered me with questions about exactly what types of snakes I was likely to see and the father, Claus, translated road signs and gave me instructions for routes ahead. I loved how the journey was connecting with people and felt privileged that they joined me or told me of their jour-neys or dreams. 'But it's nothing like yours,' often followed. In my head they were *everything* like mine. For me, all adventures are created equal and it is about spirit more than form, about what it does to you rather than how long you go for or how hard other people think it was. Stuffing marshmallows into a mug of hot chocolate at day's end while you perch on a log outside your tent feels sweetly blissful whether you are out for the weekend or away for years. In fact, maybe the smaller nuggets are all the more brilliant for their contrast with the rest of your life. In my head, the essence of it all is the same – to strive, to seek, to find and to have fun while you are out. Walking in the fields at home recently, I watched a kestrel suspend itself above the hedge line in a static hover while watching a doomed rodent thirty feet below. Seconds later it had a takeaway and I walked home with the same, the scene embedded in my memory. It is as vivid to me as handing turtle hatchlings out to sea in Mexico twelve years ago. Adventures and experience can be memorable and life-altering wherever you are.

A few hours later, and *Hercules* was denuded of luggage and upside down. I tinkered, and then fought, with the spoke key, swearing as I tried to realign the buckled back wheel. In my naivety that morning, I had thought that the ever-wobbly wobbling had been due to my supersonic downhills. An hour in and the first proper tears of the expedition (think the all-consuming, body-shaking type, as opposed to the gentle slip-down-your-cheek type) washed out and, I realised later, with every wipe of my eyes I smeared dirt across my face. Passers-by stopped from time to time and offered help, useful or not, most of them cooing at the quirky set-up of *Hercules'* hub gears and belt drive.

Famed for bike geekery, Germany is a perfect country for a breakdown, and I felt a mix of relief and daftness amongst the universal smells of a bike shop the next day. Apparently the exhilarating off-roading through tranquil forests a couple of nights previously had not been as good for *Hercules'* wellbeing as it had been for mine. That said, I felt even more daft on another day when I couldn't uncleat my bike shoe from the pedal and so thumped onto the pavement with all the grace of a jellyfish. I pedalled into the nearest town to find a bike shop and this time

pre-empted the fall, disembarking with a knowing finesse to walk
in with one shoe on, one shoe off. That time it was just a case
of loosening the screw on the pedal and tightening another: I
was still learning.

After Germany I cycled into the Czech Republic, where food
poisoning from dodgy petrol station tap water floored me for a
couple of days, confining me to a little room above a pub as
everything I had consumed exited in all directions. Fuelled only
by lemonade after my two-day fast, I then cycled all day to reach
Prague on Good Friday, streets bathed gold in the soft light of a
gentle evening as I freewheeled down into the bustling old city,
crawling with tourists. I stayed in a youth hostel and busied myself
with a rest day of washing, bike cleaning, me cleaning, diary
writing, blogging, answering emails and shopping. But inside
air-conditioned shops, surrounded by screens and LEDs, I felt
trapped and claustrophobic and cheated of the day's warmth. Since
Calais I had been outside almost twenty-four hours a day, and
not seeing the sky made me twitchy. A deeply tanned local man,
old enough to be my father, interrupted my contented journal
writing as I sat on some old stone steps in a plaza. He told me
how he thought Prince William and Kate (days away from being
married) would only last a couple of years. Sprawling on the
steps beside me, he invited me home with an air that suggested
he thought I wouldn't refuse. I told him I would be with my
husband, the first time I had lied about being alone. In the evening
I went to a concert in a church, nourished and nurtured by the
music and the space of the vaulted roof. Bach, Vivaldi and more:
no translation needed. Walking home to my youth hostel,
wandering hordes of drunken Brits on stag and hen weekends
leered over the pavements. As I lay in bed in the fetid mixed
dorm trying to block out the noise, my phone buzzed with a
message. *My little brother. Bottled. Alive. Operation. Should be OK.*
Shit. My head raged while the drunk lads bantered, feeling very
lonely and far from home. Still weak from the food poisoning
and having barely slept long enough to confirm that the back of
my eyelids existed, I stayed in Prague to sit in different sunlit
plazas and cry it out. I was angry: at myself, at being away, that

it happened and that, home or away, there was nothing I could do. Except ride on.

I was still nervous about not making it to far eastern Russia in time for the pre-winter crossings to Japan, so unless forced to, I rested little, clocking 60 to 90 miles a day, my legs finding their own rhythm en route to what I hoped would be an increasing distance. Where I could, I pedalled on major roads, trading off prettiness for pace, remembering home as friends' playlists scrolled on my iPod. I belted the national anthem through small villages when Siena's came on, and listened over and over to 'Home is Wherever I'm With You!' by Edward Sharpe & The Magnetic Zeroes. It echoed my feelings about *Hercules* and my changing backdrop of sleep spots. I slept in blossoming orchards, shady forests, empty campsites and cropped fields, alongside hedgerows and on riverbanks, tucked down leafy lanes and in quiet grave-yards. I even slept in the shower room of a campground on one wet night. My goal was always to sleep wild and accept hospitality if offered, and to find a hostel or hotel when I needed a shower for me and my kit. On occasion, if it felt like there was nowhere safe to camp, I pulled the 'security card' I had agreed with George, the team accountant, and ducked inside for whatever sort of night I could find. My experiences ranged from the salubrious to the slimy and I am sure one of them was a brothel.

In my tent I tried to tuck out of the way behind walls or hedges, under trees or hidden beneath bridges. Unless there were lots of people about: then I knocked on doors to ask for local advice about camping permissions and was sometimes invited to pitch on their lawn. Sometimes I even asked if I could. My sleeping set-up was my anchor, the repetition of routine as important as what the tent itself represented: the walls drew a line around me and metaphorically shut out whatever had happened that day – be it one to be forgotten or remembered. It gave distinction from the night outside. Though ironically, one of the reasons I love camping is that I feel that little bit closer to the moon. Some of my most memorable 11,000 nights on this planet have been ones when I have slept outside. Like the time my dad tried to convince my five-year-old self that he needed a hammer to set up a new sleeping bag in the garden, when he had actually just bought us our first tent. I have slept out for weeks in the garden every summer since, in various tents and even a home-made hammock, which would have been stellar if it weren't for the insects. In winter we slept out with hot-water bottles, the back door always left open just in case. Through secondary school the ups and downs of my teenage friendships were heightened and memorialised on the two-, three- and four-day expeditions for our Duke of Edinburgh's Awards. That I spilled our porridge on two consecutive mornings has never been forgotten by Claire or me. And nor has the time another Claire fell up to her armpits in a bog.

From the Czech Republic to Poland and on to the Ukrainian border.

'You're going back. Ukraine not allowed,' said the sludgy green uniform, pointing at my bike, his gold tooth winking at me from beneath a thick hedge of moustache. No foot passengers here. They offered me a lift in one of the beaten-up Ladas waiting to cross to Ukraine just a few hundred metres away beyond the barriers. 'Or you go to Medyka, 40 mile.' Apparently not all borders are created equal, so I got back on my bike. The guards laughed as I cycled away, shouting my plans to the queues. Tree lines stitched neat silhouettes against pastel skies. Birds chortled to get all the chat in before dark as I cruised down lanes busy with commuters recently home from a day's foraging or nest building and others readying for a night hunting.

In villages en route, storks clattered their bills atop their telegraph poles, which looked like towering flowers with their crowning nest of branches and straw. I came alongside a grandmother on her bike and took off my sunglasses to smile. I mimed and fudged Polish for what I imagined were answers to what she was asking me, which I imagined were the pro forma questions that most people wanted to know: Where are you going? Where have you come from? What are you doing? We laughed at our efforts and she called over some children to translate. Apart from English hellos delivered with something between pride and shyness, they either didn't know what I was talking about or were not confident enough to bust out their skills. Suspicious older sisters and accompanying boyfriends, a mother in curlers and dressing gown came out to watch and an English–Polish dictionary was brought out to help. 'It looks like rain,' said a child, reading from the dictionary and pointing to the clouds. Panni, the smiling bike lady, insisted she take me home as it was late, apparently not going to take no for an answer. Ukraine would have to wait until tomorrow.

After a bath, Panni fed me a rich feast of thick ham and deep slabs of bread which she cut on her stomach like my mum told me that her mum used to do. After dinner we sat in the lounge with her husband. 'My father asks what are you doing here in our small town?' their son translated down the phone, while Panni and her pink-cheeked husband waited with eager patience for the return translation. I showed them pictures from home, and showed them the map of my route. France, Belgium, Netherlands, Germany, the Czech Republic, Poland, Ukraine, Russia, Kazakhstan, China, back into Russia and on . . . Panni did the same with her family albums. Meanwhile, a picture of Jesus looked down at us from his cross in the front room and later I slept with another picture of him looking down at me in the back bedroom. It's the closest I'd ever been to that man. The next morning they brought out their elderly neighbour to watch me pack. Her weathered hands held on to my gloved ones while she gazed hard into my eyes through clouded cataracts, crossing herself as she said something I guessed was a prayer. I nodded and thanked her, assuming in my sample size of two households that religion must be important around here. Russian Orthodox churches had started to appear recently on my ride, the distinctive domed roofs and emblem of the two-barred cross standing out as new. Kalnikόw had a beautiful wooden Russian church which I wheeled round for a quick look on my way out of town, wondering at the stories of my hosts. We had glimpses of each others' lives and that was all. I reckoned that this is all it ever could be for me on this journey – vignettes.

I made it to Medyka and into Ukraine that afternoon, feeling more of an anomaly than I had on my ride so far. It was my first official border checkpoint; until now I had only pedalled through an imaginary line, sometimes marked by a road sign, sometimes not. Shifty-looking men tried me for money, offering exchange. A horse-drawn cart went by. Then a Mercedes. In some places the roads were more pothole than road and in others it was smooth and swift. Both within the country and between others, my two-week trek across the middle of the country was one of contrasts. Rural life was manual and labour-intense, a well and a bucket in the garden for water, along with a bearded goat. The odd scatter of cows chomped here and there but I don't think I ever saw a sheep. Whole families bent double in the fields tilled and planted seeds in strips, grandparents alongside youngsters, collectively stitching a collage across the landscape. In contrast, massive fields stretched for hundreds of acres, worked by the latest sprayers and tractors, one man and machine doing the work of many manual labourers. Only latterly in 2015 when politics flared in the eastern Ukrainian region, stopping its exports, did I learn that the country is known as the 'Bread Basket' of Europe, a major exporter of wheat in the area. Old women with tired eyes and wrapped in thick woollen tights, layers of cardigans and pinafores, shawls and headscarves, stood on lonely sentry duty at roadsides selling eggs or bottles of milk. Shops reminded me of black-and-white pictures of 1940s shops at home, shopkeepers standing behind a wooden counter with a glass front stretching across or around the shop, fetching whatever you wanted from rows of jars or boxes on shelves. Yet in one shop I was handed my purchases in a plastic bag from Sainsbury's.

The Cyrillic alphabet had appeared and turned road signs into wordscapes to be studied like I do the night sky, learning single constellations and recognising patterns as a handle to finding my way around the whole. 'Львив, Тернопил, Кхмелнытски, Виннытсиа, Кировохрад, Днепопетровск, Донетск, Луханск' – Lviv, Ternopil, Khmelnytskyi, Vinnytsia, Kirovohrad, Dnipropetrovsk, Donetsk, Luhansk. Town names were announced in ostentatiously huge 3-D concrete blocks at their perimeter, often accompanied by the prettiest bus stops I have ever seen, their walls mosaicked or painted with stories of life under the scythe and hammer of Communism or in blocks and curves that reminded me of art deco windows. I jumped on any chance to practise my fledgling Russian. Outside a shop one day, a young lad pointed out how I should be pronouncing Ukraine itself, laughing at me as he shouted '*Uuuuuk-raiy-EEEEEnah!*' while pointing on my inflatable globe to where he lived, repeating it again and again until he was satisfied with my pronunciation. As I stood eating biscuits, a toothless, smiling elderly gentleman in a faded suit and braces, with worn-out shoes, doffed his black cap to me and almost stood on my toes to look at me through smeary thick specs. He didn't understand my Russian and so I showed him the Ukrainian translation of my 'Magic Letter', which outlined the basics of my journey. He screwed up his eyes and furrowed his brow in concentration or confusion, and I guessed that he either didn't know how to read or couldn't discern the words with his short-sightedness.

Riding eastwards on a dappled road in the late morning sun, a scruffily dressed guy flagged me down and asked for directions. I was surprised because I clearly looked like a traveller, likely with no idea of where he wanted to go. He shifted from foot to foot as his eyes darted around him and he pointed on the map at this and that distractedly. A car rushed up and its driver jumped out to ask unconvincingly for more directions before shooting away. His wallet bounced to the pavement and I picked it up and shouted after him. Guy number one grabbed it from me, excitedly showing me all the notes inside before shoving it into his trousers. 'Fifty fifty!' he whispered, miming that we could share the money, waiting for me to say yes. I had a sense it was a set-up of some kind, and a police car sidling past at that moment convinced me. I spun away as quickly as the pedals would turn. Every time I saw a patrol car for the rest of the day I did my best to look as casual and invisible as possible.

The traffic police officers in Ukraine must have been especially bored as I seemed to be waved over every other day as I pedalled onwards. Sometimes they checked my passport and sometimes not. Only one lot asked for money, but the fluffy green dice on their dash reassured me that they were just pretenders and I carried on without waiting to hear their answer.

Then there was the night signalman who let me warm up and cook dinner on the wood stove in his cosy signal box. He wanted me to sleep in there too, rubbing his thick hands together and stroking his leg, face twitching while we ate. I firmly stuck to my tent outside and fell asleep uneasily, my subconscious chuntering 'what ifs' through the night. I woke the next morning to him showing me off proudly to his friends who had just arrived for work. I pedalled off trying to reconcile my conflicting instincts, glad I was alert but keen to continue trusting people and keep those perspectives in balance. Being solo was more of a worry to me than the fact I was a woman, for the simple fact that in duet there is someone else to watch your back.

There was a lot of kindness, too. A gentle old man in a suit bought me some biscuits, handing them to me without saying a word, and another gave me a rose with a big smile. A shopkeeper gave me some free sweets and another insisted I had a big cup of coffee with his two patrons, which I was grateful for even though I can't stand the stuff. A teenage lad cycling past with friends pedalled back to me with a bunch of pretty wild flowers on a day when I needed that lift.

Mosquitoes were a different matter. They invaded my personal space on a daily basis, heralding the start of many months of torment and strategy. I had repellent, a fine-meshed headnet, a long-sleeved shirt and a lot of swear words in my armoury. A forced camp on a moonlit marshland could have been peaceful and still, but for the lilting, burping, farting chorus of croaking frogs at all depths of field. The high-pitched screams of mosquito armies bombarded my tent wall in search of my blood through the night, scooting in before I managed to zip the door shut or track down the tiniest of tears in the fabric to tape it closed. Before long the pale tent inner was blood-smeared and spattered with splatted mosquitoes. On slow uphills I was easy prey.

I felt my most vulnerable to dogs on the slow uphills, too, and came to learn there were a lot of bored strays in Ukraine. Both lone dogs and packs of them took me and, I assume, anyone else on a bike as fair and fun game, sprinting after me, yapping at my heels. I became skilled at squirting my water bottle at them while still pumping hard on the pedals until I realised that stopping and barking back at them was the most effective rebuttal. It also made anyone watching chuckle, as many of my biking antics seemed to do. That was certainly the case on the day commemorating the end of the Second World War in Ukraine after an entire memorial service turned to wave at me as I pedalled past.

At the Russian border outside of Luhansk, the Ukrainian guards were unflinching in their outsized hats, ignoring an old lady's tearful, writhing request to use the loo. There were endless rules about what was banned or allowed in Russia, including satellite devices. A muscled Alsatian pulled at its thick chain, snarling and barking as I wheeled *Hercules* towards the Russian checkpoint. The guards stamped me in with barely a look at my documents. Relieved, I walked towards the final barrier, and saw a traditionally garbed group dressed in military uniform and pretty dresses. They started to sing, their swords at salute.

'Welcome to Russia, Sarah. I am Evgenia,' said the petite lady in civvies. I was being given a traditional Cossack welcome, complete with a cat-sized loaf of beautifully crafted *klep*. This was the Rostov-on Don region, southern Russia, with rich Cossack heritage, and Evgenia, a government official, had arranged our welcome. I had expected to meet her for a coffee – not a full-on fanfare, and I was touched by the effort. On the pedal into town, as I worked to keep up with Evgenia's car and police escort, I marvelled that such a high-level official had come to greet me, before realising over a bowl of *borscht* that *she* had in fact laid on the escort for *me*. We stopped at an incongruously Egyptian-themed hotel for a Russian dinner with the owner and various of his friends, who introduced me to vodka, local style. Apparently this meant toasting everything in shots, multiple shots. I was squiffy after four of my most enthusiastic *Nazdarovya!*

Cued by Evgenia, arrival committees in the next couple of regions gave me costumed welcomes, presentations of books, flowers, flags and more vodka and loaves over the following three days. Near Morosovski I was given flowers to place at the foot of the vast Second World War monument and asked to say something while translators translated to a small crowd of local officials. At School Number 5 I shared some tales of the journey with teenage students, my first talk of the road. 'What are the children like in England?', 'What do you think of Russia?' the students quizzed me, and I was impressed by their English and embarrassed that I didn't have more Russian yet. I planned to bring adventure into classrooms either by in-person visits or satellite calls from the field and an online resource bank, encouraging young people outside. Physically outside and beyond their comfort zones, I wanted them to explore the world and be unafraid of new challenges. A Russian flag stood outside the school and in the classroom and soldiers stood at the gate. Apart from that, it felt much like any other state school at home.

A changing brigade of police cars escorted me for those three days, and on one of them I had three in procession, feeling embarrassingly conspicuous. The officers rode *Hercules* around car parks, commentating to their counterparts, and made me pose for photos every time a new officer rolled into the duty squad. Only one scowled with a determined persistence, looking thoroughly and theatrically bored each time I caught his eye in the rear-view mirror, clearly feeling that I had disrupted far more important duties or, I suspect, a quiet afternoon of his own choosing. Still, it was a fun gig for the most part and I especially enjoyed them carrying my bags. I had no rules about who carried my luggage, only about who did my miles, which had to be me, whether I cycled, walked or crawled. If I took a lift I marked my spot and returned to the same place. At railway crossings, where traffic backed up for hours to wait for mile-long trains to trundle through with their procession of carriages, the policemen would signal that the barriers were to be lifted and we nipped over. I had enjoyed the advantages and circus of my official stint, but I was glad to solo again, mistress of my own day once more. I had about a week more in which to cross Russia, before Kazakhstan beckoned.

Before my journey, it had been Russia that people were most wary of. I was advised that someone should always know where I was and warned of being drugged and raped and killed or mugged and disappeared, generally by people who had never set foot in the country. I don't know if the same can be said for the guy in the Czech Republic who asked if I would be carrying a Kalashnikov, but my first few days set the tone for the rest of my time in Russia. Vodka, hospitality and warmth.

I pulled off the road into a small town whose name I can't remember, a dilapidated factory and its pipework welcoming me bluntly. I asked a dozing taxi driver about finding a cash machine and he beckoned for me to leave the bike and get in the car to take me there. I did so, hoping my instinct was still reliable and that *Hercules* would be there when I got back. An icon and some beads swung from his mirror.

'*Ruski?*'

'*Nyet, Angliski.*'

'*Moushna?*' I pointed at my bike. The driver laughed; he had asked if I was married. Of course they should wonder, given that I was twenty-five and didn't have a gaggle of children about my knee. Here, young women were married off as teenagers and started having children straight away. Chauvinism followed me as closely as the hospitality at times. I had barely left the shop when two ladies, arm in arm and giggling like schoolgirls, marched up to me and simply said, '*Chai?*' Why not? I wheeled my bike along after them until we reached one of their houses – or both of theirs – I had no idea how they were related to each other yet. Propping *Hercules* up under the porch, I took my shoes off at the door, enjoying the boundary between the outside heat and the inside cool. The blonde lady pointed at herself and said 'Natasha' and then at her friend and said 'Natasha', saying 'friends' a few times to make sure I had understood. Natasha pointed to the sofa and mimed sleeping: I was being welcomed for the night, not just for tea. Natasha got the rather dangerous-looking immersion heater going in a tank of water over the bath and taught me the etiquette of the long-drop loo in the garden. There was new reading material for reading and old reading material for wiping, along with spiders networking in the corners. The Natashas had known each other for ever. Teacher Natasha was a young widow with a son and the other Natasha was married to Pasha, with two teenagers. We prepared dinner together while Natasha kept climbing into her cellar through the kitchen trapdoor to bring up jars of pickles, fruits and jam. When the gregarious Pasha came home he opened a bottle of red and knocked it back in shots. We laughed and laughed and ate and drank, *Koushet!* on repeat, as they gently ordered me to *just eat*, as mothers are wont to do. When I left the next morning the Natashas gave me a hand-knitted Russian doll and we swapped socks knitted by our respective mums.

The dusty roads of the Russian steppe felt slow as what felt like every other car stopped for a photo, or to give tea, water or vodka. It was very touching but sometimes frustrating as miles slowed beyond my expectation. I was realising that trying to reconcile the 'linger longer' part of me with the quietly ticking clock counting down to winter in the far east of Russia would be a recurring theme of my journey.

A group of teenagers on roadies, mountain bikes, jumpers and BMXs escorted me into the historic 'Hero City' of Volgograd, named after the Volga River, on whose banks it was built. It had been Stalingrad before that. Local man Sergey, a devoted Beatles and Harley fan, took me under his wing after finding out about my journey through the news and contacting us to offer his support. He picked me up from my hotel, which he had arranged, to take me to his house for dried fish and vodka, then out to bars for more of the same. Reps from a local youth organization took me to Mamayev Kurgan, where the striking statue *The Motherland Calls* stands proud and tall, concrete robes flowing and her sword outstretched over the city. Below her, friezes and statues depict scenes of bravery from the 200-day Battle of Stalingrad in the Second World War. This was the battle that finally defeated the German forces, at a loss of two million lives.

Next I rode south into the Volga delta. Rivers and channels rolled beneath my wheels as I pushed eastwards through the mid-May sun, sticky tarmac shimmering and pine forests filling my nostrils with the scent of resin. Bird-life was rich and varied, from herons and egrets to eagles and kingfishers. Scores of crushed snakes and tortoises littered my route. I saved as many tortoises as I could and was happy that the snakes tended to slink off when I approached. I still didn't know which ones were poisonous – some said blunt heads and some said pointy, some talked of yellow stripes and others of red patches. My tactic remained simply to avoid encounter.

But one night something, or something and friends, was under my tent. I was too scared to investigate and so, instead, I just lay very quietly and very still, waiting for it to leave or go to sleep. The next morning I awoke to another something, or something and friends, outside my tent. I unzipped the fly and peered out, wiping the sleep dust from my eyes. A flock of raggedy sheep, nuzzling and rootling for forage, seemed unbothered by my tent. Their shepherd, quietly patient or unbothered, old cap sitting on the dark hair which matched that of his placid horse, Chocolat, wandered over for a few questions. As the ensemble drifted on I drifted into my morning routine of dismantling camp and repacking *Hercules* amid mouthfuls of bread and jam. Lifting the tent I discovered the something of the night before – a shiny dung beetle clinging defiantly to his giant ball of manicured poo, trundling it on stoically now that I had exposed him. I wished him well; in relative terms, his load was far greater than mine.

In Astrakhan there were more local ad hoc tours lined up on my behalf. I met the provincial governor in his swanky wood-panelled offices, joking over polite teacups that it was the first time I hadn't been offered vodka. Astrakhan has an impressive Kremlin, built a few centuries ago by Ivan the Terrible. I enjoyed standing in front of the ornate frescoes, with a compulsory floaty scarf draped over my head, in line with Orthodox traditions. The procession of hatted priests and menagerie of altarboys and officials wafting fragrant incense, holding lanterns or raising gilted crosses and ornately framed pictures above their heads to honour whichever icon was being remembered, was mesmerising. The rich oranges and reds of their outfits painted them in bold contrast to the stark white of the fortress walls.

A group of young riders who had been messing about in the plaza when I wheeled in the night before were keen to escort me out through the busy city traffic in the cool of the following afternoon. The mountain bikes jumped over potholes that I skirted around and bunny-hopped onto balustrades, literally jumping in and out of conversations. Dusk cued the lads to prepare to turn around for home. Amazed I would even consider camping, they insisted on finding me a local home to stay at. I was inwardly relieved and outwardly very grateful, because there was a lot of swamp and thus a lot of snakes within any given radius. I was intrigued that they cast off some saying they 'were not good homes' in favour of others, and I soon got frustrated, wondering what nuances I was missing. I suspected my instincts and tolerance were just different because it was I, and not they, who had been on the road for nearly two months, and they had local knowledge. A babushka in her nightie answered the knock at a small wooden house. Understandably, she seemed disbelieving that there was a (woman) biker. Her husband looked nonplussed as he stared at us through the kitchen window in his white vest and leggings, droopy fag trailing a wilting ash. A slender blond boy peered from behind his grandmother, mouth agog as though he, too, couldn't believe that there was a (woman) biker, as my escorts claimed. They welcomed me in and I wondered if the same would have happened at home. I handed over glow sticks and a spare light for their pedal home, and went inside.

My legs and mind were restless as I lay on a sofa just across the room from the snoring grandfather, wondering why the grandmother and young lad were in a separate bed in the sparse kitchen next door. I drifted off to sleep hoping I wouldn't need to use the long-drop at the bottom of the garden in the night, as it backed right onto the river. The next morning I gave them some snacks and a bar of chocolate which I had been saving, and thanked them for taking me in. I was glad that the Czech Kalashnikover and the nervous experts from home had been wrong about Russia.

3

Tea and Snakes: Europe and Asia

Kazakhstan | Bike | June 2011 | 2,500 miles

'*Nyet doroga!*' shouted weather-beaten truckers in the Kazakh mid-west, 'No road!' They hung through open cab windows, reluctantly accepting my reassurances that I would be fine before rumbling off, weaving between and across ruts to find the best bit of sand or dried mud. It was all relative. Hurricane clouds of dust rolled out behind and I followed on my own weaving course, remembering the expat who told me, 'If you can make it across Kazakhstan, you'll be fine.' I was pretty sure that I would, even if I had to lug *Hercules* and my gear piecemeal for miles. It was more about whether I could do it and stay roughly on schedule. I awarded the country the Golden Pothole award within a day and wished I had put a beefier tyre set on, dreaming of agile suspension forks as *Hercules* rattled me along. Troughs as deep as my knees and stretching 50 metres across, or smaller versions of the same, linked together to form what could only be described as a road in the loosest sense of the word. My forearms ached from holding my handlebars on course, through juddering and jolts, especially as I crossed the southern reaches of the Aral mountains, bleached orange escarpments chopping the landscape momentarily before they rolled and flattened into miles of unending steppe. But I enjoyed the concentration and focus that it demanded, the contrast in rhythm and flow with the smoother stretches. Where it was too rough to ride, my legs enjoyed being upright and the stretch which came from walking. One of the expat's warnings was about how, if it rained, everything would turn to mire and I would get stuck in the mud. The rain must have been ahead of me, because there was one patch in the lowlands where I slid and trudged with feet that looked more like snowshoes made of mud, and dense clods jammed *Hercules'* forks so that I had to carry him and the panniers in relays over a couple of miles. Mosquitoes took advantage of my relative stillness and I swatted them constantly, turning my white shirt black with bodies.

Heat haze jostled the boundary between land and sky, beckoning me to more space beyond. Solitary oil wells nodded all day long and static pylons ran for miles in lines. Camels stood in slivers of shade, grinding their chew, shaggy humps flopped sideways as flies did lazy laps. I cycled past their curly eyelashed stares, basking and baking in June's long days, tracking eastwards. From Atyrau to Aktobe, down to Aralsk and on to Baikonur, Shymkent, Kyzlzorda and Almaty. The roughest roads stepped away into memory, reappearing momentarily alongside more cyclable surfaces. A new motorway was snaking from China to Europe, managed by an Italian contractor, their engineers and project managers flashing by in new 4×4s. Stretches of this newly or partially laid black magic tempted me to have a go. Slipping around rubble blockades, I raced my shadow, teasing it to midday before it teased me into the sunset. After the plodding gains on the early miles of the *nyet doroga* west, my weekly averages accelerated. Starting in the soft space of dawn, bike and body warmed up in the blazing sunshine towards a sweet spot of flow, mind and muscle and machine in repetitive meditation. Tailwinds chanted me on and miles gave way graciously. If I had enough water at day's end I rinsed my shirt and shorts in my saucepan before cooking something starchy, while listening to all the noises of the quiet and empty. Troops of ground squirrels popped up from burrows to yell to each other. If there was any wood about I had a small fire, or I just boiled up my pasta and tomato paste and retreated into the tent as quickly as I could, evading the mozzies.

One evening I had camped on a pitch of newly laid road and was just rolling out my mat and sleeping bag when a man wandered up and invited me to come closer to the camp of vehicles further down the way. He was a night watchman for one of the construction crews. I accepted the invite and moved between the diggers and rollers and haulers. Instead of my normal rinse with the saucepan, I was treated to a thundering shower beneath the stop-cock of the water tanker. I had seen a few construction workers sleeping out alone on a rolled out mat underneath or beside a truck, way, way out and miles from anywhere. During the day orange jumpsuited teams of them stared or waved at me if they noticed me from their work. With white T-shirts over their heads, tiny holes cut for eyes and mouths, we joked that the other had a tough job on the road. They filled my twelve litres of bottles and bags from their supply tanks and trucks, and I gave them melted Mars bars.

With empty stretches of 50 to 80 miles along the dusty roads, my favourite punctuations to the miles were the *chaikanurs*. These dusty café outposts were oases of shade, chat, bottomless teapots and platefuls of whatever the gold- or gap-toothed owner was cooking that day. *Plov*, made with camel meat and rice, wrinkly boiled dumplings, fried eggs, soft naan breads, battered potato *pirojoks*, rich in fat and carbs. Owners often appeared from dark backrooms, wiping sleep from their eyes or stretching as they pulled themselves from slumber. I wasn't especially surprised, therefore, when one lady served me in her white nightie, her dyed copper hair a vivid contrast to the bright blue sky outside when she waved me onwards in her flip-flops and painted toenails. Cockroaches patrolled floors, lizards zipped up walls and there was usually a dog and some shabby chickens. We all sought shade. I did the same on the road using whatever I could find in the miles of open. I envied lizards who pattered silently to a statued crouch beneath the shade of my pedals, slowly lifting limbs in reptilian tai chi. I, too, tried to sit in *Hercules*' wiry shadow, the sun bragging at me from its midday zenith.

Often in a *chaikanur* there would be calls of '*Anglichanka!*' from the other punters, who waved me over to their low tables where they sat or lay on the floor, before waving at the owner to bring me food and *chai*. An enamelled teapot with a cavernous belly of velveteen stewed tea would be set down before me, and someone shunted the sugar bowl to follow. Milk was offered because I was English, until I learned *sin moloka*, 'no milk'. I have always preferred herbal teas but now, heaped with sugar, I was converted. So long as I remained, the pot was topped up and I sank cup after cup of the sweet brew. In Russia it was vodka, vodka, vodka. Now it was *chai, chai, chai*. I knew which I preferred. A few times I got up to pay and the owner would signal that someone had already covered my tab, even if I had been sitting alone and not spoken to anyone.

A bush telephone told *chaikanurs* and drivers further ahead about the *Anglichanka* on her *velosiped*, meaning that sometimes strangers greeted me with smiles of recognition, as though they had been expecting me some time. People gave me numbers for Qyzlorda, Shymkent or Aralsk, urging me to call their aunt, granny or friend. Others stopped on the road to give me food and water. Everyone posed for photos on their smartphones. In one village I knocked on a door to ask for some water and was invited inside to the delectably cool inner room to sit on the richly patterned carpet. The young daughters beamed at me with deep brown button eyes and milk-toothed smiles. The woman fingered the collar of my grubby white shirt, tutting gently at my general grunge with the affection of a mother. A spread of food was laid out and we ate together. I promised myself that if ever I saw a laden biker I would give chase and force them to take a fiver and a banana, or bring them home for a night to wash their clothes, whether they liked it or not.

For now, I stuck to sharing food and water with fellow travellers and gave a few notes to people who looked like they might need it more than me. I would choose my person, dash in quickly, hand it over gently with a smile before cycling off. Who knows what they made of it, but I hoped it would be useful to them in the same way that others' gifts to me had been helpful. Some of the best gifts I received were the simplest – smiles and good wishes for my safe passage ahead and, of course, pots and pots of *chai*.

Some gestures were not so welcome. I quickly learned that the Kazakh men were rather forward. Or desperate. Regularly a driver wound down their window telling me 'Kazakh men very good!' and I had a few offers of marriage and many more of 'sex, very good sex!' I always shouted at them before pedalling off, pointedly ignoring them if they pulled up again. They never felt threatening, just cheeky and annoying, though, of course, the truth is that it was still sexual harassment. Mostly I felt more frustration at them having held me up. I wondered if they actually thought that if they asked enough white women on bikes, that someone might say yes.

One lambent morning, while I packed up my tent and ate my watermelon breakfast beneath whispering trees, I was suddenly surrounded by a herd of hungry cattle. I shooed them on only to discover that they had shooed a black snake from the long grass, which was now winding over to *Hercules*. Effortlessly pulling up through the wheel and around the frame, it lurched for the open pannier. Shiiit! Watermelon, tent or snake? A cowboy ambled over, chivvying stragglers with cracks of his whip. '*Svir! SVIRRR!*' I shouted as I shooed the cows to no avail. The cowboy seemed amused and rather blasé and dropped down from his horse with a swagger. He drew back suddenly, which I understood to mean it was either venomous and he was scared, or that he hadn't believed me and was startled. The whip thwacked and the metre-long squatter slid swiftly into the scrub. I gave the cowboy the rest of my melon in thanks and he just stood there, watching me, before following his herd as they meandered on. I rushed to get packed, stamping rather than walking around to ward off any snakes. I am fascinated by these creatures for their amazing biology (I am in awe of anything that dislocates its jaw to have a chunky snack), but prefer not to share my bike with them. The cowboy returned, which I thought odd, and said something I didn't understand. He said it again and still I told him '*Ya nie ponimayu.*' Then he made a lewd gesture which couldn't be misunderstood and I yelled at him to piss off.

On the top of a grassy hill the next morning, I had another run-in with a snake. Stamping my feet in case I was intruding, I weed in a scrubby area near my tent. As I was turning to go back, a brown snake leapt up from my feet to waist height, flaring its head and sending me running back to my tent. I flipped the screen on my video to record and, out of the corner of my eye, spotted an even thicker, dappled grey snake S-bending across the grass. I declared, pantingly, that 'I haven't been this scared since yesterday.' I geed myself up to head back down the narrow track to the road to pedal on, imagining all the other snakes in the grass before I reached the relative safety of open tarmac.

As I cycled along a rough track in the Syr Darya river basin in the south, I felt *Hercules'* back wheel pop. Part of the metal hub had cracked around one of the spokes and a piece came off in my hand. With one spoke down, a lot of weight and an uneven surface for the foreseeable, I needed to find a welder. Sitting with my back to the road to avoid the dust, I was studying my map and running sums in my head when a chunky SUV pulled up and a Scottish voice called out. Paul was project managing a local construction team and was with his local driver and translator Yurlan. I stood with my head through the window enjoying the cool of the air con. Teasing me about my commitment to pedal on instead of taking a lift, he said that there was a welder in Baikonur, where they were staying tonight, and invited me to stay. I rode on, buoyed by the bed, conversation and shower which awaited and enjoying the placid traffic of wild horses along the road. Paul's driver returned to pick me up, reeking of alcohol, and I wondered whether or not I should get in. Built to service the space station missions which launched from the steppe some miles out, Baikonur was a closed town to anyone without the right documents. The guards would not accept my Russian visa and so Paul came out to meet us, assuring me that going over the fence was the next best option. Many of the locals do it, apparently, and so, feeling a bit like a naughty child, I stood on the driver's shoulders and scrabbled up and over. As I walked towards the car someone yelled 'RUNNN!' and, not knowing which direction they intended me to take, I raced back to the fence and hurled myself over. I sat quietly in the first car as the police moseyed by on patrol. Second time and I was over, scurrying into the pick-up car where Paul and Yurlan were waiting. A drunken Yurlan and his equally sozzled girlfriend fondled each other in the back of the car beside Paul, who clutched an open bottle of beer and offered me the same. They wanted me to go on to a nightclub with them, but it was late and I was barely awake, keen for a shower and bed. They drove me to their rented apartment in a block of Soviet-era flats. Graffiti led us up a stark stairwell that stank of urine and alcohol. The tiny, airless flat was dirty and the bath tub was cracked in two.

Paul explained how locals give up their flats for paying incomers to patronise the nightclubs, and I wished I was back in my tent with the horses and moon, asleep hours ago; I am sure I would have felt safer. In the small hours Yurlan and Paul crashed onto the one bed in the house, draining more beers when they woke up in the morning. I much preferred this more sober version of my host, the one who explained about the special hotel where the cosmonauts are kept in pre-flight quarantine and how the launch happens way out on the steppe. Unfortunately, after a long wait in a pretty mosaicked courtyard, the welder appeared and declared *Hercules* needed someone more specialist because his hub was made of aluminium. Yurlan's brother lived in Kyzlorda, a city on my route down the road, and he arranged for me to meet him in a few days' time so that he could help me find a welder. I don't remember his name, but I remember how he proudly showed me the painted wooden house where he lived with his new wife. He fed me attentively and strummed a guitar-like instrument and sang local songs. Over tea, of course. *Hercules* got his weld and I rode on.

Mountains appeared to my south, becoming companions at my side until I was upon them, climbing up and up. Watermelon sellers lined verdant roads and I stopped regularly to gorge at their huts, grateful for the variation on meat and dough. Justine had flown out to Almaty to film me for a week and we met on the road; she would ride all the way to Ürümqi, a week away in China. I gripped her in the sort of hug I hadn't had for months. We spent a full couple of days running errands in the city. She had brought me new gloves and *Hercules* a new wheel. I pushed long hours at the keyboard and tinkered with gear, breaking to shop for supplies, piling a basket with fresh fruit and carbs. We watched a performing baker hook out a soft naan from the coals of a glowing tandoor and celebrated day's end with the champagne a friend had sent out to mark the MBE I had recently been awarded for services to charity and rowing. On one day a local conservationist took us high up in the mountains, which welcomed us with their silence. I drank in the crisp clean air, soothed by the glacial lakes, inspired by the craggy peaks which rose from them. Birds of prey wheeled above, and tiny bright flowers shouted bold greetings. It was a blissful pause before returning to the dust and heat of the road and heading into China at Korgas.

4

Gao: 'I am happiness': Asia

China | Bike | July – August 2011 | 2,000 miles

My first impressions of western China could be described with the following words: noisy, intense, dusty, busy, hot, crowded, people spitting, I had a sense that stuff could happen quickly here, and that you would be left behind if you didn't, or couldn't, keep up. Bridges reaching across valleys that looked too wide to be spanned. Brick factories where countless hands sorted and carried millions of bricks. Market traders shouting that I should buy their pig snouts. Old men hauling buckets of water, bent double in a yoke. People defecating at the roadside. The blaring horns of beat up old trucks – China followed Kazakhstan loudly and boldly.

I was in a petrol station drawing out my snack choice so that I could enjoy the cool air con just a little longer, when I glanced out to check on *Hercules* and saw a young Chinese guy studying him. Moments later, he was at my side, his hair even fluffier than mine. '*Ni Hao*! Excuse me. My name is Guang, Gao yua Guang – you can call me Gao. Is it your bike? I am so proud of you. What you doing is—is—uh—brilliant,' he said nervously, and then asked where I was going.

'London.'

'Oh, wow! Cool. I am so proud of you.' Eyes wide. 'And where are you coming from?'

'London.'

'Wow! I want—I want to do a bicycle ride but, uhh, but—it looks really difficult. How do you do it?'

I told him that I thought the most important thing was starting, just getting out and having a go. Pedalling on, I hoped that one day he would email and tell me of the adventure he once had.

Half an hour down the road, a car horn honked and pulled up on the other side of the road. Running out, Gao told me that he wanted to come with me.

'Sarah, Sarah, you—you need a companion! I ride with you to Beijing!'

I had not expected that and stood, baffled and impressed, as he traced his finger along the coloured lines of the road atlas telling me 'You be the leader, I be the guide.' I had a date with my sponsor Accenture in Beijing in early August, just a month and 2,000 miles away. Then there was the Gobi Desert. What if I had to call his mother to tell her that her son had just expired on a bike with a random British girl he had met in front of the wasabi peas? I didn't want the responsibility and so tried to put him off as politely as I could. Gao just rattled on, telling me how we would ride at night, buying 'foods and waters'.

'Have you done much riding?' I asked.

'Uh . . . not really very much,' he said, omitting to tell me that he didn't even own a bike.

Somewhere amidst Gao's excited chatter to Justine's camera (for we were not quite at the end of her week) I decided to say yes. So many people had helped me in the days when I didn't know how or where to start, teaching me and letting me make mistakes. People still did. The potential was huge and the risk no bigger really than the shape of Gao's fear. I knew that Gao was scared that a ride would be too challenging, and I later found out that his parents wanted him to stay and study instead. But by saying the words out loud and committing to having a go, Gao had already overcome the biggest obstacle in his way. So I wrote him a shopping and finding list for what he'd need, underlining 'tent' to peg out my feelings of team mate: yes, tent mate: no, and we arranged to meet in Ürümqi, a day's ride away.

Two days later, Gao arrived and Justine flew home. I had just finished cropping my bowlish mop with my penknife and I opened the door to my hotel room to see that Gao had also been shorn. Unlike me, he probably hadn't done it himself and so hadn't been left with a rat's tail like I had. I had missed the extra lock of hair because I couldn't get the hang of holding a mirror behind my head to see it in the one on the bathroom wall. Top to toe in red-and-black lycra, he beamed and we went for some lunch with his brother and cousin. 'I was too nervous to sleep last night,' he giggled, and I asked if he was excited. 'I am always excited!' I felt fond of him already and looked forward to the insight he could offer into his country. I hoped I could do the same for him on mine.

The shopping list had worked and a new red-and-black bike, loaded with bought, rummaged or borrowed gear leaned against the wall, a huge Chinese flag hanging off the back and a little line of them pegged on the handlebars like candles on a birthday cake. Gao later told me how his brother had loaned him the money and I could see from the way he told strangers about his little brother's route to Beijing that he was proud. Maybe he wished he could ride, too. As we posed for our first team photo, I asked Gao about the flag. 'My brother, my brother, he said, "You need a Chinese flag, but, uh, it must be bigger than Sarah's!"' and he burst into impish laughter. My British and Chinese flags were the size of postcards. They had been mistaken for me being American, Italian or something else and I had tut-tutted that I had ever assumed our small island's flag was universally recognisable. The Windsors, however, were different: all through Europe people had asked me about the royal family, one chap in Poland asking if I was 'looking out for the marriage of my Prince'. That is to say, was I going to watch the wedding of Will and Kate? (I had thought he was coming on to me.) That had stopped somewhere in Russia, and through Kazakhstan I noticed that saying I had come from England garnered less reaction than saying I had cycled from 100 miles down the road. It was all a question of perspective.

Almost out of the city as we approached the turn-off to our road, I noticed a car on the hard shoulder and small red things on the floor that looked like airport landing lights. Gao's brother and cousin were waving and shouting madly ahead of us. Gao appeared at my side, yelling at me to ride faster, just as the line of landing lights exploded at my heels, swirling white smoke into the traffic. Firecrackers: of course, a traditional Chinese bon voyage. Once safely out of the firing line, we stopped to say goodbye to his brother and cousin, who passed round a bottle of something with the alcoholic potency to blow your head off.

We rode off into the desert, asking each other questions. Gao apologised for lying to me about having recently graduated. Actually, he was only here in Xinjiang province with his brother (who ran a business of their father's) because he had quit his business course in Heinan 'to do something more meaningful' with his life. Even as an outsider I understood what a brave statement that was; I had gathered that out here the pressure of family expectation can be crushing, especially for sons. I later read of a government edict making it illegal to neglect filial duties to one's parents. Perhaps that is why he didn't tell his parents of his spontaneous cycling jaunt until we were nearly two weeks down the road. Contrastingly, he was amazed that I could be away for a few years on an expedition, with acceptance and encouragement from people at home.

My main goal for the first few days was to ease Gao in gently, which by definition isn't an easy thing to achieve on the fringes of the Gobi Desert when you have never cycled more than a few miles in one go and you now have a fully laden bike. But by the end of the first day, things felt good. Gao had learned to fix a puncture. His bike had a name: '*Stranger*, I call my bike *Stranger*.' We had good miles on the clock. I seemed to have convinced him that his jumping jacks and lunges during breaks were un-necessary in trying to impress me – I was already impressed. And we were still both smiling. That first night was Gao's first ever in a tent and it was nearly his last because he had lost his tent poles within the week, setting a theme for all sorts of losses. The tent poles weren't too much of an issue until later on in the damper mid-north of the country, as initially it was generally too hot for anything but sleeping on top of our sleeping bags under the stars, side by side between the bikes. And we only did that when our raw saddle sores or lactate-jammed legs shouted so loudly that we had to listen. Otherwise we rode on as long as our eyes stayed open, making the most of the cool before the wind started to pick up with the new day's warmth. Ideally we rode town to town so that we could treat ourselves to a shared room in a trucker's hostel for a few yuan, excited for a shower or jug of water to rinse the dirt and grime away. So long as we were sheltered and shaded for enough time to top up on rest and fill our water bags and bottles, we were unfussy.

In the hottest regions around Turfan, where temperatures topped out at 50 degrees Celsius, we had to plan more than I had done in previous miles, trying to judge whether we could make it to the next petrol station or settlement before we ran out of water. We carried 15 litres each but back-to-back days of 50 to 100 miles in searing heat and fierce headwinds made short work of it. 'I ride like a dog!' said Gao as we pulled up a hill. 'What do you mean, buddy?' And he panted like a dog. I often rode holding a mouthful of water for as long as I could, eking out its usefulness. On one of the few occasions when we had both run out of water, thirst gnawed and then squeezed at my brain. I would spread the last sip of hot water around my gums, willing it to multiply and imagining what it would feel like to lick the last remnants of flesh from the discarded melon skins on the roadside. My tongue looked like a dry river bed, and it reminded me of why I had chosen WaterAid as one of my supported charities. Arriving at a tiny café, we sank bottle after bottle of drink from the fridge before we did anything else.

The famed Xinjiang vineyards of these fiery red-stoned valleys loved the heat, but for us it was a daily battle to push the miles I needed to stay on schedule and stay alive. By midday it was impossible to be outside, what with the heat and the headwinds screaming off the mountains. If we were near a petrol station or a town, it might mean stretching out in a storeroom or under an awning, or paying for a few hours in a hotel. Mostly we were out in the 80-mile stretches of nothing where shade meant crawling under low-hung spans of drainage channels under the road, which the locals used as makeshift toilets. Having taken a sleeping mat and water, the first goal was to search for a spot between remnants of used paper. Once installed, every movement had to be considered for fear of waking to someone else's toilet paper on our face. In the western provinces, it was sad to see the (road)side effects of what felt like a lack of government investment in something so simple as decent sanitation for everyone. This meant that if the wind was blowing in the wrong direction, we smelled villages before we saw them. People squatting to defecate at the roadside in full view of passing traffic was not an uncommon sight. Even at apparently well-kempt petrol stations there was often no designated long-drop. The clean and efficient long-drops of Russia and Kazakhstan were a distant memory as I balanced over tiny trenches, holding my breath. No one seemed to mind if children crouched in the street and babies and toddlers had no seat to their trousers. Plastic bottles carpeted roadsides and ditches, and plastic bags wallowed and waltzed in the winds before getting caught for a while in whatever happened to get in the way.

When I asked Gao about it, he said that people just didn't care, saying that within a village, for example, where there were shared conveniences, that it was no one's responsibility to keep it clean and therefore no one did.

Our miles took us right across the mighty dust bowl in the north. At night it would still be high twenties or thirties, but, along with the drop in headwinds, to our parched bodies it was bliss. Generally, gritty winds charged off the mountains and beat through wide valleys blaring a static white noise which sand-papered us as it scoured the landscape; clocking just a few dragging miles in every hour was not unusual. In these conditions, desert which had been blasted and blown from untold miles away crept into every crevice of our bikes, through every gap in my clothing, and found places to rest in my eyebrows and on my eyelashes. Sometimes I felt like I was half desert, half human. Even with Buffs pulled up high over our noses, we ended up filthy. We rinsed our clothes wherever we could and once I took mine to a laundry where they turned my socks away for being too awful. Bare-chested road workers did the same, waiting for their turn with towels tied around heads, their vests rolled up. It didn't take long for clothes to dry to cardboard.

We were growing into a team where both of us had roles and were the better off for the other one being there. We bantered through the heat, headwinds and kit failures. Gao called me

'Potter' because I could magic anything out of my bag that he needed. He called Brits lazy for using teabags instead of leaves. Gao teased me for my sweet tooth and I made him eat his first Mars bar, just as he made me eat my first chicken's foot. It seemed ironic that this same foot could have come from England, exported because at home we don't eat them.

The difference in our respective cultures was mutually interesting on more fronts than chicken's feet. Gao was surprised, for example, to learn that there are summary executions in China when I asked him about what he thought of them – information being harder to come by in China. One night we met and rode with Andy, a peaceable American touring cyclist who had left his hairdressing life to pedal around the world. Gao teased me afterwards, declaring his surprise that he thought all Americans were loud and all Brits quiet and unassuming. 'But Sarah, Andy is quiet and you talk a lot!' He bowed when he met other Chinese people older than himself, and when he spoke to my mum on the phone he was adamant about calling her 'Miss Helen'. He seemed unbothered when we saw a young child being thrashed for doing something he had been told not to, and didn't bat an eyelid when a mother punched her boy in the face. He was amazed that people feed garden birds in Britain. I was both surprised and not surprised to hear from him that Party membership is needed for many jobs and how, in Xinjiang, there is a palpable dislike of the marginalised Uighur people by the more numerous Han Chinese, who consider them second class. Gao was thoughtful after chatting with a Uighur restaurant owner one day, learning that his life was especially hard because of his ethnicity and the local racial tensions. Before that, Gao had derided the government policy that allowed Uighurs to sidestep the one child policy and bear more, just as celebrities also escaped levies on extra children.

The yawning chasm between the increasingly well-educated and burgeoning middle classes of urban areas and the rustic, mostly ageing, populations of rural areas was stark. Recent decades have seen a massive and non-returning urban migration, stranding grandparents who look after the tiniest of the grandchildren while sons and daughters earn money in the cities to send home and support them all. Family groups sat under trees or in communal courtyards playing board games and cards. I couldn't help but compare it to home. Walking around the estate where I live in Oxfordshire, most front windows frame people in front of a television, invariably heads down on a separate phone screen of their own. That said, cellphones and phone masts were as ubiquitous here as anywhere else in the world, a beacon of empowerment and connectivity.

One of the most memorable meetings (probably for both parties) came outside a shop in a tiny village somewhere in the hills of Gansu province after a dusty, ponderously slow but beautiful 30-mile climb. Small houses sat squatly in rows and the tiered and terraced fields of rice made a striped patchwork of curvy burnt reds and greens. After downing a few bottles of icy water Gao helped the owner change a motorbike tyre and I felt proud of his evolution from not knowing how to patch a puncture on *Stranger* to helping strangers fix theirs. As I sat in the sun taking photos I soon found myself surrounded by a gaggle of old women who had the same ideas as to the meaning of personal space as the snake cows in Kazakhstan. They discussed me loudly and asked questions which I tried to answer, shouting to Gao for translations: 'They ask if we are married.' 'And what did you say?' 'I said yes and that we met on the internet!' Roars of laughter. Then one of the ladies at the front asked something and it all went quiet for a moment as she casually reached forward and squidged my boob, as though she greeted strangers like that all the time. I definitely didn't know how to answer that in Chinese.

I accepted that I was the odd one out and therefore prime studying material, though I wished it didn't have to happen right in my face. In a country of 1.4 billion souls, I suppose there's no such thing as personal space. People regularly prodded my thighs or squeezed my biceps to see what I felt like and I often fixed tyres with a gathering of spectators or turned around from market stalls to see people opening the panniers, testing the brakes and even getting up on the saddle. So maybe I shouldn't have been surprised to have part of a crowd peel off from watching a dancing display to follow me like a flock of sheep. The day an old chap unzipped my tent at 6 a.m. to peer inside summed it up – people just wanted to see and feel what was going on. In the same way that groups gathered and winnowed grain together and people squatted in 360-degree open plan toilets alongside strangers, life out here was communal, especially in the rural middle and west. Something reminded me of reading about the harrowing public denunciations under Mao Zedong, not because my treatment was anything like that inflicted by the erratic and terrifyingly dogmatic era, but because it felt like China's past had left a sense that there is nothing personal about a person, not even their body. But the upside of that same communality was that we were treated to touching and humbling hospitality, too.

Like the cycling fanatic who arranged an impromptu feast for us with his friends in Ordos, let us sleep in his bike shop over-night and then escorted us out the next day with his club of young riders. He had only met us a day before in a service station. There was a café owner who opened up on his afternoon off to cook us platefuls of noodles and then insisted he gave it to us on the house. And Chow Lee who helped us pitch our tents on his petrol station forecourt, and then sent me text messages telling me he missed me. Truckers offered us lifts (which we didn't accept) and drivers offered us water and watermelons (which we did). There were the policemen who escorted us off the motorway because it was illegal and then treated us to lunch. In fact, the police were very good to us: off the top of my head I can count four occasions of troops pulling us over to load us up with food or drink, to invite us home or escort us to a safer road. And then there was the farmer and his wife who invited us into their bare home to share a deep wok of rice with them and their young son by candlelight. They couldn't afford electricity at the moment because the husband had a broken leg and could not work. I sang nursery rhymes with the four-year-old from his English book as Gao talked with them. The next morning I left a fistful of notes on the table.

Sometimes I think Gao enjoyed the chance to chat in Chinese, although at other times he got frustrated by people's questions. My reasoning for always answering the curious was that you never know what it might inspire, although maybe if I was the one with the local language I would feel differently, too. I was certainly grateful for his translations and explanations. There was one man, however, who was glad of us being able to tell him about another traveller who had passed through his little roadside house in 2004. One handwritten note amongst the little cards he had collected over the years stood out for the scale of the journey and the effect its French writer had had upon our host. It read: *Josephe Capeille – 85 yrs old – Cycling around the world five times for 25 years*. His black eyes shone as he described how he had come to look upon Josephe as a son during the weeks he had stayed with them, nursing him back to health. He said that he hadn't heard from him since. I Googled Josephe on my phone and found a bronzed rider with outsized sideburns looking back at me. I was reading his obituary. We all sat silently for a moment, each contemplating and one mourning as he absorbed the news that he had died just three weeks on from here. In this little house Josephe's story – and those of the Dutch guy walking across Asia or the British lady Megan Lewis riding horses from Shanghai to London – would go on inspiring and energising riders limping in from the heat.

Out through the deserted west and into the industrial badlands of the mid-north where factories belched acrid flows into the sky and river beds lay rubbled and empty. We pulled ourselves up through the mountains of Gansu where people once lived in caves and serpentine trucks now backed up in 40-mile jams. Weaving on through the twists and turns of the Yellow River valley, where I stood transfixed as teams winnowed methodically, tossing piles of grain into the air to separate wheat from chaff. In the final couple of weeks to Beijing I fretted about not making my date with Accenture. Gao fretted about *Stranger's* mechanicals, which took hours to fix. He suggested I cycle on alone, which I wasn't ever going to do.

After a sweaty 124-mile day on our final ride to Beijing, Gao was wistful that this was the end, that his one month on the road had passed 'soon, too quick'. As I filmed his thoughts on the last thirty-five days on the road, he told me that even though 'every day was hard it was not very hard enough', already the tougher

bits slipping away into the middle distance. On *Stranger*, he said
he realised 'on the first day, that you should learn to it, you
should know it and you should let him know you,' and I realised
he could have been talking about us, too. Finally, I asked him to
sum up how he felt in three words and, after pausing to think
about it, with head on one side he said, 'I . . . am . . . happiness.
No, I just can use one word: happiness.'

Gao stayed in the city to work for his uncle before going home
to Hebei and I pedalled on towards Russia. Trekking eastwards
from the megalopolis dust bowl of Beijing through the increasingly
affluent hot flatlands of the east and into the humid forested
mountains of the north, I settled into the silence of solitude and
listened to my iPod, which Gao had often borrowed on our ride.
Scrolling through the playlists I happened upon Queen's 'We are
the Champions' and hit Play. It was our team song and we had
belted it out together from Gao's first miles in Ürümqi. Except,
we sang: 'We are the looooosers!' laughing at our punctured
tyres, our naps in shit-smeared tunnels, the ridiculous headwinds
and dizzyingly tired nights. From there I went to 'You are My
Sunshine', remembering a day of pouring rain where fields of
carnivalling sunflowers had cheered us down our road for hours.
I sang it to Gao and he made me sing it again and again and
again while he learned the words. Now, missing his jokes and
his thoughtfulness, the image of him riding along with no hands,
confident and carefree, made *me* happy and I sang the song again
and again. For what Gao did and how he did it, I am proud and
grateful; not only did he enrich his life and mine in those two
months, but his story has inspired and continues to inspire people.
During my school visits and talks, and in blogs, Gao's example
of having a go is the one people remember, and his message of:
'If you want to do something, just do it. Don't worry about
anything, just do it.' Not long after I left Beijing and Gao had
started working with his uncle in the city, he posted on my blog
about the effect the ride had had on him, ending: 'I look for my
future and I not scared now.'

I did feel a little more nervous without him than I had done
before as a soloist, as my Chinese was still very limited and I

knew that I missed nuances. That was certainly the case one night somewhere west of Dunhua, on the outskirts of a town whose name I couldn't pronounce. I had spent the day on muddy tracks which passed me through villages nestled in thickly forested hillsides, and the contour shading on the map suggested more of the same beyond it. I hadn't seen anywhere to pitch my tent – everywhere was stuffed with crops or people, and I wasn't keen on camping in maize fields where I knew people went to squat or anywhere that someone might come and unzip my tent door at 6 a.m. to have a look. Hoping for advice I could understand, I showed a trucker my map and, naturally, I ended up with a crowd of people's input. It was unanimous: not safe, no people, and wild animals who might eat me but there was still no suggestion of where to pitch for the night. Given that the only wild animal I had seen in China so far was the shrivelled tiger penis on a street stall in Beijing, I thanked them and headed off to see if the outgoing road was different on this side of town.

Ten minutes down the road and it wasn't. Straddling *Hercules'* crossbar to make a new plan, the put-put-put of an approaching motorbike grew louder and closer until a motorbike was right by my side. It quickly didn't feel right and I was not surprised when sex was offered. 'China man very good,' I was assured. As the man grabbed my leg I busted out my schoolmistress routine just as I had done to the presumptive Kazakhs, and sprinted off. I heard the engine approach again and so swung *Hercules* around, to return to town, just missing the ditch. He was soon at my side again and then in front of me. STOP! Shove him away. Shouting. Racing back now, pissed off and crying, wishing Gao were still here and wishing more that I had listened to the locals. It is sometimes hard knowing when to choose others' instincts over your own.

'Is it safe?' is a common question, particularly from women, and I know from emails and questions at talks that many women are held back by the perception that solo travel as a woman is not safe. Yes, you can be unlucky, and we've all heard of horrible, shameful things being done to travellers, but we have heard of equally heinous things happening to people at home, too. Running a quick web search will show you that hundreds of women have and do solo all over the world with nary a blink of trouble. Ninety-nine point nine per cent of people will want to do well by you, wherever and whoever you are.

5

No Roads, Only Destinations: Asia and Europe

China – Russia – Japan | Bike and kayak |
September – October 2011 | 2,300 miles

I cried for all six miles of the journey from the Chinese border at Suifenhe to Pogranichny on the Russian side because I wasn't allowed to ride my bike. Everyone has to take the bus. Tired and frustrated by the officious border guard telling me once again that my journey was stupid as he watched me load my luggage, I wished that my silent tears be swallowed back into my eyes. He had just made me wait a few pointless hours in the terminal, apparently only to taunt me; mostly he wanted ego-stroking and agreement as to his and China's brilliance. I was glad of some peace when he was called away to something else. He returned and ordered me to go the bathroom: 'You have something wrong with your face.' I asked what, but he just kept repeating that I go. I turned to the friendly guard sitting quietly nearby and asked him. 'I am sorry. You have some mango on your face.'

Having arrived at the Russian checkpoint after the fastest few miles of my journey, holding *Hercules* in the aisle of the bus, I cleared the queues and customs. I was glad to be back in Russia, imagining that this far eastern region would feel quite different from the western regions I had pedalled through all those months ago. Pedalling away I left the tears behind. Pulling into an unre-markable sideroad to camp amongst tall, swishing grasses, I was thinking how quiet and spacious it felt compared to China when a rusty Lada rumbled up in a plume of dust. Its driver told me that I shouldn't camp there, 'You come home with me,' and he phoned his wife to ask her. My tired brain screeched at the effort of trying to find Russian words again as we bumped down winding tracks to his house and I tried to mentally map where I must be. Music thrummed from the back garden from which people clutching glasses came out to greet us. I asked if it was a wedding. 'Yes, I marry my wife today,' said Darrell, the guy who had just brought me home. One of Darrell's guests swayed too close to me and Darrell pushed him away. The second time it happened he threw him sideways to land on his back with a thud. '*Champanski*' and vodka were flowing freely. There was a raffle and some very bad but enthusiastic singing before a family took me home for the night and I joined in with more shots, toasting everything and everyone. Their glasses were charged with all the warmth and hospitality I had remembered from all those miles ago. 'Do you think we are always drunk?' one of the ladies asked, and everyone paused to listen to my answer. In one evening I had already drunk more alcohol than I had done in two months crossing China.

She also told me that 'In Russia we have no roads, only desti-nations,' and I let that thought meander round my head as I pedalled towards Ussyrisk and then north 700 miles towards Khabarovsk. She had unwittingly summed up my journey perfectly, and I think, life. There had been no route to the start of my journey and no set path lay ahead, no givens, nor guar-antees at any stage. By the same token, the only thing we know about our lives is that one day, at the end of the road, is death. The idea that life's road is finite clarified for me at age twenty-one when my dad died suddenly. He was fifty-three. Having already been planning a row with a crew from Australia to Mauritius, Dad's death was the impetus for changing course and going solo, on a journey which I used to fundraise for arthritis charities and help me chart my way through grief. I arrived on the other side, physically and metaphorically, in 2009, three years later. Having seen my dad live and suffer from rheumatoid arthritis since I was a toddler, I credit his quiet stoicism and positive attitudes for showing me how to live even when you can't choose your own path. I don't believe in any higher being or afterlife, but I do believe that the spirit of a dead person lives on for as long as those of us who remember them; my father is still with me in my journeys.

Just weeks before my arrival in Russia we had been dropped

in the proverbial when the shipping company discovered that *Nelson* was too long to fit on the plane in his six-metre wooden crate. Justine scrambled to have a detachable three-piece kayak made so that it could be transported as hold luggage and bolted together on the other side, while the rest of the team scrambled to find a solution for *Nelson*. Sponsored by the lovely Welsh company Rockpool Kayaks, I was honour-bound to use him and knew that we fitted and worked well together. But even if we got through the first 'Could you ship a kayak?' question, we generally found that shipping companies fled at any mention of Vladivostock, the far eastern outpost to which he would be shipped. At the last minute DHL came on board, confident that they could get *Nelson* all the way from England to the city of Khabarovsk, where I would be meeting up with Tim and Justine sometime in September. I was running a couple of weeks later than we had originally planned, which was frustrating at the time but now I see it wasn't too far out at all.

I pedalled north through pastoral scenes of small wooden houses, tin-roofed wells in gardens full with harvests of veg. Honesty boxes for produce sat outside garden gates. Babushkas with their thick woolly socks reminded me of their Eastern European counterparts from all those miles ago. I crossed sweeping rivers bulging with recent rains, glad that the bridges were just about intact, wondering if they would be up ahead once communities became fewer and further apart. Locals were surprised when I said I was sleeping in my tent and warned me that I would be eaten by bears. Often I stayed awake long into the night – or woke myself up – scared they would eat me, wondering, too, about the handful of endangered Amur tigers in this region. In reality I was only eaten by mosquitoes, fatter and more determined than any I had seen before. I found them squashed in my pants. They fell out of my hair. I blew bodies out of my nose and I scraped them out of my ears. They drove me mad with itching and turned me into a swatting machine, wishing that I was as unbothered by them as the bands of mushroom pickers foraging in the forest appeared to be.

After the hubbub, bustle and in-your-faceness of China, I enjoyed the relative privacy and gentle curiosity of Russia, as well as the return to a language which felt increasingly familiar. My sweet tooth also enjoyed the sugar and I had my fill of blinis, jam, bread, chocolate and cheese. I hadn't had cheese in months.

The road to the tsarist-era city of Khabarovsk tracked north for 500 miles generally following the Ussuri River, which, at that stage, marks the boundary between China and Russia. South of Khabarovsk the Ussuri joins the mighty Amur River which itself runs north-east to the sea towards Sakhalin. The white and gold of the Orthodox churches struck an impressive contrast against the city skyline. Benetton, Starbucks and Gap sat alongside other familiar high street names in the open boulevards of the city centre. People milled about and skateboarded in the squares, and cycled and walked down the decorative riverbanks, everyone enjoying the lazy September evening.

For over a year we had been working on the logistics for the upcoming biking and kayaking on the Russia to Japan leg, which we nicknamed the Far Eastern Question for its complexity. The first stage was for me to pedal 500 miles north from Khabarovsk to the tiny coastal town of Lazarev, the closest settlement to Sakhalin. This island was essentially a stepping stone down to Japan. Tim, Justine and the kayaks would follow me from Khabarovsk to the coast in a 4×4 from where Justine and I would kayak across the Tatar Strait to Sakhalin. Tim had already been out to the region on a recce the year before to find various local fixers for advice and support. Vladmir Chebanov was our man for Khabarovsk, and while waiting a day for Tim and Justine to arrive he helped me with errands. He also organised a press conference and talk at his outdoor shop, followed by a bike tour around the city with some local riders. He said it would have been a car tour but he thought that my journey rules meant I had to cycle *everywhere*. I also had a sports massage from a guy who, as he dug his elbows into my tight hamstrings, recounted meeting a friend of mine, Al Humphreys, on his world bike trip nearly ten years before, when he cycled this way. *Small world*, I thought as I lay there in my standard-issue paper pants.

Justine and Tim brought with them a rush of home and I was excited to see them again. I was also glad that they could take over some of the admin and logistics. All thoughts of having a couple of rest days in Khabarovsk together evaporated when they asked if I would be biking straight away; I got the sense that they wanted me to get going. We all went to the DHL depot to release *Nelson* from his wooden crate and, as someone crowbarred the lid off I cooed at seeing my little blue-and-white boat again, surprised he was not even tied into the crate. Noticing some gaffer tape over the front deck I pulled it off to reveal a scruffy hole in the fibreglass, presumably from being crushed at some point on his journey. Quietly livid, I got ready to pedal on the next morning, leaving Justine to advise on a repair job by a local workshop and Tim to elucidate onwards logistics. As I was clipping into helmet and pedals, Tim explained why they were keen for me to get going. A mishap in visa admin meant they hadn't been granted the three-month business visas we had planned for, meaning that he and Justine now had to be out of Russia by October 7th, in less than four weeks' time. Losing a week could be a deal breaker – given that there was nearly 1,000 miles of mostly off-road biking and lots of technical kayak crossings ahead to get to Japan. Pedalling off into the raw taiga as I headed north to Lazarev, my frustrated grumblings stewed around with angst at whether I would even manage the kayak crossings after so long off the water.

Tim and Justine had hired a local driver named Igor for the journey to Lazarev, and after a couple of days on gravelled roads the jeep caught up with me. They trailed me to take photos or film or went ahead to lay out lunch or find good places for the night's camp. I sometimes got discombobulated by not being totally in control of my own daily plans, but I was glad of the support and extra thinking power and I enjoyed the company. At night I enjoyed the fact that with lots of us around there was less likely to be any bear incidents, now that we were deep into the thick forests of the taiga. One night we were all invited to stay with a buxom lady called Nadia and her family after she stopped to take a photograph with us on the road. Apparently they didn't get too many cyclists through there normally. Igor was very excited at her insistence she would light the *banya* for us and we understood why later that evening, as we beat each other with birch twigs and poured hot water over ourselves in the little wooden steam room. Fire crackled in the stove, which hissed when we poured water over it. I hadn't had a proper rest in weeks and I was physically and mentally tired. I promised my body a break in Japan, once the work was done. Crowded around Nadia's kitchen table with her family, we toasted the night away with fresh-caught fish and fish eggs, home-made bread and pickles and, of course, vodka. Sleep came easily that night.

Waking before the others to give a live interview with a radio station back in England, I wished I was still in bed. Instead, after a breakfast of pancakes and more fish, we started the ride with vodka shots and tears from Nadia, who was worried I might die. She waved her Russian flag and toasted us, shouting '*Pi eckola*' [*sic*] as every other Russian did, wishing us luck.

At the same time back at home, the core team was also working hard on managing and planning, with regular emails nipping this way and that as we worked towards Japan. At times this led to mixed communications, missed expectations and frayed tempers. Later on, both George and Sara said that during the first six months of the project, as the team found its feet, it got to the point where they felt like they were having an affair with me, emailing me secretly so as to avoid conflict from the others in their lives.

In comparison with logistics, the physical effort of cycling seemed straightforward as I headed north to Lazarev on gravel and mud tracks between swathes of birch and spruce that marched for miles over the hillsides. *Hercules*' bottom bracket (the bit that the pedal crank sits in) had other ideas as it rattled to a crescendo and then ground to a halt a day's ride from the city. 'ARRRRRRRRRRRGGGGHHH!' I shouted into the silence of the forest and my echo shouted back. I had felt something amiss some weeks ago and had since paid various mechanics more qualified than me to check that all was well – and all had said nothing was wrong. Stupid bearings. A truck pulled up a few minutes later and they offered to drive me to De-Kastri, six miles away on the coast. Happy for the ride, I accepted and bundled into the cab with them. They showered me with questions: why on earth was I out here on a bike, and how on earth did I think we were going to kayak to Sakhalin? (Lots of people had already told us we were going to die.) With no bike shop for miles around, we decided that Justine and I would start kayaking from De-Kastri, rather than Lazarev 80 miles on. The weather forecast said that we had to leave the next morning, which meant no break, no breather, no practice runs: just go. Tim and Igor would return south for Tim to catch a ferry to Sakhalin and find a fix for *Hercules*, adding to his already bulging jobs' list. I got a ride back to the point where Hercules had bottomed out and then walked back to town, joining up my human-powered dots. It was the first time I had walked for more than a couple of miles and the only time that *Hercules* hadn't made the distance. Some people had asked why I bothered, saying no one would know if I skipped a bit. But, to me, that wasn't the point. I knew, and as long as I was able to join the dots myself, then I would.

In a tiny two-bedded room in a rig workers' hostel, Justine and I sorted our gear for a week in the kayaks, a task that can befuddle at the best of times. Having spent six months packing my bike, not a boat, I probably resembled a stunned sloth as I sorted through the various boxes of gear sent from home to choose spare socks, thermals for night-time, extras just in case, wash kit, camera gear, sleeping gear, food and water to stuff into waterproof dry bags. I hadn't even considered that this would be mind-jumbling in the planning and made a note that for future legs it would be handy, if possible, to increase transition times. (If it was foggy for me in preparing my kit, I imagine it must have been more so for my mum and Sara some weeks before as they did the same in my mum's front room, sorting through boxes which I had labelled before going away.) I didn't sleep well that night on account of the adrenaline and all the time spent sorting gear.

Cranes and wharfs in the middle distance reminded us of the oil industry's part in the local economy (timber and oil) while we packed the kayaks on the beach the next morning. Dense forest carpeted the cliff tops in green, stretching away up the coast. I was very conscious that I was the slowest to get ready as Justine nipped her stuff away into hatches in twenty minutes while I fumbled to get things stowed, trying to make a mental map of where I had put my spare top or waterproof jacket and which hatch the snacks were in. I wondered how I had convinced myself and others I was capable of such a challenge, because right now I felt quite useless. Pulling the top half of my drysuit over my shoulders I popped my head out through the rubber neck seal and Justine zipped me in. Having pasted my face with suncream, I zipped up my buoyancy aid, which felt like a weights' jacket, its pockets stuffed with snacks, a reservoir of drink on my back. I double-checked the rubber hatch seals and declared myself ready while demons paraded around inside me, shouting that this was ridiculous, that I was ridiculous. With no reference point and a confidence base not much above zero at this stage, I was relying on Justine's confidence that I would be OK out there and hoping that time on the water would reboost my confidence. The map we were using warned that it was not to be used for navigation purposes and was peppered with symbols for wrecks, casualties of the shallow Tatar Strait. We would be totally alone, crossing to a sparsely habited coastline, with no local boats that we could contact for assistance. We had to make safe decisions and hope that luck, and my muscles, were good to us.

We waved Tim and Igor on their way as they waved us on ours, pushing out from the beach into the calm morning. The first 20 miles following the coast on the mainland took us past sunbathing seals lying in U-bends on the shore. Some slid into the water to peer at us as we, too, slid past and peered back into their glassy eyes. White-tailed eagles sat haughtily on high bluffs, and waterfalls ribboned down to the sea. The wind picked up and rain and hail showered us in shifts. Eight hours later I paddled into the widely curving beach to finish off my first day of paddling since we had crossed to Dover 10,000 miles ago. Relaxed and happy at having stayed upright, my eyes were busy scanning the awkward heaps of driftwood high above the tide line when Justine shouted 'Saraaaaaah!', just as a curling green wave picked up my kayak and surfed me sideways, almost tipping me in. Shit: must stay focused.

Our landing routines were always variations on a theme. Surf in and land. Carry boats up the beach enough to be out of the way of the waves. Empty all the gear into our Ikea bags and head up the beach to find a camp spot. We had to construct a sleeping platform for our tents at the back of the beach, moving large pebbles to make space for them. Snack. Get changed. Carry boats up above the high-tide line. Cook dinner and sit quietly on logs while eating, watching a rainbow reflect in the wet sand, cutting through the moody skies. Get our gear ready for the morning, filling up reservoirs and pockets of snacks. Zip into our tents. Wind down and sleep.

The forecast was for north-west winds, which would create rolling side-on waves, and there would likely be tide rips ahead – not ideal conditions for my first big crossing. When we rafted up at the final headland and Justine asked if I wanted to go on and start the crossing, the sensible part of me said we should carry on up the coast to a narrower crossing point, but instead I said: 'I think we should go.' Metre-high waves rolled into and under us from the side and I tried to think about anything other than the distance to go, instead checking in with every part of my body in turn. 'So toes, how are you doing down there?' and I wiggled them, working up methodically towards my shoulders, unclenching my fists around the paddle, clenching my butt cheeks, flexing my hamstrings, rolling my shoulders.

'How are you doing?' asked Justine, patrolling nearby. She made paddling look effortless and graceful, flicking her hips in tiny movements to steer. Given that I normally chat and sing (whether she is listening or not), my quietness had already told her that I was scared. My short 'Fine' in answer to her question confirmed it.

A few hours in, and as a convincing chunk of miles slipped behind us, I realised that I had relaxed a bit and was even enjoying myself, skills coming back to me as I braced into waves. I always trusted my endurance but I had less faith in my skills. Confident enough to divert my attention from concentrating on technique to singing, I started to make up songs about Justine's little red-and-white boat and how I followed it everywhere. (Little did we know that this tradition of singing would still be alive and well five years later.) In my head, Justine was the queen of sea kayaking and I trusted her completely, questioning her decisions to add to my knowledge rather than because I doubted anything. Eight hours after striking out from the far side, a couple of miles offshore, I shouted 'Land ahoy!', the low-lying spit just visible. We rode in to Sakhalin on gentle, hushing waves – finally here after eighteen months of planning and 10,000 miles of journeying. As I pulled the grab loop of my spray deck and leaned back in the cockpit to free my legs one at a time, my hand on the deck for balance, I couldn't believe I had made it without a capsize, surviving the side waves, slaps and tide races. Justine had already hopped out of her boat and was pulling it up the beach by the toggle, camera in hand to record my triumphant landing. As I put one leg down to get out, a small wave pulled me out to sea in its backwash, tipping me off balance and rolling me out into the shallows. If only I had just spent eight hours practising my get-outs!

Over the next few days we paddled southwards along the sparse, weather-beaten west coast. Stunted trees grew at right angles to the ground as though fighting for every half degree of uprightness. Occasional wooden, weary-looking villages and fishing huts hugged low cliffs, tiny buildings peering out to sea over the edge. In the early hours of our third morning I woke to thirty-knot winds flapping the nylon tent sides onto my face. Peering through the tent door onto what could have been a different beach from the night before, I now saw a grubby white field of foam drifts, which were being flung up the sand by feisty surf. Out to sea the waves were also mostly white, thanks to the tail end of a typhoon to our south. Shouting over the wind to Justine in her tent, we agreed to a rest day and I snuggled into my nest of sleeping bag, jackets and gilets, unable to remember the last time I had had a lie-in. I even read a couple of chapters of my book, which I hadn't managed for months. After gorging on pancakes, which we cooked on the little gas stove, we wandered inland over the dunes in search of a village marked on the map. Amongst the long grass which led us in, we found abandoned chairs, a lone table, old tyres and the odd rusty vehicle resting on its axle in the sand. Only the chickens seemed brave enough to chat to us as we walked along narrow lanes between houses in search of a shop for treats and someone to talk to. A dog on a chain barked; the few people we saw just stared. Clad as we were in brightly coloured Gore-Tex and arriving on foot with no clue as to where we had come from or why, I am not that surprised.

After more sleeping and eating we were ready to paddle on again the next morning, and so was the weather. We watched occasional fishermen in wooden rowing boats tending the gill nets for salmon: pickled, poached, jarred, roasted, dried and smoked, this fish is the mainstay of the year's larder. It looked like a wild life up there, remote and raw in both weather and economics, as both danced with the seasons. I imagined that Sakhaliners must feel very far away from, even foreign to, the government in Moscow, on the other side of the continent.

The lowest depths on our map marked shoals, and paddling through the rusting hulks of giant shipwrecks confirmed it. In disappearing they were blending into the island's narrative, their long-abandoned insides now a part of the land and sea which had eroded them. What was it like to have been on board one of those ships? To fish these waters and make a living from these seas? I regretted being time-limited, wishing that I could stay longer to understand lives and cultures through their own stories rather than perceptions and assumptions from snippets of conversation and observations. Even though I had more Russian than any other new language of my journey so far, I also wished that I had bought 'teach yourself Russian' audiobooks before going away. Feeling that I couldn't afford them and yet buying various other things which I had latterly sent home, I decided that next time language would be higher up my priorities.

When we reached Alexandrovsk, now about halfway down Sakhalin and 600 miles from the capital in Yuzhno-Sakhalinsk, it was time to transition again. Through kayaking contact Greg Balyiakov, who Tim had connected with in 2010, we hooked up with local couple and outdoor enthusiasts Alex and Yulia Yemchenko. They had kindly offered to be our local fixers on

Sakhalin and drove up from Yuzhno in their 4×4 to meet us from the water and swap *Hercules* for the kayaks and return south with Justine.

They tracked me for a day while I slipped and slid my way up and down hills that were more like rivers of thick mud, cutting through the autumnal forest. Head to the floor, I bore down into sore muscles as I pushed *Hercules* on the up-slopes and tried not to let him run away on the downs. It was as much fun as it was tiring, far more exciting than a straightforward tarmac road, and I enjoyed the peace and quiet of being alone again between meetings with the wagon. As the track hugged the high-cliffed coast I looked down on the blue sea, rippled and flecked with waves and white horses, memories of similar views over different seas bringing home to mind. That night we camped in a meadow, the nearby river chattering us to sleep after an evening with our kind new friends. The next morning I struck out alone and Justine, Alex and Yulia headed to Yuzhno. I felt flat saying goodbye to Justine, even though I should only be a week behind them.

Autumn leaves cast exquisite reflections of warm reds, yellows and oranges across the peaty ponds of the marshlands. I wished my head-space was as calm, but uncertainty on the final plan for kayaking out of Russia before the visa expiry was stressing us all out. A negative monologue whirled in my head, pinning me in the tent each morning, lethargic and lacklustre. I cursed myself for sending the stove back with Justine in my bid to be fast and light, instead eating cold food and water. Of course, it felt better once I pulled myself outside and breathed in the morning, hooking panniers onto racks, rolling up my sleeping bag and taking down the tent. It is always amazing how something as simple as just getting out of the door can be the hardest part of the day, whether you are remote and alone or not.

I found it difficult to accept that I should be finding the solitude hard, annoyed that I hadn't settled into the transitions better and then getting more annoyed again for being so critical of myself. Being around others cheered me up, especially when it happened spontaneously. Like the two ten-year-olds who rode out of town with me on their bikes, goading me to keep up.

After getting talking to another family of bored teenagers who were hanging out in a bright yellow bus stop on the edge of a town, I even swapped a ride on a motorbike for a ride on *Hercules*, while a teenager barely tall enough to see over the steering wheel of his rusty clapped-out banger drove noisy, dusty laps around the block. In another sleepy village, I bought ice creams for a group of children who were playing football outside the little shop where I was stopping to stock up on snacks. The boys were eager to ask questions and the girls too shy to come close. By coincidence, that evening, while camped off a gated track some way in the forest and feeling rather down with worries at my recently low mileages, I met the grandfather of one of the ice-cream boys. He was a security guard on night patrol and had just invited me into his truck for tea.

On my final day to Yuzhno I had 170 miles to ride. I knew that if I made it, I wouldn't need to pedal the following day, and so I set my sights on it, accepting that it was going to be a long and ridiculous day but motivated by the idea of a dry bed at the end. My legs were like lead and my fingers soon grew numb in gloves already wet from the night before. Muddy tracks quickly turned me brown as passing traffic zoomed past. Early in the day I decided I wouldn't sit down for the rest of the day, afraid of losing momentum if I did. I ate standing up or squatting down while I stamped my feet to return blood to my toes, biting hunks of cheese and slurping spoonfuls of jam as I did so. It took me six hours to escape the mud and arrive on tarmac so smooth I actually knelt down to pat it. The road swung out to the east coast where a languid grey sea batted the coast like a bored teenager and I flew along. At dusk a madly waving figure at the roadside flagged me down and Yulia and Justine grinned at me from under their hoods. My toes melted into fresh woollen socks, and I layered them with plastic bags inside my shoes, my feet warm for the first time since the day before.

'Are you sure you want to keep going?' asked Justine, looking concerned, 'You can always carry on tomorrow.' I nodded through mouthfuls of cake. Breaking my rule of not sitting down, I was glad to let the car seat hold me up for half an hour after twelve hours' riding and standing. I pedalled on and on, up and down hills, my body on auto-pilot. My tea fairies delivered more goodies at the roadside a few hours later as I spun along rhythmically in the dark, *Hercules'* brilliant dynamo front light making me look like a car, apparently. My feet had screamed with cold all day long, forcing me off the bike to march my toes back to life when it became too unbearable. My legs enjoyed the stretch from the new movement. I was using a pair of dry bags as an extra layer over my gloves for token insulation, wishing that I already had the neoprene pogies that would keep my hands warm in the North American winter and boots far more substantial than my cycling shoes.

Somewhere in the middle of the night as I reached the top of a hill I heard a dog barking stage left from the buildings. Louder, closer, louder, closer – it was obviously in protection mode and taking it very seriously. Not wanting the dog to chase me, I decided to stop and stand still, talking to it as calmly as I could as it snarled and growled its way to my side, grabbing at my leg. It had its jaws around my calf when the owner appeared to investigate the ruckus and, both reassured that I was just a tired, wet cyclist, I was allowed to carry on. On and on into the depths of myself, pulling out every trick I knew to keep my legs spinning. At times I was a robot, unconscious of how I was even staying upright. At others I fought with myself just to stay on the seat, shouting rowing calls into the night from my days on the river at Oxford. I also gathered together all the people I knew and loved into an invisible peloton to help me through the miles. Being that not everyone in that group is a cyclist, I let whoever wanted to walk walk, the swimmers swim and the paddlers float and so on. Claire was on a bike. Justine was paddling. My parents were walking. My old rowing team were in an eight. As I wandered through them all, I shouted out their names to the sky and listened to their returning voices, feeling comfort that I wasn't fighting those miles alone. My peloton dissipated with the last traces of night and I was glad to have found I could call on them to such great effect. They had been as real to me as the weird psychedelic shapes and bright lines which had flown across my field of vision for the last few hours of dark. I clung on to consciousness, shaking my head to stay awake and reciting snatches of remembered lines from poems, feeling sick with lack of sleep. No wonder sleep deprivation is a form of torture.

As the earliest commuters headed in and out of Yuzhno to their day, Justine and the others arrived to escort me to the end of mine. I was euphoric at having successfully punched through the night, clocking nineteen hours riding since I had first started pedalling from the muddy roadside. After a steaming shower, I fell asleep in the armchair of my hotel room, mug of tea still in hand. In bed, I fell into that very best sort of unconsciousness that swallows you after such frazzling effort. Brutal as it was, that big ride was one of my favourites for exactly the reasons that most people might think it miserable: the 40 miles of mud at the start, the screaming toes, the single-minded focus on getting through, where everything else falls away as surplus. In those sorts of battles you can often feel the most alive. After a run of down days in which I had bashed myself for low mileages, it was also a confidence boost: I had pushed beyond endurance and I had also found a way to tap into my invisible peloton, increasing my pedal power many times over. Often it is that lightest muscle of all which pulls the strongest – the mind.

The next day I watched the snowy blanket knit itself over *Hercules'* luggage and frame, before wiping it off to uncamouflage the dark colours of my clothes and panniers so that I could be seen. Trucks and cars flew past, slinging wheelfuls of heavy slush at me in brown sideways thumps, and I lived for the bus stops where I could shelter and warm my hands on the tea flask. In between sips I returned blood to my frozen toes with lunges and jumping jacks. It didn't seem that long ago that Gao had been doing the same in China, trying to impress me on his first day on the bike. This was my last day of riding on the wild island of Sakhalin, two months on from the Gobi.

I kept on moving, hoping the weather wasn't a harbinger of things to come. Influenced by Siberian airstreams from the mainland and wet air from sea on all sides, it would not have been surprising to Sakhaliners to have spent the last four weeks with

snow. We still had two serious open water crossings to make –
one from Sakhalin to Hokkaido and another from there to Honshu
– for which we needed settled conditions. I dried out a bit towards
day's end as I turned off onto a coastal track of mud and sand,
the 4×4 following with Justine and the kayaks. The next morning
the inside of my tent fly cracked like sheet glass as I unzipped it,
layered with ice and frost. Diamonds danced on the water under
a fresh sky as we packed our kayaks on the beach. I worried that
I wasn't quick enough at getting ready and Justine confirmed it
as she paced around, sighing, fiddling with toggles and stretching.
Or maybe it was in my head. I wanted to be as quick as her one
day, but for now I had to accept that I would battle daily to
remember my routine from the day before and that all gains were
useful. Pushing away from shore felt good.

From time to time as we paddled south towards Cape Krillon,
at the end of the island, we came across the last camps of the
salmon season, the only signs of people for miles around in this
verdant wild stretch. Outside the huddles of wooden buildings
hung lines of pink and silver fillets drying in the sun like laundry.
Men worked nets in the shallows at river heads, looking up to
wave as they clocked us, or else they stood and stared, scratching
their beards and rolling cigarettes. On our first night we pulled
ashore at one camp and asked the lone fisherman if we could
pitch our tent, hoping that increasing our population would mean
that bears were less likely to bother us. Petrov said no, as he was
worried that we would get eaten by bears. Instead, the gentle
old man quietly insisted we sleep inside the little cabins. We didn't
even need to look at each other to accept the kind offer – the
idea of removing tent packing from the morning routine clinched
it. He showed us through to a room of simple bunk beds and
rough woollen blankets where pictures of scantily clad ladies
competed with each other for the attention of fishermen who
had been here before and would come here again. This was the
only sort of 'bare' that we had seen – so far there had been
nothing more than footprints in the sand. He walked us outside
to show us the little long-drop and to stare out to sea, the silence
between us as natural as the land around us. It was a gentle cap

to our day of banter and chat and I wondered at the storms that must lash his solitary outpost. Sporadic, considered questions showed that he, too, wondered at ours. My sense is that we were both outsiders, of sorts, at least for a part of our lives, and I asked if he was the only one here, and if he was married. I couldn't work out from his explanation if his wife was dead or living some miles away, or whether he wasn't married at all. Any of the answers seemed plausible as many men up here in the north lived a double life of home and away, working on oil rigs or living out in the salmon camps for months at a time, leaving their families in rural villages. Watching him throw corn for the hens and top up the hay for the milker, I sensed that these were his family for now.

We went through to the wooden kitchen with our stove and food bags to cook dinner on one of the long benches which divided the room up like swimming pool lanes and, without talking, Petrov lit the gas ring hob and nodded that we should use that instead. Smiles said as much as words and he returned to his book, reading by the light of a paraffin lamp. He gently declined our offer to join us for a bowl of pasta and salami and I wondered if his usual evening company was a shot or two of vodka. The next day, after porridge and fresh milk, we ferried dry bags and boats back to the water's edge, which was some way further out than the night before. Petrov helped and observed, testing and tapping our kit, which I guessed was quite different from his own boat rig in material and form, if not in function. He rubbed Gore-Tex between his fingers, tested the sharpness of our knives which we kept cinched on the front of our buoyancy aids, tapped at fibreglass and held our feather-light paddles. Wading out into the shallows to help us launch, we thanked him and paddled away as he stood quietly with hands in pockets. I looked over my shoulder every couple of minutes to wave and the last time I did he was still there, standing on the beach.

After weeks of being told that bears were going to eat me and of wanting to see one, we were finally rewarded. The first was pawing through the tangle of seaweed on the tideline, unaware that we were watching, masked as we were by the stiff offshore breeze. An hour later, I spied some black lumps on the beach in the distance which looked like more. As Justine and I put on a sprint for a better view, the black blobs grew legs and then started to scramble up the muddy cliff into the forest, for berries or shelter, I guessed. It was a sow leading her two small cubs, who both seemed more intent on playing than going home. Bears the world over were preparing for hibernation, gorging on salmon and berries to gain fat reserves which would power them until spring. Like many mothers in the animal kingdom, the sows would work hardest of all, still suckling young cubs. The more weight they put on now, the more likely they were to survive. For that reason, we were pretty sure that they wouldn't be too interested in us, but still we obeyed good bear routines and kept food and toiletries away from our tents and cooked downwind of our camps. We had pepper spray just in case and only fired a bear flare once when we spotted eyes reflecting in our torch beam. It was probably just a fox.

I have always loved the boundary between land and sea, glimpsing both worlds from both directions. Being in a kayak allows you to explore the nuances of the meeting point and spend time on each side of it. We threaded between rocks to have lunch in tiny coves that bigger boats could not reach, or hauled up on to shingle beaches below sheer cliffs which meant you could only come in via the water. At the end of the island, at Cape Krillon, Russian guards held lookout from ageing watch-towers for people doing just that. Japan was only 30 miles south and they had never been easy neighbours. Therefore it shouldn't have been surprising that a guard was waiting for us on the shore as we picked our way through the channels at low tide, trying to get around to the west coast. He was young, maybe we were his first ever passport check, and I suspect he, too, was glad that his superiors radioed that he could wave us on. The watchtower pivoted around in my field of vision as we rounded the cape, doing a very good job of reminding me that this was a military zone and I was glad to be clear of it, sweeping past towards a curve of white sand. We surfed in through rows of short, fizzing waves, aiming for the two 4×4s which waited for us, the fire burning a warm welcome. Through our fixer Alex, we had hired local adventurer Max and his pals to drive down to meet us and then take us northwards to Korsakov, a port of entry. This was the only place that we could officially stamp out of the country, which we planned to do as soon as we got there. Meanwhile, Alex and Tim were chartering a boat that would carry us from Korsakov back down to Cape Krillon, and drop us outside Russian waters. From there Justine and I would paddle back in towards shore, intersecting a GPS point which we would set the following day with a morning paddle out to sea. This was all in the name of joining up my human-powered dots en route to Japan, which lay just across the water now. (I'm sorry if the logistics have confused you; it took us many months and brains to figure out how to make this work too.) That night we feasted on a cauldron of stew and celebrated the fact that we were there – not just at the end of Sakhalin, but also that magic mix of sharing food under the stars and the moon with the warmth of friends and fire.

The drive north the next day showed us a different view of the land we had just paddled past. Max guided us with boyish energy through left-over warrens of bunkers and rusting artillery rigs the size of minibuses from the world wars and Japan's previous occupation. Graffiti in both languages told stories of unknown lives and I was grateful that a knee injury at nineteen had put paid to the army scholarship which was due to lead me to military service post degree.

Further up the coast, after lots of off-roading and sliding down muddy tracks we stopped at a tiny hamlet to look at more rusting metal which told another story of neighbourly struggles. Orphaned by a hunter's shotgun as a cub, an adult grizzly bear as big as a horse sat on its haunches in a cage while another padded and circled in a cell next door. This one had been retired from a circus and, like the orphan, being accustomed to humans it was unsafe to rewild it. Just as we had paddled through rusting shipwrecks, I now looked into eyes where bears had once been, their hulls now empty. While the orphaned bear slurped noisily from a bowl of soup that a local lady held for him, his long claws and huge jaws redundant now in this canteen, the circus bear padded its fetid cell. The thin bars underlined the fine line and huge chasm between freedom and captivity, and I was glad that we had seen so few bears in Russia. The more that bears avoid people, the longer the two will coexist.

Tim flew to Japan ahead of us, accompanied by *Hercules* and the gear, having organised the charter boat with Alex. I wasn't convinced by the boat owner's politician answer about how prac- tised the crew were at dropping small boats over the side at sea. 'These men very strong,' he kept saying, and I hoped that it would be calm the next morning when we planned to start paddling. I gave Alex my expedition jacket and hugged him in thanks. As for so many expeditions, local knowledge is gold, and he and his wife Yulia, and friends Greg and Max had been so supportive from the very start of our planning. They, too, wanted to kayak to Japan one day, and I recognised that sense of living vicariously through helping another on their way.

Once we had chugged out through the port, we busied ourselves with preparing for the La Pérouse Strait, the stretch of water between Sakhalin and Japan's north island of Hokkaido. The Japanese call it the Soya Strait. We aimed to be halfway across at slack water, when the tide switches and is at its least powerful, so Justine worked out headings based on the direction of the ebb and flow and the weather forecast, to maximise the useful pushes and reduce zigzagging. Having not actually found anyone who had kayaked the strait, we relied on whatever data we could find from bigger boats and buoys, confirming again that wedding guest quip from my first night in Russia: 'no roads, only destinations'. We talked the captain through our plans, working out how close to the border of the Russian waters he could drop us to reduce the mileage we had to paddle back in for our GPS fix. Then we went out on deck to check and sort the kayaks so that they were ready to lower into the water when we got there the next morning. As I packed a food bag and a clothes bag into my forward hatch I noticed that the internal waterproof bulkhead separating the cockpit and the front of the boat had been shoved loose, perhaps an aftershock of the crush injury in transit. In that state, a capsize could mean a sinking and so I spent the last hour awake with my head inside *Nelson*, jamming it back into place with almost everything sticky and waterproof that I could find in the repair kit. The epoxy would have to wait until Japan.

The next morning we got up, got dressed and went over the side into our kayaks. Thankfully it was millpond calm. Now just over 12 miles offshore from the cape and west of our waypoint, which was 3 miles out to sea, we headed off into the mist, aiming to use the south-east-setting current to help get us back for our GPS fix (the charter boat returned north). We were alone now with 40 miles of paddling ahead, probably a twelve-hour paddling day. Kudos to Justine for being up for it – not only were we paddling extra miles on an already serious crossing, but twenty of them were illicit. Five years later, I wonder if it was worth the risk, just for the sake of joining up dots and sticking to my human-powered plan. Still, at the time it felt like it was. 'Do you know where we are?' shouted Justine after four hours of paddling in choppy conditions. We yahooed and laughed for a moment before turning around. I was feeling more settled as a paddler, if not as a trespasser, as we headed back out to sea, pointing south-west to counter the east-setting current.

Invariably Justine paddled ahead of me and I plodded on behind, imagining a line tying me to her so that she could pull me forward. I recited poems or composed blogs when I wasn't concentrating on just staying upright, whereas Justine said she favoured number-crunching imaginary sums. So for a lot of those twelve hours we were each in a world of our own, coming together whenever one of us felt we wanted it or if Justine thought that I needed it for a confidence boost. Every hour marked the ritual raft-up to eat and wee, compare notes and celebrate or curse the GPS track, depending on progress. 'We need to paddle faster,' mumbled Justine through mouthfuls of cheese while I daubed more suncream on my face. I was glad that out in the middle we had no landmarks to remind us that we were being dragged backwards in every rest break and repad-dling the mile just lost. We could paddle side by side for an hour and barely talk to each other or we could chatter for a few. I generally narrated the day with singing, though Justine might not describe it quite so politely. I jukeboxed through every song in my memory and made up new ones, mostly around an absolute earworm of a crap tune.

I often visualise my mileage as a meter of something like an old weighing scales, with the entire crossing divided into smaller chunks, rounded up in case of needing to paddle further. As each mile falls away, the dial moves on and, once chunks of fives or threes or whatever makes sense are complete, that whole block clears. Literally imagining a shortening chunk of miles to run and seeing the stack of covered miles clearing is really powerful and gives me tangible goals to hang my toil on. Snack breaks stand as oases and I plan what I am going to do and in what order as my clock approaches the hour, for I am the self-appointed Mistress of Snacks. Justine often says she doesn't eat much on the water, and yet somehow manages to nibble through Snickers and granola bars and count out the final handful of cranberries into equals. I think the memory mismatch is down to her being eleven years older than me, and frequently express this opinion to wind her up.

The final quarter of those twelve hours had dragged as we had been pulled away from land and out to sea and I used everything I could find to keep my shoulders turning. 'COME. ON. OOTS!' I would shout into the air, pedalling my feet against the footplate to try and add some rotation and extra power to my stroke. 'Push, pull, push, pull, push, pull' was a rather boring mantra compared to the 'Shit and fuck and bloody hell' one which I had made up as a teenager in some cross country race. 'You are weak, they are strong!' had come from my racing days at Oxford, and 'Master of my fate, captain of my soul' was taken from a favourite poem, 'Invictus'.

Rounding the wall into Wakkanai harbour, we pulled ashore onto a concrete slipway amongst rows of small wooden upturned boats. Justine and I high fived and hugged, both glad that there was no more singing for now. It felt like everything in me creaked as I got out of my kayak, and even Justine the Machine conceded that she felt a bit tired. We pottered about with food and boats until Tim and a welcoming party from the local town hall arrived a couple of hours later, greeting us with flowers and a banner, apparently as excited as we were that we had finally made it to Japan.

6

'We are all one': Asia

Japan | Hokkaido to Honshu | Kayak, bike and preparation time | Autumn 2011 – Spring 2012 | 1,000 miles

Arching my back to try and stretch out some of its protests about the lack of rest, I wriggled down into the warm hug of my sleeping bag. Knowing that I would wake later with excruciating pain, I had already popped a couple of ibuprofen or 'vitamin I', as I have heard them called. At this moment it was the only way I could stitch together the miles, in the same way that the fishermen on this north-west coast of Hokkaido were patching up their windows ready for the winter storms. With a single day presenting itself as a possible clear weather window for our final kayak crossing to Honshu in six days' time, I was sprinting south on *Hercules* to try and make it. Given that I hadn't had a proper rest day since the windswept day on the beach on Sakhalin and had now been on the go for over six months, it felt like a sort of survival. I sensed it did for Tim and Justine as well, for they, too, were tired and ready to be home now. Having only got married a week before leaving, Tim had currently spent most of his married life with us. I would miss them when they left, finally getting my head around the transitions even with the challenge of no sleep and continued complexities in onwards logistics. For now, Tim and Justine buzzed ahead of me in the hire car, laying out picnics of Japanese rice balls, fruit and granola bars and filling up my water bottles. All I needed to do was ride.

Through the pastoral rolling north of Hokkaido I was reminded of my childhood in Rutland, now nearly half a planet away. Seaweed hung from washing lines and I envied its stillness. White-gloved traffic marshals (both human and mechanical) bowed as I entered and left the sulphur-lit tunnels which blitzed through cliffs. Looking for distraction, I busied myself noticing contrasts between Japan and Russia. Perfectly manicured fields versus the taiga hillsides exploding with autumn. Neat little houses stood quietly by themselves, and in crammed streets thick power cables slung loosely between buildings in webs, threading buildings and lives together.

Six days after arriving on Hokkaido I arrived at the wooded bay of the small boat harbour at Hakodate, at the southern end of the island. It was late, the surrounding hillsides aglow with the lights of small buildings. Tim had already pitched our tents amongst the driftwood and salted paraphernalia of boats and boat things, and I got ready for bed wishing that there were more hours between sleep and paddling. Justine projected a five-hour paddle across the Tsugaru Strait the next day, our biggest challenge likely to be avoiding being run down by the frequent ferries and fishing boats which zipped this way and that. How wrong we were.

Firstly, I had crashed. It felt like I had nothing left to burn and was literally rolling from snack to snack, food input and energy output in sync. The next morning we set off paddling due south to counter the strong east-setting current, aiming to avoid being pulled out to sea, missing land. After the first five miles the current changed and we were pushed northwards, essentially backwards, almost faster than we could paddle. Our hourly stops were even more hurried than normal as we were pulled away from our target. This meant the first part of the next hour was purely making up the lost ground, clocking on average one mile made good per hour, three times slower than normal. Cargo ships, fishing boats and ferries charged out of the mist in front of us and birds wheeled here and there or sat in small groups on the water, waiting, watching. As we had hoped, the current weakened in the final couple of miles and we straightened our course towards shore and the squat houses which sat behind concrete breakwaters.

Soya Misaki, Aomori prefecture of Honshu. We were there. I rolled out of my boat to lie motionless on the floor for a few minutes, staring up into the flat grey sky. My drysuit felt clammy and my hair was soaked. I inspected my sloughing wrinkled palms and relaxed into the idea that, for all the challenges and changes, collectively we had solved the Far Eastern Question in one of the most extraordinary team efforts I had ever been a part of.

By sheer luck we had managed to come ashore outside a B & B and, being out of tourist season the fishing-mad owner had space for us. Tim arrived with the car and *Hercules* and we spent a night feasting on a Japanese smorgasbord of soup, rice, fish, pickles, scallops and jellied things. The owner proudly showed us black-and-white photos of him posing with 400 lb tuna that hung from gaffes to stand taller than he was. We sorted gear, racked the kayaks and I caught up with admin, looking forward to a less frantic final few weeks of the ride. My goal was Choshi, on the east coast in Chiba prefecture, about halfway down the island. This is where I planned to launch from in my rowing boat the next year on my Pacific row.

Setting off on my bike again, I was soon in the mountains of Towada-Hachimantai National Park where roads looped around slopes ablaze with the bronze and golds of beech, oak and bright cedar. I enjoyed the contrast with the mental and physical swamping I had felt in recent weeks. Swims in mountain lakes purged any tensions and amused the locals, who seemed surprised that anyone would do such a thing, preferring instead that their lake experiences be observational at this end of the year. My sense was that here, nature was something to be afraid of, to be packaged and delivered in manageable, safe chunks. Everything that could be neatly railed in or chained off seemed to be, perhaps as a way of imposing order and control over something which is, at essence, inherently uncontrollable. I prefer my nature, wild and free, unspoiled and unpeopled; more like the Russian version, I suppose, bleak and rugged. People's fear of bears up in the mountains was tangible, and perhaps not surprisingly so, given that warning posters around campsites were of cartoon snarling, salivating bears with demonic eyes. Hordes of overdressed hikers piled out of buses to follow ordered trails through forests or along riverbanks, their bear bells jangling from backpacks. I preferred to stay away from so many people and imagined that the bears would, too. I camped one evening near Tazawa-ko with two

Japanese guys out for a weekend trip with their inflatable kayak. As we sat round the campfire, toasting marshmallows and singing tipsy renditions of Beatles songs, they tinkled their tiny bear bells as a heads-up to any would-be man-eater.

Mostly I camped alone. Under pergolas, in fields, on picnic tables, campsites and car parks I slept in or out of my tent. One night I inadvertently checked into what I later found out was called a 'sex hotel', which could be rented by the hour. As I clocked mirrors hanging from the ceilings and noticed that the drinks cabinet didn't contain drinks but sex toys, I understood why the attendant had looked so confused as I assured her that, except for *Hercules*, I was quite sure that I would be alone for the night.

After the mountains I turned east for the coastal region of Tohoku, curious to see what life was like there now, what had happened and how things were changing. It had been devastated by a huge earthquake and tsunami in March, just before I started out from Tower Bridge, its effects reaching far inland in some places where the land was flat and the water unchecked. It had caused a major nuclear incident at TEPCO's Daiichi power plant near the city of Fukushima rendering acres of land an evacuation zone due to radiation concerns; people had even asked me if I would avoid Japan because of it.

I cycled out to the coastal city of Ishinomaki and rode quietly along the seafront and through town, swallowing silent tears. It was frightening to think of being caught up in such a catastrophe, or indeed to be a survivor, trying to carry on. Many had fled, never to return. There were high suicide rates. Pedalling past vast piles of twisted, ruined vehicles which formed something like cliff tops along the seafront, adding ugly metallic relief to a once flat plain, I reflected on the humbling potency of nature and our insignificance as humans. It was a bleak contrast to the damage and destruction I had witnessed so far on my journey in the opposite direction; that of humanity wreaking disaster on the natural world. Cranes and diggers moved about on massive tips, loading and piling and sorting. Queues of trucks shifted rubble from ruined sites, taking it on to cities that were being forced into accepting some of the load, local services overwhelmed. Tiny impromptu shrines with photos, pinwheels, flowers and fruits memorialised lost loved ones. Many bodies were never found, either washed out to sea or buried beneath the sludge. Houses stood silent, rotting, clocks stuck in time; skeleton reminders of communities which once thrived in this busy fishing port.

I sat cross-legged on the sea wall looking out to the ocean that had rolled in again and again and again on that early March day. The timelessness of the sea against the long-lasting devastation it had left behind sat in painful juxtapositon. Whole classes of children had drowned with their teachers as they tried to escape the flooding, caught out by their own guidelines of only needing to reach a certain height above seawater by a tsunami which had exceeded all recent norms. Everywhere, sea walls had been overwhelmed and, in some coastal areas, waves had swamped thirty-metre high cliffs.

Belongings without owners were scattered throughout the damaged areas of town, waiting to be found, buried or carried out to sea again. Trees had been uprooted, cars upturned and buildings twisted in odd, awkward poses like metallic driftwood. Lying on its side in the central reservation of one road was a giant red cylindrical tank which I assumed had ended up here when the water receded. Someone had painted a mural on it of a floating bottle with a label saying *We are all one*. Whatever the intention of the artist, it spoke to me of togetherness, equality and connnectedness.

The tsunami had reached as far south as Choshi, and from Tohoku I headed back inland for a few hundred miles before turning east to dip my toe in the ocean. At Choshi Marina I wheeled between and underneath the hulls of the yachts and motor-cruisers tied to the floor – these were the ones that had survived. Elsewhere ruined boats lay in crumpled heaps, ready for removal or repair. Nearly every one of the floating pontoons had been removed from the water.

The day before I had arrived at the town hall in Choshi after 100 miles of riding in sheeting rain. A welcome committee all dressed in red and yellow silks had clapped me in and wrapped me in towels. When I met with the mayor, he asked me not to die on the ocean. I said I would do my best. I cycled to Tokyo to pause and rest. By now it was the middle of November, meaning I had about five months to recover and to prepare for the Pacific. This had always been the plan, given the seasonal constraints of getting from Russia to Japan in the first place. Joints in my back and legs needed to be massaged and stretched back to full function after such a swift run of miles from England on a heavy bike and loaded kayak – especially given that I had been woefully lax in my stretching.

I spent the first month in the mountains west of Tokyo in a cabin loaned by a friend of a friend from home. Each week I went into Tokyo on the bullet train for physio and massage and also spent a week with George, who flew out to visit, and another week with one of the young associates from Accenture, who had won a fitness competition as a prize as part of our engagement programme with the journey. We made some team changes, too. Having learned a lot through the first year of the expedition, we revised processes and budgets, plans and roles. Tim moved on and we also brought on a new media manager in the spring, Jenny Ellery.

In December I returned to Ishinomaki to volunteer for a week with the NGO It's Not Just Mud, who support various local clean-up and recovery projects as part of the ongoing efforts to support community regeneration. It was an international melting pot in the volunteers' house; some people like me were there for a week, while others like Yannick and Colin had been there for months. We bleached and scrubbed and power-washed ruined but still standing houses, treating the wooden frames for mould or removing stuff that was beyond repair. We shovelled dust and dried mud into bags to be taken away. We helped host a Christmas party for children and their families.

The most profound day of all was the one we spent kneeling in the silently falling snow helping Matsumura-san create a flower garden where her house once stood. The flattened residential area was now a condemned zone. Matsumura-san wanted to frame the colourful plants in a heart-shape made of rubble, a mark of her hope for the future and commitment to carrying on. She told us how her eleven-year-old daughter had been at home alone when the tsunami struck and had rung her repeatedly to ask her what she should do. Busy in their sports shop in town at the time, Matsumura-san and her husband hadn't heard the phone. With no answer as to what to do, her daughter had run from their house to the school evacuation point at the bottom of the hill. Incoming waves had shoved cars half a mile inland and up into the school, causing a huge fire which forced everyone to flee up the hill. With nowhere to run, 80 of 100 children perished along with their teachers. Pairs of little shoes and boots sat obediently in rows along a scorched wall in tribute. It took Matsumura-san and her daughter some hours to be reunited. After finishing the flower garden at her house, Matsumura-san went to where her elderly neighbour's house had been. She knelt alone as she scooped out earth, pressing it around some pansies and wiping tears from her eyes. Her neighbour hadn't survived. Buildings would never be built on that particular stretch of land again, and as with many other places, it seems they should never have been built there in the first place. All along the coastline ancient stone tablets had been found marking maximum water levels of previous tsunamis, cautioning against building near to the water again.

Meeting Matsumura-san, seeing people's efforts to rebuild their lives and hearing tales of the increasing suicide rate as people couldn't face asking for help or leaving their homelands, I felt humbled. I felt privileged that people like Matsumura-san had shared their personal journeys and found myself looking at my expedition as futile, questioning if I should just stop and go home and do something with more direct tangible benefit to other people. It felt selfish, somehow, and it took a while to reaccept that the journey was spreading good energy in its own, small way. I still believed in it and so I carried on.

In January I moved south of Tokyo to the Miura Peninsula, into another cabin. This old harbour master's office at Kasa Zima Marina was just twenty steps from the sea, overlooking Saigama Bay. Mount Fuji was my neighbour and my hosts were the gentle and genteel Mr and Mrs Ootake, whom I had been put in touch with via a kayaking contact who had stayed here on his circum-navigation of Japan a few years ago. Being so close to the water but with no obligation to cross it just yet was refreshing, but it also meant that if an earthquake struck close to shore, I wouldn't stand a chance. During earthquakes I froze while everything shook. Here, too, they had suffered damage from the tsunami back in March. For my few months by the sea I came to think of the Ootakes and their children and grandchildren, who visited regularly, as my Japanese family. In an interview for the BBC, Mr Ootake was asked what he thought of me and I nearly cried when he told the reporter that I was like a granddaughter. A warm and smiling man, he still went into the main Tokyo office which ran his various companies every day, being chauffeured an hour or more each way by one of the marina staff, Nori-san. I sometimes went with them and we sat in the back together, exchanging quick notes on how we both were. 'Fine, Sarah-san, but it's a little chilly today.' Content that all was well, we both slept all the way to the city.

A knock at the door to my cabin often meant a summons from Mrs Ootake, via her home help, to join them for dinner in their luxurious flat, which overlooked the marina. Holding on to my arm or using her walking stick, Mrs Ootake hobbled to the balcony across the lacquered floor and threw bits of apple to the black kites who circled practically every bit of sky that you looked at on this stretch of coast. Often when I was out in the boatyard I would hear a faint 'Sarah-san, Sarah-san' and look up to the balcony to see her diminutive hunched frame beaming and waving at me, beckoning me up. Once my rowing boat *Gulliver* had finally been delivered in February, she stood and watched even more often, with her binoculars trained on me. If she ventured down to visit the boat, Mama-san, the yard manager, helped me translate. I never actually knew what Mama-san's name was because the other workers also called her this. I can see why, too: she mothered everyone in whatever way she could. Unlocking the door to my cabin after a packed week of travelling talks and admin, one of the marina men said something in Japanese.

Mama-san translated: 'He says welcome home, because we miss you when you go away.' I assured them the feeling was mutual.

Home has meant different things to me throughout my life – an ever-changing roll of people, places and, perhaps, ideas. On the ride my home had been wherever I was with *Hercules* or in the kayaks with Justine. I loved my home by the sea in Japan, both for the relative space and quiet and the fact I could go from my door to being on the water in a matter of minutes, and for the people, too. I enjoyed watching the comings and goings of fishermen in the bay and often saw them peering from their boats into a glass-bottomed bucket in search of sea cucumbers or raking seaweed and doling it out to neighbours in bucketloads. The fish restaurant underneath the Ootakes' flat grew ever busier as the months grew warmer and the marina staff themselves, mostly ageing, pottered about cleaning and fixing boats.

I went up to Tokyo fairly regularly to give school talks or meet with new friends. I had met Mike through the embassy and his love of cycling, and I met Kelly and Kaz through Mike. At the international Christmas dinner that Kelly and Kaz hosted, I met Tari, a gregarious and caring Indonesian expat. We all cooked and drank gin together, rode our bikes, visited *onsens* and went on hikes and snowshoeing trips. I was glad that being static meant I had more time for new friends – so many times in the journey so far I had wished I could have hung out with people for longer, seasonal pressures forcing me onwards all the time.

I trained in an old glass-fronted room overlooking the marina, where I sweated long hours on a borrowed rowing machine and repped circuits with some basic kit. Out on the water I did laps of the bay on a sit-on-top kayak or rowed *Gulliver* himself, once he had been shipped out to join me. All the shipped kit and equipment needed sorting, too, and happy, absorbed hours floated by while I tinkered and tuned this and that in the gentle, satisfying way that boats need, running through different scenarios and set-ups to find the best solutions to storage or operation. Doing some capsize drills one day, we realised that the forward cabin door had been jammed locked by errant kit careering out of the bungees, meaning that we needed to drill through the internal locking pin to disable it and ensure it wouldn't happen at sea. I wanted a door that I could shut tight, not one that I couldn't open.

I spent equally long hours at my desk on admin, both on the rowing stage and even on onwards stages all the way to the Atlantic leg. Even though that was a projected year and a half and many thousands of miles away from now, we anticipated that this would be the most static time and head-space I would have for a while. Finances needed to be spreadsheeted, jiggled and magicked out of nowhere as we calculated that current and projected income would not be enough to get home, given that my insurance policy had been many times more expensive than we had first thought and the Russia–Japan leg had been, too. This meant finding new sponsors or persuading existing supporters to renegotiate. The machine needed to make the journey happen was an ever-growing puzzle of supporters, inputs and learning.

Based on historic weather data and previous North Pacific rowing attempts which he had managed, my weather router Lee Bruce and I had decided we would aim to go on standby from April 20th. That is to say that the goal was for *Gulliver* and me to be packed up in Choshi Marina, ready to leave at the first suitable and safe opportunity thereafter. Through all the arrangements for transporting *Gulliver* up to Choshi from my winter marina home in Miura, and importing my food into the country and then having it released from customs, I learned that Japanese bureaucracy is almost as slow and frustrating as ocean currents can be, spinning you around in circles to dump you a few days (or weeks) later in the same place, or even backwards of it. Hierarchies played a part, as did the oddity of my imports and plans – and the very Japanese trait of not liking to say no or disappoint. There were all sorts of diversions, delaying tactics and silences which, for someone brought up to ask and answer direct questions, was rather frustrating. Still, in the end, it eventually worked and we had rower, boat and eight months' worth of food and supplies stacked in pallets at the Choshi Marina ready to be melded together into a self-sufficient unit.

Just weeks before Justine had been due to fly out to Japan to support my final departure preparations she punctured her lung in a biking accident. At short notice, Ricardo, who had been my weather router for my Indian Ocean row in 2009, flew out to join me for ten days of splitting up, sorting and waterproofing all the food that had arrived in the crate, before packing everything on board. Ric took care of my phone to help ease pressure and made sure that I did basic things like eating and drinking, too, or shielded me enough from interested folks to let me get on uninterrupted – leaving me to focus on getting my head ready to go. In the build-up to leaving I recognised the familiar swinging emotions and adrenaline that come with a departure and I tried to make the adrenaline my friend, letting fears have their voice and nagging noises do their bit in a controlled space, letting the excitement drive me on.

Another British rower, Charlie Martell, was preparing to leave Choshi at the same time as me on his own North Pacific rowing attempt, in a sister boat to mine, *Blossom*. We had collaborated on the boat design after my Indian Ocean row and our two boats sat on tyres or trailer in the marina near each other while we both worked hard to be ready. Charlie's brother-in-law Adrian had helped me with PR for my Indian Ocean row and so it was doubly good to be able to have a beer or two with them and talk about the rows ahead with someone in the same position. I knew that I would enjoy being in contact while afloat, that having an ally on the waves would feel positive and connecting.

I was in daily contact with my weather router Lee as he sent projections, looking for a departure window. This meant a stable pressure system with a gentle offshore wind for a few days, creating the safest possible window for *Gulliver* and me to get away safely out to sea. At this time of year it was not a given, as spring storms, described by locals as 'bomb low pressures', were still whipping through. It didn't surprise me when the standby date passed. I focused on trying to get decent sleep and rest and on tying up final things from land, but I found it hard to switch off, knowing that I could only get close to that once I was out at sea and settled into the rhythm of the ocean. April 29th looked like an opening to launch and everyone rallied around to get me ready to leave, Ric now back home in Portugal. Local fixers Kay and Kaz drove me for a few hours to the passport office to stamp out of the country, as they had done with two other British rowers a few years before. Choshi Marina manager Kawasaki-san presented me with a tiny plaque he had made which said *Team Choshi*, to remind me of the nickname I had given his team. The customs officials and coastguard came in their uniforms and hard hats to inspect my boat and equipment and a shower of press photographed us as they did so.

On my final full day ashore, my closest friends Tari, Kelly, Tracey and Mike came out from Tokyo to stay with me and we visited an *onsen* overlooking the sea. I was warmed, calm and excited all at once, glad to be sharing my final night on land. After dinner we sewed on British badges to my clothes, fuelled by gin and giggles, while I wrapped lists of emails, phone calls and boxing the last load of things to send home. I checked my inbox at midnight, just before I went to bed. There was an email from Lee with *Gale forecast* in the title. Previously forecast to blow itself out to the south of me, it was now due to blow right over the top of Choshi in a few days' time, making it unsafe to launch. Heading out knowingly into such rough conditions would be reckless, so there was no choice but to postpone. Kelly wrapped me in a hug and I breathed deep, feeling bad that lots of folks would appear at the marina first thing in the morning expecting to wave me off over the horizon.

After a fitful few hours with my eyes closed, if not asleep, the new day was strikingly bright with sunshine and the sea calm. We arrived at the marina to find the crowd of well-wishers busily taking photos and admiring *Gulliver*, who waited for me next to the jetty. I felt nervous about telling everyone of the decision, even though, of course, when I did so it was relief, not disappointment, that greeted the news. People just wanted me to be safe. I invited everyone to join me for rides on *Gulliver*, padding down the wooden gangway in bare feet to climb aboard my blue boat.

Throughout the day I showed people around the boat and took many of them aboard, smiles and questions aplenty. I explained the three main parts of the boat: the back cabin with electronics panel, storage and a sleeping bunk just as wide as I am, and a front cabin for storage. The deck in the middle was where I rowed on a moving seat and there were storage hatches below that, too. The cabins were covered in solar panels. For some children it was their first time on any sort of boat. Children sat on the cabin roof with legs dangling or stood with their heads out of the open hatch at the back of the boat, waving at parents on shore. I rowed with little ones on my lap, letting them hold the oars, their hands inside mine, dwarfed by the wooden handles. Others powered us along while I manoeuvred the rudder lines. One gentleman handed his four-year-old grandson over the rails for us to take out and he leaned over the gunwale, trailing his hands in the water and licking the salt from them as we paddled, totally at ease. An autistic teenager pulled hard on one oar, relaxing into it in a way I hadn't seen him do on shore. I was glad and grateful that the weather had changed my departure plans for that day.

7

Stormed: Pacific Ocean

Pacific Ocean | Row | Summer 2012 | 800 miles

The carbon-fibre safety rail dented my shins as my toes gripped the gunwale edge, my calves enjoying the stretch as I dropped my heels into the air and dipped a toe, and then a foot, in the cool water, swirling it about. Even my breathing sounded loud. I was naked but for a spit-smeared swimming mask and the fish-hook necklace that I always wore on a leather string around my neck. I played with it in my lips, pushing my chin into the leather band, just as I had done for thousands of miles and many months up to now. I had bought it from a wandering soul from his blanket in a park in Australia, just before I set out on my Indian Ocean row. The Maori emblem was to keep me safe at sea.

'Bloody hell, Outen! Why are you such a wimp?' I shouted at myself as one foot and then the other landed back on deck so that I could clear my mask and find my courage. I had been poised to leap for nearly half an hour: I was trying to have a swim. So far only my head had made it over the side, owling around under the surface to check for Things From Below before sliding back through the safety rail to yelp with delight at my brief bravery. *Gulliver* rocked at the movement in proud approval; the water rippled gently in applause sending concentric rings across the mirror-like surface. An albatross flapped languidly with M-shaped wing beats in the middle distance as I caught my breath and salt water tingled my lips. I was living out another cliché – this was the calm before an incoming storm. Within twenty-four hours we could be in survival conditions: Typhoon Mawar was currently hundreds of miles to my south, over the Philippines, tracking northwards. Lee's most recent forecasts projected that it would be downgraded to a mere tropical storm by the time it reached us, losing power as it recurved out to sea. He predicted that from the evening of June 6th through the 7th, the wind would rage at 55–60 knots (over 70 statute miles per hour), gusting higher, while the centre of the low passed within 100 nautical miles of me. It was now the evening of the 5th and Typhoon Mawar had already claimed three lives in the Philippines.

The last few days couldn't have been more different. *Gulliver* had glided eastwards under the light zephyrs at the centre of a high-pressure system, pulled effortlessly by a powerful arm of the Kuroshio current as though towed by graceful swans, most of the work happening without my help. The day before had seen my greatest progress on the log yet, at a stonking 91 nautical miles in a 4–5 knot current; recent daily totals before that had never dropped below 30. Prior to that I had already bagged a few negative mileages. The first couple of weeks since casting off from Choshi had been rough, nauseous and tiring as I settled into my dynamic new world. Having pulled steadily away from the jetty at 7 a.m., hugged away by friends and locals and even watched by my mum via live web feed, I rowed out to sea with following winds which pinwheeled a squadron of wind turbines on the cliff tops. Besides squirrelling precious tiny minutes lying down inside the cabin, instantly asleep and then instantly awake with my alarm, I had rowed through the night, on high alert for local fishing boats which worked the inshore waters, keen to get away from the unforgiving coastline.

The breeze stiffened and a low pressure bombed through on my third night. Torrential rain slammed into steep seas over the continental shelf drop-off, hurling *Gulliver* over in a violent capsize, thudding me into the walls, as if in brutal tango as we rolled back to upright. It had taken me by surprise, as I hadn't been strapped into my bunk and it had hurt. It had always been a case of *when* rather than *if* I capsized out there, but that was a sharp shock to go over so soon, making the dark feel even darker that night. Being upside down in any boat is one of my least favourite things to do, especially in an ocean-rowing boat. Perhaps this is because it is an entirely passive act as the boat will reright itself, providing hatches are watertight and weight safely distributed.

My five-kilogram waterproof Peli case had followed my tumbling that night, colliding with the air vent beneath the main hatch, breaking an apparently useful and non-fixable part of it, which left an extra gap for water to slosh through when waves broke over the cabin. Said water usually poured straight onto my bedding or my feet, which hung over the end of my not quite long enough bunk, adding to *Gulliver's* general damp.

The next week we went through a charging 45-knot gale (or rather, it went through us), *Gulliver* being jerked about like a rider on a frightened mustang as he was pulled through irregular seas by the current, which ran against the wind. In those conditions *Gulliver* would be hanging off the end of a sea anchor from his bow, a bulky set-up rigged back to the boat by stainless steel shackles. This 4-metre-wide parachute at the end of 50 metres of rope adds drag, which holds the boat to the waves and slows it down, meaning extra stability (and less risk of capsize) and reduced drift from windage (and therefore fewer lost miles). During those first three weeks of the voyage I had already quickened my routines for setting and retrieving it. Multi-tool looped around my wrist and safety harness round my chest and middle, I would nip out of my cabin as nimbly as I could, clipping on my line and shutting the door behind me in one go. Hand-railing along from my cabin over the three steps to the forward cabin, I eased the stiff hatch handles to open and reached inside, slipping the keen bungee cord so that I could heft out the two buckets and one bag that I needed. Taking care not to get wrapped up in rope, I unpinned the bridle line which ran from the towing ring at the bow and checked it was over the safety rail. Simultaneously grabbing the end of the parachute line to join it with the bridle, I twisted the shackle shut and tightened it off with the multi-tool. I then threw the bag overboard and let out the line, watching *Gulliver* swing round into the waves as the billowing yellow and red parachute sank and ran out, the speed varying, depending on the sea state. I did the same with the floating retrieval line, which I lashed back to the boat, before stowing the empty buckets as quickly as I could and scooting back into the dry, trying to time hatch openings with the waves.

Even in winds of 20 knots, being on the sea anchor could

make for a rough night if the wind opposed the current. In wilder sea states I had lain on my hip-width bunk, strapped down by the four-point racing harness. Through extended periods of incarceration, I braced against boredom, too. At first there is gratitude for the extra rest and sleep, then enthusiasm for reading or listening to music through headphones and finally a steady resolve to zone out in a sort of meditation, keen to avoid negative energy which can easily spiral downwards when you are alone, tired, possibly scared and lacking the balancing perspective of another team mate. I generally find that forty-eight hours' forced lying down becomes an effort, rather than a pleasure, around about twelve hours in, especially as an overhead sun starts baking the cabin like a greenhouse and my lower back starts to scream from immobility. On other days I rowed from the dewy dawn into the first speckling dew of night, only to gain handfuls of miles in a useful direction before being returned by opposing currents. Suffice to say, the Pacific was testing and teasing me already.

It was all a matter of the zoomed-out perspective and accepting that sometimes I would go backwards to go forward, rowing when I could and waiting when I couldn't. It wasn't always easy to do, but my philosophy has always been one of averages: if you can be positive and grateful about things more times than you are negative, then it should be OK and you will move forward, metaphorically and physically. Every day I chose 'good things about today' to focus on and be happy about, even if it was as basic as being OK in body and boat or even more basic things such as being thankful for the day's end. It didn't matter what it was – it just had to be something. The negative energy just needed an outlet and, sometimes an ear outside the boat.

Thankfully, the ocean showed me many diamonds amid the rough, often spoiling me with choice for my good things. Dawns and sunsets doused wide skies in vivid, streaking blushes with all the artistry of a painter at her easel, and clouds chased each other, whipped on by winds, or lolled lazily in cauliflower puffs. Pancake seas on clear, bright nights sandwiched us between stars and their reflections. I always used 'us' with *Gulliver*, in the same way I would have done with any other team mate: we were each responsible for the other. It might have been psychological, too: saying 'we' made me feel less alone, which in turn made me feel stronger, probably.

The wildlife certainly felt like company, albeit mostly fleeting. Sun fish ogled at me, gawping mouths and goggly eyes rolling as fins gyrated in a stroke somewhere between rotation and finning, shades of dark grey making their uppermost fin look like a shark's in colour, if not form, as they periscoped along the surface. Dolphins cavorted in bubbling loops, clicking their appraisal of my boat between themselves in whistles and melodies loud enough for me to hear through the hull, meaning that I often heard them before I saw them, sending me outside on eager lookout. No one can be uncheered by a dolphin. Whales of varying shapes and sizes and species cruised gently by, harrumphing lungfuls of air in and out with rasping, smelly gasps. Sperm whales and humpbacked whales breached or dived at varying distances from us, the thrash of their leviathan forms booming out across the waves, especially on silent days when all sounds were in high definition. Sleek albatrosses sailed gracefully on outsized wings or sat politely on the water, paddling softly and nodding silently to any gathered congregation. They never bickered or screeched like the terns or shearwaters, nor did they harangue like the skuas. Petrels twittered and chattered all night while dancing with the beam of the navigation light.

While the Kuroshio current had taken care of mileage, I spent some time catching up with myself – topping up on sleep, cooking noodles and pancakes on my single-ring gas stove, scrubbing myself and my clothes and drying both in the sun. I had even thrown tipsy birthday parties for myself and the Queen, who was celebrating her Golden Jubilee back home. I got out my Union Jack and paper chains, balloons and a bottle of cider, recording spoof phonecasts of my own Jubilee pageant, feeling proud and a bit emotional to be British as my tiny speakers belted out 'Rule Britannia'.

Which brings me back to where I started: trying and failing to take a swim. The idea of Mawar lurked uneasily, both real and abstract as the depth below. I grabbed my safety line and tugged sharply at its red-and-yellow braid, clattering the shackle against *Gulliver*'s bulkhead, testing one lifeline against another, shouting down remembered cries from others about how absurd it was to leave my sanctuary voluntarily. With all the elegance you would expect of a lone rower who is scared of deep water, I manoeuvred myself onto the smooth flat of the gunwale once more and hesitated for a moment as I leaned into the rock of the boat as he leaned over to deliver me to the water, as a parent might crouch for a child to climb down from a piggyback.

Certain that the next three days would be scarier than the next few minutes, I dropped in with a 'Yahoo!' The bubbled rush and crash of the splash filled my ears and head. I spun around jerkily with a drive of my legs and arms, throwing my face into the kaleidoscope below the surface, just as I had done in the deep end of the school swimming pool, convinced that a shark was going to explode out of the filters. Unending blues morphed through shades of brightness and danced with shafts of light, crowds of tiny creatures and flecks of whatever entrancing me as I peered beyond my toes. The throbbing, pulsing, drifters and swimmers against the vastness of outwards and downwards was beguiling and it reminded me of the quiet hours I had spent as a biology undergraduate sifting through petri dishes of plankton for my dissertation. I pulsed my arms and legs breathlessly as I tried to relax and let the salt do the floating. Pulling myself along the grab line which looped like bunting across *Gulliver's* side, I arrived next to the rudder at his stern. Looking down, I inspected the gathered troupe of black-and-white pilot fish who had followed me in various rank-and-file forms for a week now, their barcoded bodies in popping contrast with the turquoise sea as they kept lookout for friend or foe or food. Jellied barnacles hung limply from the side while their feathery arms wafted. There was an elegance to it all ruined only by my naked writhing. I breaststroked as far from *Gulliver* as my line of courage would take me, my safety line waiting patiently in coils, never likely to be used to its full 15 metres – I was not brave enough for that. Not on my own, maybe not even if I had a human team mate. I pulled the camera up from its loop around my wrist and licked the salt from the lens before taking a selfie with *Gulliver* posing smartly behind. The picture shows a benign prologue to the tempest ahead: a woman alive with the energy of the moment and the twenty-five days and forty minutes of perching it had taken to get there, in front of a very smart boat.

As I swooshed my hands and screw-kicked my feet to turn me back towards the boat, bubbles spiralled upwards in a cloud of white behind me, and I catapulted myself under the safety rail in my best attempt at a flying penguin impersonation, convinced something was about to eat me. Heavy breathing gave way to chuckles as I realised that the bubbling predator had been my very own hands and feet.

During my spring time in Japan, a child asked me whether I would have a boat following me across the Pacific, in case there was a problem. 'No,' I said, and he furrowed his brow. 'So, you've got to be careful, then?' he said, wide eyed with concern. I reassured him that this was exactly what I was going to do, explaining that it was my main goal to come home safe and well afterwards. Sometimes it would be my *only* goal.

The impending Mawar felt like that. Deciding whether to stay put or request assistance for a pre-emptive evacuation from passing shipping had been a heavy decision. If I was picked up ahead of the incoming storm before things got too rough, I would probably lose *Gulliver* in the process as I would be the priority. Losing *Gulliver* would mean I would not be able to carry on my journey. There was also a chance that the system would recurve sooner than forecast, heading out to sea to burn itself out before it reached our sea area, doing nothing more than giving us a good shake. If I stayed put, I would have to storm-ready the boat, batten down hatches, hunker down and hope for the best in what would be the roughest conditions that I had ever faced. Beyond that, there would be little I could do except keep as calm and focused as possible and stay strapped in to my bunk so that I would be as safe as possible. The ultimate risk was death, which, though unlikely, could happen in a number of ways according to my logic and even more according to my imagination. Long ago I had decided that you never can tell with oceans and boats – the unpredictable is very possible. Lee answered my questions on wind speeds and wave heights and past experience with rowers, and I sat on deck trying to find the right answer within me or on the waves. The team psychotherapist Dr Briony Nicholls always says that there is often no right thing to do, but rather that it is just the thing you do or choose at the time. I had known Briony since we started working together in preparation for my Indian Ocean row, exploring the psychology of soloing, of risk, of dealing with uncertainties and stress. She has become a friend and valuable member of the team ever since, and we had a shorthand for experiences and lessons from my journeys and I know that even when we didn't talk, through reading between the lines of blogs or emails, Briony often pre-empted my worries before I told her about them. I call it Bri-fi.

With thirty hours to go until the storm hit, my project manager Sara checked in on my decision:

From: Sara
Date: 4 June 2012 17:09 BST
To: Sarah boat phone
Just checking you want to ride out the storm rather than have me arrange a pick up.

From: Sarah boat phone
Date: 5 June 2012 08:45 BST
I have faith in *Gulliver*. I'll stay.

That was it. We were now committed, and my team were too — we would all be riding this out together, albeit remotely. I sat out on deck with my back to the hatch and phoned Charlie, now just over 100 miles away. It was curious to think that for the next two days we would be the closest people in the world to each other and yet probably feeling more alone than we had ever been. Charlie had also decided to stay and we swapped our version of events ahead. 'Good luck then, mate; see you on the other side. Be safe over there.' And we returned to readying our respective boats and minds.

Crouching over the footwell, I prised the bung from the hull and the two from the ballast tank wall. Azure sea rushed in through the hull and gurgled as it flooded the adjoining tank, the breather hole sighing as the water inside balanced with that outside, adding extra weight and stability. I untwiddled the pins on the gates and pushed the oar handles up inside their fibreglasss storage tubes, tucking the ends under the gunwales. I lashed them securely around a thwart so that even in capsizing they would be safe. I set the water-maker to filling my 5-litre water bottles and tied them into the footwell. I filled some extra water bags and added them to the hulk of the forward cabin, stowing them low amongst the other gear beneath a web of bungees. I wheeled the seat down its runners to release the rollerblade wheels which made it move, unclipped the tether and added it to the forward cabin: I wanted the deck clear.

In my cabin I aimed for the same, to reduce injury risk to myself and the boat by flying bulk. I stuffed away clothes and gear that was not needed in dry bags which in turn I shuffled and shoved into hatches. Tipping out a bag of food onto my bed, I sorted boiled sweets, nuts, chocolate bars and granola bars, dried fruit and jerky for my storm rations. For water, I wished I had a better way to store sufficient drinking bottles close to me, but wondered how much I would be able to eat and drink anyway, given that using the bucket would be impossibly dangerous. I wondered about adult nappies and kicked myself for never investigating it further on shore. As I tied my camera bag down, I wished that we had screwed in more lashing points for gear to be inside the cabin but safely held in place, worried that my yellow Peli case would fly again at some point.

I smiled at the photos of friends and family taped to the wall, and their messages of motivation and humour. *Hold fast* or *Give it the beans* sat alongside quotes from Winnie-the-Pooh, Gandhi or messages to stay safe and come home soon. Leaning back against the cabin wall, I opened a bag of trinkets from home. I rubbed the smooth thumb stone that my mum had given me, breathing and relaxing into the adrenaline which was adding to the weird mix of calm and nerves. Tucking the stone into my bra, I pulled out the hunched wooden yogi that someone had given me and rolled it around in one palm. It was supposed to carry your burdens for you. And then there was the six-inch wooden boat which the young and sickly Robert Louis Stevenson had made, given to me by my friend Patrick. He was living with motor neurone disease, fighting his own big storms.

I cooked outside in the early evening, enjoying the fresh air and warmth of what would be my last hot meal for a few days. I set the sea anchor, checking and rechecking that the shackles were all as tight as possible. I put the bulky red bag of my survival suit and life jacket in my cabin.

Preparing my mental boat and safety lines was just as important. I wrote *No storms last for ever* around the metal rim of the hatch outside with a marker pen. I wrote *Smile* on my left hand and *Breathe* on my right, hoping they would remind me to stay present. Moment by moment, that was my goal. Mawar would later show me that it is impossible to smile when you are terrified, but it was all about intention. I wrote out the forecasts on my whiteboard so that I could wipe each hour or section away as it passed, and tucked it into the netting at my bunkside.

Anticipating a few days without refreshment, I brushed my teeth for a bit longer that evening, enjoying watching the soft seas, wondering if the pod of dolphins which jaunted past knew what was about to happen. I made the most of the stillness to hang upside down across the cabin roof to let my back stretch. And then I stepped into my cabin to sleep and wait, sticking a strong anti-emetic patch on my chest before finally settling. The thought of vomit flying around the cabin in capsizes was almost worse than being thrown around it myself.

To my surprise and relief I had a good night, waking period-ically to check for shipping before rising early with the new day. *The* day. Although the early morning wind was only 15 knots and the waves no bigger than *Gulliver*, the descent into chaos was frighteningly swift.

From: Sarah boat phone
Date: 6 June 2012 08:00 BST
To: Sara
2PM   ALLOK. WIND INCREASING. STRAPPED IN

Good luck. Stay safe.

THANKYOU MY FRIEND. I KNOW THIS STORM
ISNT JUST STRESSFUL FOR ME. HERES TO THE
OTHER SIDE

We had agreed that I would let Sara know every hour by text
message to her email that I was OK. As the barometer plummeted
and the winds became shrieking harpies, waves a seething, tumul-
tuous mess, the brevity of my messages belied my fear. I didn't
want to go into detail, in case it pulled me out of the rational
into the emotional. The phone writes in capitals by default – I
wasn't sparing any energy in changing it, nor with attempting
any proper punctuation.

09:27 BST   530 OK. SCARYBUTOK
10:31 BST   630 OK

My memory of what happened over the next few days exists
mainly in images and feelings. The order is jumbled and staccato.
As I write this book, four years later, I am still careful not to get
pulled too deeply back into where it overwhelms me. Sitting here
at my kitchen table watching fat pigeons hop about the lawn, my
chest is tight as I remember what it felt like. Lying on the sheepskin rug and sleeping bag on my bunk, I was pinned there by the
chest harness and leg strap, prone but protected, less than one inch
of foam and fibreglass boat wall separating me from the chaos
outside. The peak of the conditions coincided with darkness, which
arrived late, it being almost midsummer. Before night fell the main
hatch window at my feet, which looked across the deck and bow
of the boat, showed a world of white – spray, foam and waves,
meaning that I couldn't distinguish sky from sea.

11:31 BST   730 OK

As the system front went overhead, ballistic clouds pelted rain
so loudly down onto *Gulliver* that, at times, it obliterated the roar

of the waves. Lightning lit up the cabin like exploding shells light up a military target. Waves laid down heavy fire from all angles, sending tonnes of water charging into and over the boat due to the swift rotation of the storm system. Lee's forecast put the waves at 10 to 15 metres and the sustained maximum winds reaching 55 to 60 knots with gusts well over. In the UK we drive down motorways at those speeds.

12:30 BST   830 OK

Sometimes *Gulliver* raced down waves before juddering to a halt as though running into a wall, before being bulldozed over from upright. Other times flight lead straight into a lurching, heaving spin, pivoting on the groaning parachute anchor, G-forces pushing me backwards into my harness as though being swung around by my arms. Squeezing my eyes tight, I tried to deepen my shallow breathing and find whatever version of calm was possible. Unjamming my teeth, I flexed my leg muscles and unclenched my fists.

13:20 BST   930 OK

Then we would be slammed onto the concrete-like water, throwing me back into my frightened, living version of rigor mortis. I had never heard anything like it before and I worried for my little blue boat, alternately pleading with him to keep me safe and thanking him for doing so. I don't remember the first of the capsizes, but I remember they were violent and clocked in multiples, sometimes happening in close succession and at other times more sporadically. Waves thundered into or over us, either surging us along in the break or toppling us immediately. Thrown upside down, I hung in the harness, bracing my arms onto the cabin wall or clinging onto the straps. Time stood still in those moments. 'Come on *Gulliver*! Come on *Gulliver*! COME ON *Gulliver*!'

17:02 BST   1AM OK

My pillow and blanket escaped to follow my yellow Peli case, drinks bottles and survival gear, which crashed off the cabin walls to land on top of me as we settled. So did the water which streamed in through the vents, soaking me from both ends of the cabin, both as the waves first hit and then as we rolled around again. Water that had collected in the footwell or lockers below me found its way out to soak me again and again as it sloshed around the cabin like a washing machine.

18:03 BST   2AM OK.HORRID BUT OK

The groaning sounds of *Gulliver* straining against the sea anchor lines had changed. It was daylight when I realised that we were being held side on to the waves, capsizing and slamming more regularly, meaning that the main line to the bow must have been ripped away. With each slam and roll, the retrieval line wrapped around the boat or some part of it. Shocked gear popped off with bangs.

00:56 BST   0730 OK. MAY NEED PICK UP. ALL LEAKING
            CONCERNS ME. AERIALS BOTH DOWN
            TOO AND RUDDER DAMGD. LETS WAIT
            TIL CALMER 2 DISCUS

Through the hatch on to the deck I saw the satellite dome and other antennas explode off the forward cabin. I heard the antennas rip away from my cabin roof after a clattering effort to hold on by the final threads of wire which connected them to the electronics inside. The rudder jammed and hammered noisily on the transom of the boat, just inches from my head. Water streamed into my cabin through the seal around the main hatch as waves crashed. I assumed that the hatch door must have been warped by the extreme forces exerted across that bulkhead.

01:00 BST   9AM OK. CANOT WAIT4 CALM. WISH I
HAD TAKEN PICKUP

It hadn't taken long for the cabin to warm up with the new day's sun on it, softening the ache of weary muscles, if only minutely. I hadn't slept since before the storm system but I closed my eyes from time to time, trying to relax. My lower half was chafed and soggy from lying on a urine-soaked sheepskin rug: I hadn't been able to use the bucket since the start of the rough and so had had no choice but to go where I lay. The retrieval line strained with the full drag of the sea anchor sideways to the boat. I heard a massive bang and saw that the carbon-fibre safety rail had disappeared into the waves.

01.50 BST   10 SAFETY RAIL JUST BEEN RIPPED OUT

I cursed myself for clove-hitching the retrieval line there before the storm. The sea anchor was now attached to *Gulliver* via whatever tangles and loops the various lines had wrapped and held around the boat. I was nervous that the safety rail's removal had put another leak path into the forward cabin: I could see the hole in the bulkhead where it had been ripped out. Boat-builder Jamie assured me that it should not have been pulled all the way through but it felt like I couldn't rely on *should*. It felt like normal supposition was out.

I suspected *Gulliver* had sustained too much damage for me to be able to repair him and carry on safely after Mawar had passed. With the main hatch into my cabin leaking and the potential for leak paths into the forward cabin, his righting ability was compromised. Separately, the water-maker and electronics gear were soaked and most of the boat's aerials and antennas had been ripped away. I scrolled through the contacts in my satellite phone and rang Sara. Voicemail: it was 1 a.m. at home. I rang George to tell her I would need a pick-up once the storm had died down. Protocol in a non-life threatening situation dictates that Falmouth Coastguard first be notified (as I am a British national), and they then coordinated with the Japan Coastguard about a plan. They asked that I activate my EPIRB, my emergency satellite tracking beacon, and so I unclipped my harness and moved, somewhat dizzily, to the end of my bunk so that I could undo the hatch and grab it from its fixings outside. I did so as quickly as I possibly could, my feet ankle-deep in water as I did, pulling my head back inside and slamming the hatch shut. It, too, had been taken by the waves and I cursed myself for not having brought it inside.

Thankfully, I had a smaller version, called a PLB (personal locator beacon), and so I studied the instructions carefully, twice, before pulling back the safety tab, uncoiling the metal antenna and pressing the small rubber button. A white light flashed in Morse code and I secured it in the wire netting by my head before lying back down on my bunk and strapping myself in. Just as I was reading a text message from home *Gulliver* was thrown over into a violent capsize, sending water crashing through my cabin and kit careering after it. As I fell forwards out of the harness, stubbing my toes into the cabin roof, I realised (rather painfully) that I had forgotten to tuck my feet underneath the webbing loop over my legs. I rubbed my sore toes, before trying to kick things back into the footwell. Between them Sara, George and Jenny escalated our crisis plan – informing the team, my family and friends, our sponsors and supporters and my friends in Japan.

03:01 BST   EVERYTHING RIPPED OFF G. NUTS. BIT SCARED. FEEL SILLY FOR RIDING STORM. IMSORRY

A logical, sensible voice in my head quieted the regretful one and calmed me again. Even though surviving in a rowing boat is a passive act, the mental control is active and critical. The team at home knew this, too, and also tried to gee my spirits and reassure me. A maelstrom of media interest erupted, following a leak from the Japan Coastguard to the national press, adding to the pressure on the team at home.

Within an hour I had spoken to the Japan Coastguard, who told me that they were sending a plane out to monitor my drift. Given that I was 600 miles offshore and drifting south-east, this would take three hours to arrive. They were deploying a patrol vessel from Sendai which had an ETA of thirty-six hours, putting them on track for an early evening pick-up on June 8th. I felt relief on the one hand and yet it also felt like a long time to wait. I was battling to keep it together and hoping that *Gulliver* could. Meanwhile, my phone buzzed with incoming messages from home – a mix of team and family. Having limited my texts during the storm to my hourly messages to Sara in a bid to conserve battery and also head-space, it felt like a mental seal had been loosened and I replied where I could. It was a bizarre mix of the real and the surreal – texting is such a second-nature activity in just about every sphere of modern life, and yet this was such an otherworldly context.

For me and for the folks at home, the days of the storm and the wait were a blur. I had no sleep and the team had barely any. Afterwards George wrote:

> It was a shitty night and a pretty grim week. There were lots of decisions to make and people to call and then we just had to wait. While we were waiting to hear that you had been picked up your mum ironed and I did the VAT return. Sara and I swapped shifts through the night so that you always had one of us alongside you, sending supportive messages. We were just on autopilot. During this time my elderly neighbour broke her leg, my cat died and my family needed me. I even missed my brother's birthday.

For Jenny, the rescue collided with her being bridesmaid for a best friend's wedding. The only place she could find reception was in the bathroom at the very top of the house where she was staying, meaning she spent the best part of two days in there fielding calls and emails from journalists.

I heard the plane before I saw it, and tried calling them on my hand-held VHF radio. The line was too crackly to hear and so I got up gingerly from my harness to be able to use the fixed VHF unit on the control panel at the end of the cabin. As I was egging myself on to undo the harness, an albatross soared over the boat and made me smile. I wished I was above the waves, too.

7 June 05:52 BST SEEN PLANE. HUGE WAVES. MOUNTAINS

I had to guide the plane in to spot me, my 7-metre-long boat hard to see amongst the 15-metre-tall waves. Sticking my head out of the hatch I got a delicious, if momentary, burst of fresh air, and I closed the hatch door as a wave crashed over the cabin roof and into my cabin. I was just turning around when a wave pounded into us, sending me careering into the cabin walls as *Gulliver* rolled. Time crawled as I lay on the cabin roof and pleaded 'Come on *Gulliver*. Come on *Gulliver*. Come back around. Come back around. Pleeease *Gulliver*!' Turquoise water frothed and whirled outside the hatch as more sluiced out of lockers inside to soak me and streamed through the main hatch.

7 June 11:57 BST CAPSIZD. HIT HEAD. OUCH

Up to that point I hadn't cried. Now I couldn't hold back the tears. I sat and sobbed, my chest heaving.

7 June 06:53 BST ANOTHER VIOLENTROLL HERE

People often ask if I had ever thought of giving up and my answer is always no; I hadn't but I had often wished that bad experiences would finish. The hours to the pick-up ETA dragged and I counted them down, just as Sara had predicted I would get through the storm, hour by hour. It seems strange that moments seemed like years and yet it was only a three-day clip of my entire journey.

7 June 07:53 BST FEEL RATHER VULNERABLE

I lay back on my bed and strapped in as fast as my tired, fumbling fingers would allow, not even bothering to sort out the bedding beneath me. My head throbbed. I noticed a wave of sickness rolling within me and lunged for the plastic bag I had stashed to hand. Green bile soon filled it and I searched for a water bottle from beneath the disarrayed gear to drink from before lying back down again with a mint humbug to suck. Before the storm I had planned to listen to music but I hadn't played anything beyond the first few hours of building waves so that I didn't mask the sound of them. Briony later explained that this was to give me an illusion of control, given that there was nothing else really that I could change amid so much uncertainty.

7 June 09:21 BST   TRYIMG2 KEEP CALM

I found the satellite phone under my mattress, specked with water and with a damaged aerial. I wiped it dry with my damp top and typed a message but the phone turned itself off before I could send it. My spare was not within reach. Tears slipped down my cheeks. I felt even more alone now. As the evening sun dipped my body cooled, and I pulled on hats and Buffs to keep as warm as I could. I even wrapped myself in a paper-thin Union Jack, my addled brain choosing that over my sodden sleeping blanket, which was in the footwell. I knew that I needed to eat and yet I didn't.

7 June 14:06 BST   TIRD, SOQE HEAD, NERVOUS

The regular thrum of the coastguard plane at thirty-minute intervals stopped in the early evening, while it returned to base to refuel. Having requested evacuation a few hours after I had, Charlie was also being monitored with flypasts and he, too, was all over the news. I later learned that the majority of it was positive and concerned – many expeditions are not always so lucky and instead are slammed for their risk-taking.

Before night fell I flicked up my grab bag from the bottom of my bunk with my feet and pulled out the red survival suit, sliding into it awkwardly as I lay down. I tied the arms around my waist, not wanting to get into it fully. The extra, though minimal, warmth was welcome to my frigid limbs, which now shivered occasionally.

My wonderful friends in Japan worked hard on arranging land logistics, helping with translations and informing local contacts, pulling together some clothes for me to wear ashore and, in true Tari fashion, asking me what I would like to eat.

7 June 16:05 BST   PANCAKES PLS. COLD OJ. GRAPES

They also planned to meet me off the boat in Sendai, six hours north of Tokyo. I swung between not daring to think about being ashore and safe to visualising it, the warm and smiling Tari wrapping me in her warm hug, Mike making jokes. I imagined myself wallowing in the bath at Kelly's house and waking up with the nose of their dog Patch in my face. My team and family at home were reassured that they would be there to scoop me up, too.

7 June 19:32 BST   DAWN HERE. STILL ROUGH. SLAMMED LOTS

I dozed a bit during the night, still waking up with every new noise and the occasional roll. Daylight heralded pick-up day and the final twelve hours of waiting. I hoped the coastguard boat would be early, just as I knew Japanese people to be. The plane continued to circle me every half an hour and even sent a photo to Sara. I was given no news of Charlie, despite my regular questions after him, and I hoped that he and *Blossom* were OK. I later found out that no one knew much about how he was doing because his comms had been wiped out for a time and even the surveillance plane hadn't been able to hail him.

Daylight dissolved some of the fear and disorientation of the dark, which always seemed more frightening and chaotic than the light. Through the night condensation had dripped onto my face from the hatch above my head and I had wiped it onto my lips to soothe my parched mouth. My head still thrummed from the head-banging roll of the day before and, I suspected, dehydration.

7 June 23:23 BST   ROLLD AGAIN. HATE THIS. WANT
IT OVER. GUESS 20 ROLLS THIS STORM

As the sun climbed higher the wind and waves bayed and
bowed the low-pressure system on its way. My heart rate fell
steadily. By mid-afternoon the golden sun made me think that,
on another ocean on another day, it would be a perfect time for
a row and a happy time to be out. Even after those three crazed
days trapped in *Gulliver*, I knew that I would be back some day.
So many things felt very abstract at that point, but my yearning
for the waves felt real and reassuring. Shit can happen wherever
you are in the world, so the risk of the same thing happening
again was certainly not a reason to stay at home.

8 June 04:12 BST   STILL IN LOVE W OCEAN. NVR
SEEN NYTHING LIKE YDAY. NVR WANT2 AGAIN

When it felt safe to do so, I sat up to wee a tiny amount of
burning liquid so dark it looked like Cola. I rolled my neck and
flexed my arms. Everything felt bruised, which was lucky because
if I hadn't been strapped in it could have been a lot worse. I have
never been in a car crash, but imagined this was what it might
feel like afterwards. I considered my gear-strewn, soaking, stinking
cabin. Lockers half full of water, their contents floating. Green
grew around the electrical contacts of the switch panel, meaning
that they had been drenched. Something buzzed. Was something
shorting? Ropes heaved on the boat. The rudder knocked. I
talked myself through tiny actions to start tidying up. In small
scoops I bailed water out of the footwell and lockers with the
hand-bailer from outside. I made a note that any future boat I
had would have a hand-operated bailer fixed inside my cabin,
within reach. More dazed staring into nowhere. More metaphorical slapping myself about the face and into action. I nibbled at
food but felt sick and so sipped at my water bottle.

Finally, I phoned my mum. She had been messaging me for
hours, asking me how I was doing and telling me to hold on. I
hadn't been able to reply, needing to keep my emotions together

without having to take care of anyone else's. Memories of my eight-year-old self crying down the payphone to my parents while I stood huddled in the crowded dining room at my boarding house have always made it difficult to share when I am sad. I think part of it, too, is that with an experience so removed from normal life, I found it hard to connect. It felt like only *Gulliver* knew what we had been through and I knew that I couldn't articulate it yet. I didn't want to either. Still, I knew that many people at home were watching and waiting to hear that I was OK. I recorded a phonecast for my website, thanking everyone, my voice cracking with emotion and exhaustion. I also let them know that *Gulliver* would be flying solo for a while as the coastguard boat wouldn't be able to take him.

As I hung up, a message buzzed through to say that a passing ship was on its way to sit nearby while I waited for the coastguard, and a quick look out of the hatch confirmed it was already here. I was dizzy from being upright and so lay down to think about what I needed to take with me. Cameras and memory cards, laptop and electricals and my yellow Peli case. I stuffed some clothes into a bag (although later I discovered I had forgotten pants) and, in my brain fog, took a bag of hats instead of the bag of trinkets from friends. I thanked *Gulliver* and boat-builder Jamie for keeping me safe: in a lesser boat the outcome could have been very different.

Japan Coastguard patrol vessel *Zou* arrived in the late afternoon, an hour earlier than they had estimated, in true Japanese style. Sitting at the end of my bunk, my feet in a pool of water, I talked to the captain over the VHF. 'We will lower a small boat for you . . . We are coming to make you safe.' I cried as I saw the grey giant lolling towards a little rowing boat, feeling as though I was watching someone else's story.

The crew winched down a small rescue boat into the still surging sea. They wore orange waterproofs and hard hats and two divers in wetsuits and masks had backpacks. I stepped over onto their boat, grabbed by their arms to be pulled into the huddle of bodies. The two divers went onto my boat and opened the hatches, checking inside the cabins. I gazed at *Gulliver*, tears trying to get out but stuck as we pulled away towards *Zou*. 'Keep it together, Outen. Keep it together,' I whispered inside. I asked about Charlie, but they couldn't tell me anything. The driver worked to keep the boat straight and manoeuvre into position alongside *Zou*'s hull. It reminded me of a coasteering day as a teenager where my brother Matthew and I had played in a nook of rock, laughing at the upswell and downsurge pulling us up and down the rockface. I suddenly felt trapped and claustrophobic. Giant metal hooks were attached to our boat and a humming winch hauled us up to deck height. More smiling faces in hard hats and navy uniforms. A camera. Arms helped me up and over the rail, and onto legs that hadn't walked more than a couple of paces at a time for a month. '*Arigatou gozaimasu*,' I said, thanking them. I turned to look for *Gulliver*, disappearing into the waves.

Safe. I was safe now. 'Sarah-san, you must eat.' I was ushered into the mess-room for a snack of juice, biscuits and a neat little Spam sandwich, my body not keen just yet, even though I had barely eaten for three days. 'Tell us what happened,' chatter in Japanese. 'When did you make the call?' More Japanese. I woke up to see Marina, the young woman coastguard, rubbing my arm gently. 'Are you sure you're OK, Sarah-san?' More questions. The two divers who had gone on board after I had left now appeared with some things I recognised from *Gulliver*. I hoped that I was imagining that I was looking at the bright yellow and black body of the YB tracking unit; that he hadn't really taken it off the boat. That actually it was still on board beaming up *Gulliver*'s position so that I could salvage him one day. I felt sorry for the guy when I explained: he had thought it was a mobile phone that I might want to keep. Charlie was picked up by a Russian cargo ship bound for Vancouver, and so I didn't get to see him, which felt like a blow. Originally, the plan was for *Zou* to pick him up after me, and I had been looking forward to a hug. After all, we'd just been through the same storm. I was glad for him that *Blossom* had made it out, too.

Preparing to leave the ship, I gave the captain a Union Jack rubber duck that had sat on top of my electrical panel. Giving me the coastguard's insignia badge, he shook my hand with a smile. 'Sarah-san, do not give up. I hope you try again. *Ganbatte!*' which means good luck and do your best.

Tari and Mike had driven up from Tokyo to bring me home to Kelly and Kaz's. Some of the Team Choshi guys had also driven the six hours to welcome me in, and I hugged them to stay upright and to say thank you. A row of press wanted to know what it had been like out there, and I tried to put words to the disjointed flashes in my head. I was glad to retreat to the quiet of the local hospital and drift while a bag of IV fluids sorted the dehydration. It felt good to be with people who knew me again, although we hadn't expected it to happen so soon. We joked with the bottle of gin that someone had sent as a welcome present, taking pictures of it upside down next to the IV line.

'So, you are going home, then?' asked the Japanese man in the seat next to me as we taxied down the runway a few days later.

'Yes, I am,' I said, and braced myself for the turbulence ahead.

PART II

Having Another Go

Pacific Ocean and the Aleutian Islands

**UK – Japan – Alaska | Rowing and kayaking
the Pacific 2013 – 2014 | 4,500 miles | Total miles from
London: 16,300**

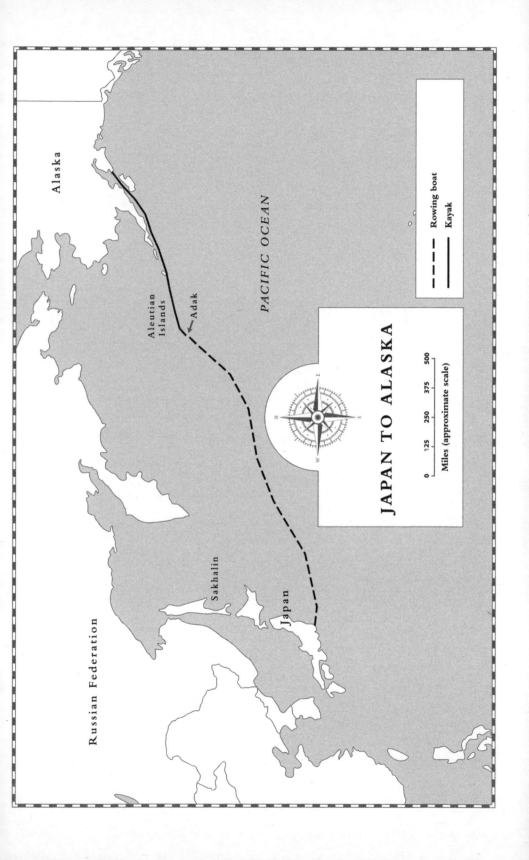

8

Fallout: UK

Recovery and Pacific preparation | Home |
Summer 2012 – Spring 2013

'Just relax', a friend had said, sure that this would transform my spluttering whale impressions into something that looked more like front crawl. Putting your face in the water when you are hungry for oxygen has always seemed counter-intuitive to me but now, session by session, reaching for glide with each stroke, I relaxed and breathed. One, two, three, breathe. Repeat, repeat, repeat. I stared at the black line on the pool floor and it pulled me forward like a lifeline as the water held me in the moment. I swam regularly to escape the noise in my head, to feel the endorphins and find some flow. Out of the water I was not really coping.

At first I didn't know what to feel or how to feel it. For a short time, 'You must be so happy to be home!' felt about right, as I was whisked along in the rush of seeing friends and family again. Grateful to move back in with my long-suffering mum, my little bedroom looked much the same except for the pile of fifteen months of mail; on some level it felt like I hadn't been away at all. And that, in part, was scary. I'm generally a positive person. I should have been happy. I should have loved being home again. I should have been able to shake it off. '*Should* is a very difficult word,' said Briony. In my logical head-space I knew there are no rules to feelings, especially after trauma, but logic wasn't really getting a look-in and I struggled to hear other people's perspectives. Gradually, a cloud of sadness, negativity and fear settled and I realised that I was trapped within the storm that Mawar had left behind.

Some mornings Teifi the Labrador boffed my bedroom door open and pushed his wet nose into my face. On others he sat outside until I appeared or tracked back and forth to see if I was coming out. Even after fifteen hours of something between sleep and lying in bed with my eyes closed, I was exhausted. 'OK fists, uncurl now, one finger at a time. Teeth, stop grinding. OK jaw, that's it until tonight.' I breathed deeply, trying to relax. Self-battering rants circled like vultures. At various times, waves booming over *Gulliver* flashed at full volume. I tried to rationalise the visions and ground myself in the present, but they often caught me by surprise. I was late and lost things (or myself) frequently, and I turned up for more than one event on the wrong day. My emotions swung like the waves and I struggled to hold on, metaphorically and physically. I became paranoid of others and afraid of myself.

Sure that if I could keep the positive moments linking up with each other I could handrail myself out of the dark, I spent hours walking the dogs. They seemed to sense that I needed company, often sitting quietly at my feet. People were more difficult because they asked questions. They wanted to know what it had been like out there, and what was next. I avoided talking about what had happened, partly because I couldn't articulate it and partly because I was afraid to – both for their reactions and to admit to myself that I was falling apart. I think the fact that I just wrote the word *admit* illustrates part of the problem around mental illness, which equates struggling to failing. And yet if I had come home with a broken leg I don't think I would have worried about what people thought of that. 'Oh shit,' said one friend when I told her my doctor had just diagnosed depression; an involuntary reaction I am sure, but it didn't encourage me to volunteer more. The fear of judgement in a head already awhirl with negative, downwards-spiralling voices can make sharing a mountain too tall to climb. And yet letting other voices in and spending time in others' heads is always going to help.

Now I can see that it was normal for depression, grief and PTSD-like symptoms to follow the trauma of being trapped alone in a boat for three days in uncertain, dangerous conditions. And I can see that I needed a time of recovery and decompression and processing, and yet even before I left Japan I had started thinking of how to return to the ocean. That is always my way – to be doing and coping and moving forward, or at least trying to feel like I am. Perhaps it is a way of dealing with the fear of not coping. Of needing to keep it together, to feel like I am doing something useful, even if the most useful thing would be to do the opposite. Like many of us do when we are really struggling with demons, I tried pushing them away and pushing on in a bid to shake them off. It wasn't very convincing, though: crying got in the way of doing anything useful; small tasks floored me; my inbox terrified me; my to-do list felt like Everest; a promised article went three months late. I was paralysed. During Mawar the idea of becoming a teacher had floated by with all the welcome signs of safety, challenges and no storms, and yet the idea of returning to the Pacific had an even stronger pull. I wanted to go back and carry on with the journey, for there was still so much of it to run, and I also knew that in the ocean I would find healing and perhaps even myself again.

Understandably, some people didn't get why I would want to go back. But many also didn't (and still don't) get why I would want to go out there in the first place. I think Mum understood why but struggled with how:

'I just don't think you could cope at the moment, sugar plum. You can't even cope here at home.'

And she was right; I couldn't. But I knew that the dark stuff wouldn't last for ever, if only I could find a way out. When I found myself frightened and disorientated in a car park in Leicester one day, not sure how I had driven there nor how I would get home, I knew that I needed Briony to help. I had frozen in the car park because I was still stuck in my boat, and so in Briony's office we dipped back into the storm. Apparently in survival situations our brains decommission the part that processes time, leaving us with snippets and flashes of the event. These generally get stored in our somatic and visual memory – meaning we feel and see what happened before we can put words and a time frame around it. By talking and remembering in a controlled way, I could start processing it.

'I'm going to pull you out of it now, Sarah. It's almost time to wind up,' Briony would say, and I would pull myself out of the chair where I had pushed myself as far back as I could go. Slatted blinds. Green digital numbers on the flat square clock in the corner. Water jug. Safe. Safe. Safe. After each session I drove home feeling like the lid of the pressure cooker had been lifted, if only for a moment. At the times I felt the furthest from myself, I considered accelerating into road bridges and considered other ways of finding an early exit. It felt so rational and straightforward, which now feels so frightening and sad, but that was the state I was in.

'What if it happens again?' many asked. That was a risk I had to accept, and while there would always be a chance of another row-ending storm, there was also no guarantee. Weather data would continue to give us the best chances of making the safest decisions and I had ideas on how to improve my (at that point imaginary) boat, which would hopefully improve my chance of making it out the other side of any other major storm event in a position to carry on. I would have to deal with my own fears of another storm happening just as I did with other scary potentials – I would rationalise it, accept it and use it. 'If you will still have me, I would love to be a part of your team,' said Lee, and other team members did too. That was a confidence boost. Not long after I came home from Japan, Sara had decided to step away to find balance in her life again after committing twenty months of unflinching enthusiasm, energy and good sense in her role as project manager. I understood and was glad for her, and yet after her being my right-hand woman since the very start, it felt like another grief. Even though various sponsors pledged their continued support and belief (even before I had announced my intentions), my negative head-space fell ever inwards and reinforced the growing idea in my head that I wasn't worth their support. Food, gear and clothes were all helpful but money was the keystone. The project had nowhere near enough for any sort of boat and it would take me too long to earn the tens of thousands needed and still keep the project current. So when, after much negotiation, our insurance broker confirmed that Lloyd's would pay out on the policy we had bought for the expedition, it felt like a parting of the seas. Now, if I could find a boat, secure some more funding, patch myself up and renew the team, I could see a way back out to the ocean.

I first met with Rebecca Rees in a coffee shop in Oakham where I had once served her as a waitress some years before. She wanted to nominate me for a national award and it had taken Jenny some time to persuade me to agree as this was the last thing I thought I deserved. My main goal was not to cry, but at the first 'How are you?' my tears replied.

'Is there anything I can do to help?' asked Rebecca, stirring her cappuccino while I cried over my peppermint tea. 'I've been in a dark place before,' she said, 'and I know how difficult it can be. I'm a coach, perhaps I could help you with something practical?' I put my tea down and let her in. After our next meeting at her house overlooking an autumnal Rutland Water, I explained, through tears, the geography of my slump. Everything was sortable, Rebecca reassured me, and she was keen and able to help. She typed while I narrated a tangential trail of thoughts for the overdue article, turning that scariest of whites into a page populated by some words which I could add to. Within a couple of weeks Rebecca had found a new project manager in local mother, accountant and sports fanatic Mel Jarrett, who joined the team on a voluntary basis, apparently unphased by our worldy goals and financial gaps. Having a co-pilot to whom I could hand over detail that I was failing at felt like having another paddler on board: I still had to paddle hard, but the boat still moved if I rested a bit. We were aiming to return to Japan in March, nine months after I had been picked up, which, even without the demons in my head, would have been a tight timeline.

My boat-builder Jamie had rung me shortly after my return. '*Socks*, John Beedon's old boat, is for sale. I've just repainted her for a guy who bought her but has now backed out; mid-life crisis or something. She's mint, Sarah. You should come and see her.'

Apart from the name (which I have always felt suited horses and cats better than boats), I knew that this sister boat to

Gulliver and *Blossom* would be perfect. After negotiating further commitment from my major sponsors and key supporters, I stretched out my overdrafts and christened her *Happy Socks*. I named her after the stripy woollen 'happy socks' my mum knits and as a nod to her origins as *Socks*, glad to be keeping some of the old with the new.

The final star to align was Jamie's diary. Over the autumn he tinkered, changed, strengthened and added to my little white boat. Floor-to-ceiling joists were added on either side of the main hatch into my cabin to support the bulkhead, which we presumed had been shifted in *Gulliver* to cause the leakage. (Charlie's boat *Blossom* had been torn open in this area under the strain of a pitch pole capsize.) A manual bilge pump was put near my bunk, so that I could empty water from my cabin in rough seas. Towing rings for deploying the sea anchor were strengthened, as *Gulliver's* had been pulled out during the storm. Extra cleats. Flexible whip aerials replaced fibreglass ones. The rudder pintle was extended for easier fixing and removal of the rudder at sea. Batteries were moved rearwards for stability. Extra tie-down loops were added to my cabin to detain errant gear in capsizes, and extra bottle holders within reach of my bunk. Alone, each added function might seem unimpressive but, like an orchestra, cumulatively they were significant. In remote and extreme conditions, ocean rowing is about survival, where even the tiniest omission or need for extra effort may be critical.

At the final shortlisting for the awards in November I saw Fiona, who was representing Accenture in their category. The black dog sat heavily across my shoulders that day and my chest hurt with tears.

'Where's your determination gone?' she asked.

'I don't know. I don't feel like me right now,' I sobbed.

'Hey. It's OK,' she said. 'I believe in you, even if you don't believe in yourself right now. The demons have latched on: the bastards are hard to shake. But you will – when you and they are ready. They're short-term features but you're in for the long haul.'

Fiona had just flicked a switch, giving me permission to let others do the believing for now. She invited me to her house to spend an evening with her family ahead of a sponsored bike ride we were doing together with an Accenture team that weekend. Being around her two bubbling, chattering children was a perfect tonic and distraction because, a bit like dogs, children don't judge and they can make you smile effortlessly.

Another important thing which had helped me climb over the wall was in learning about my inner chimp through reading Professor Steve Peters' book *The Chimp Paradox*. In it he explains his model of the brain and its distinct but interlinking parts. The animal centre (the chimp) acts based on emotion, instinct and desire. The logical centre (the human) makes decisions based on facts and reason. Your behaviour depends on who is in charge – human or chimp – and how these centres interact. Having your chimp at the helm is beneficial when a fight or flight response is needed, whereas your human will be better at steering things in a tricky meeting. For me, the idea worked in helping me understand why I behaved more emotionally or rationally in certain situations and also in helping me appreciate what my inner needs are. I have been calling my chimp Chimpy ever since.

By December the storm had passed. *I think I am finally, fully, me again,* I wrote in my diary. *I still get flashbacks but it is more controlled now. I have my sense of humour. I have my bounce. I have my belief. It's all coming together.* Getting through the post-traumatic angst and gloom of depression had been a bit like trying to get over a wall. I had been the only one who could build the ladder, but many people had helped me, fuelling me when I was tired or guiding me when I was frightened by the scale of it. People I admired had also told me of their walls, which had helped me feel less alone. Others had listened while I described mine and helped me believe there was something on the other side. That wall is still there somewhere and actually I am glad, because it helps me understand myself and others better. The blog post I wrote afterwards on the lack of openness around dark stuff was one of the most highly commented upon of my whole journey, which I think illustrates how we can all feel squashed by heavy stuff at different times and how if we can make it less scary to talk openly about it, it might seem a little bit more manageable. In the wee hours of 1 January 2013, Claire and I drove out east to a Norfolk beach to leap off the sand dunes at dawn. Running into the sea, we shrieked and hollered as the surface sparkled. I dived beneath the water, my brain stinging and skin on cold fire. Resurfacing, I felt alive again.

A week later, while I was making a fruit crumble in Claire's kitchen, Lucy walked into my life. A couple of months before, I had been ruffled by the novelty of noticing that I was attracted to women and unsettled by not knowing what to do with the feelings. I wrestled with it for a while until, with a friend's encouragement, I decided to just see what happened. 'You never know, you might meet someone who sweeps you off your feet,' she said, and I laughed it off. But Lucy did. She was studying at the Royal Agricultural College and planned to work on her family farm in Oxfordshire, while I was still in Rutland training and preparing for the Pacific. So, for the next two months I contrived reasons to be in Oxfordshire to cuddle the piglets and she drove up to Rutland after lectures, hitting the road pre-dawn to get back in time for more. I wasn't really coming out (because it was a new-found attraction for me), but my perception of what I thought other people might think meant that I had to gee myself up to talk about it. 'What did you think I would say, you daft thing?' asked my friend Roostie after I squirmishly announced that I was going out with a girl (through text message, as I had avoided telling her over lunch). 'For someone to make you smile like that, she must be amazing. I can't wait to meet her.'

Lucy and I told each other that if we met someone while I was away, we should go for it, and then we both protested that of course we wouldn't. We knew that even though I would be away for a long time, we wanted to be together. I jokingly suggested that Lucy come to Japan with me at the end of March, but amazingly, she was actually able to. Cherry blossom fell in pink drifts as we mixed up school talks with visiting friends and rowing admin, alongside trips to *ramen* bars and *onsens*. In Sajima we visited my adopted Japanese grandparents, warm and smiling as ever, and nodded to Fuji-san across the bay. Mr Ootake-san unbuttoned his pyjama top to proudly show us his stitches from a recent heart surgery, and I wondered if I would ever see them again. Tari still bounced with all the energy of Tigger and the tenderness of Kanga while Kelly and Kaz were brand new parents to eight-week-old Quinn. As we cuddled and bounced him, Lucy and I imagined ourselves as parents together one day. We hadn't known each other for very long, but it felt like we had been together for ever. 'Just bloody come home safely,' said Lucy with eyes puffy from crying, as we hugged goodbye in the departures hall at Narita Airport.

9

The Pacific Ocean #2

The Pacific Ocean | Choshi, Japan to Adak, Alaska |
Row | Spring − Summer 2013 | 1,500 miles

As Lucy flew home, my new ocean support manager Tony
Humphreys flew in for a week. I had met Tony while he was
working with Charlie the year before but knew of him through
other rowers, too. He had extensive experience working with
sailors and rowers, and it felt good to have him on board. *Happy
Socks'* delivery from the customs impound was delayed, meaning
that we squashed a week's work into three busy days once we
finally took delivery of her in Choshi Marina. Enthroned on
Gulliver's old trailer amongst the yachts and motorboats, she looked
very much like a six-year-old who had slipped into a team photo
of fifteen-year-olds.

While we worked on packing gear the marina staff sanded,
patched and repaired the local pleasure boat fleet − either for their
yearly update or rehabbing them following the tsunami damage.
Now two years on from the devastation of March 2011, the marina
was well on its way to being fully functioning again. As we sorted
and packed gear we took snacks and surplus treats to the guys
working in the building next to us, and they accepted them in
that very Japanese way of elegantly refusing and then elegantly
bowing with thanks. When it was cold they brought us cans of
hot coffee from the vending machine, hanging over the safety rails
of *Happy Socks* to chat and consider the set-up of my life at sea.
Many other locals did the same and I answered their questions
with a mix of gratitude for their interest and impatience at wanting
to get on with the to-do lists as I zoned in on the ocean. One
day a Canadian guy introduced himself and we chatted.

'I have a cousin who is about to row the Atlantic,' he said in
a strong French accent.

Launch Day, Tower Bridge, 1 April 2011, en route to the world.

A different view every night – some more beautiful than others. This was in Western China.

Through the Gobi Desert it was hot, dusty and windy. Gao's red flag
billows out behind his bike, *Stranger*.

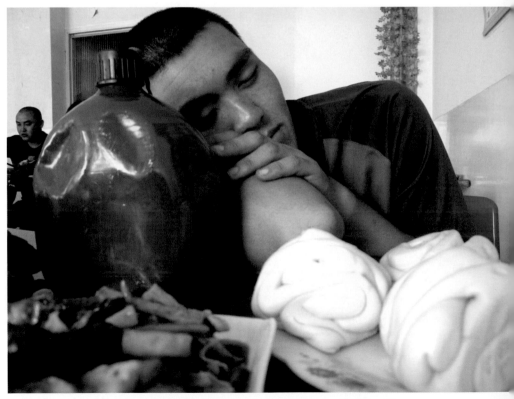

Gao often fell asleep at mealtimes, after hours in the saddle.

With *Gulliver* and all the supplies for a Pacific voyage.

Swimming in
the Pacific –
at once scary
and exciting.

Being picked up
from *Gulliver* by the
Japan Coastguard
after Tropical Storm
Mawar, June 2012.

Day 66 of the second Pacific row – engaged! I drew a ring on my finger with a marker pen.

Land ahoy! Arriving in Adak, Alaska, after 150 days at sea aboard *Happy Socks*.

Hiking across Adak Island with Lucy and Justine to join up the dots from the tracker. There was still snow on the ground.

Kayaking in the Aleutians in rolling seas.

Justine and I pull ashore on Homer Spit, 101 days after we set out from Adak, having paddled 1,500 miles along the Aleutian chain and Alaskan Peninsula.

Young grizzly bears play-fighting in Hallo Bay, Alaska. Along the peninsula we saw lots of bears, many of them feeding ahead of winter.

The first snow out of Whitehorse, Yukon, Canada – relatively warm compared to the dry, biting winds which accompanied the deep freeze of midwinter across the Canadian Prairies and American Midwest. The lowest temperature was -40°C.

Releasing a storm petrel. It couldn't get off *Happy Socks* without a bit of a launch.

A sea turtle visits my boat on the Atlantic. Most were wary of me, but this one was very curious.

Harnessed into *Happy Socks* during rough weather. Trying to remain as calm and comfortable as possible was physically and mentally testing when the risk of capsizing was so great.

Paddling under Tower Bridge, 3 November 2015, with the flotilla of kayaks.

Reunited with Lucy at Tower Bridge, ready for the next adventure.

'No way! Mylène Paquette?' I had helped Mylène in her preparations and we had each packed presents and letters for the other's crossing. Her goal was to row from Halifax in Canada to France this summer, aiming to leave some time after I left Japan. It seemed a ridiculous coincidence that her cousin should be out here working on the dock I was leaving from.

As Tony passed dry bags up and I snuggled them into *Happy Socks'* lockers, it occurred to me just how many times my supplies had been handled in their life, not only as part of my journey but also during their entire production cycles. Themed dry bags proclaiming their contents of 'Breakfasts', 'Puddings', 'Treats' reminded me of the packing weekend in January with a team of friends and family. Over the winter Mel and I had collated deliveries of electronics and rechargeable battery packs, ocean waterproofs, thermals, dry bags of all shapes and sizes, suncream, biodegradable soap, flasks and drinks bottles, canned butter and tinned meat, hundreds of freeze-dried meals, fruit and nut bars, roasted seeds, and a few Mars bars. Patrolling the supermarket, I had been shot strange looks as I cleared a shelf of milk powder and built a mountain of dried fruit in my trolley. There were kilos of oats, enough tissues for a small town's flu season, tiny bottles of bubbly and big cartons of juice, a few crates of tinned fruit, at least a bag of every grain and pasta on offer and a selection of dried sauces, spices and flavours to rival any restaurant. In a bid for efficiency and enjoyment I needed calorie- and protein-rich fuel which was lightweight and durable.

I raided the aisles for talc, lip balms, hand creams and nappy rash creams, and Doctor Caroline prescribed the more exotic items of injectables, suture kits and a 'magic lolly' of something a bit like morphine in case of a bad accident. For redundancy I had twice as much of my daily thyroid medication. 'How many soup sachets do you want in a bag?' cried a voice from behind a pile. 'Shall I split up teabag flavours?' 'Do you want me to put the cystitis sachets in the main medical bag or the spares?' My helpers squirrelled away treats and messages or drew pictures across packaging for me to discover at sea. By Sunday evening we were left with boxes of stacked zip-locked bags, each filled with a few days' worth of snack bars, or variations on a theme of salted nuts or soups.

'Well, you're not going to go hungry out there,' Tony joked, and it was true. After basing my Indian Ocean rations on cheapness rather than enjoyment, I had learned my lesson and added extras, just in case. During the row, Tony would monitor and manage my tracker and advise on kit issues on board. If there was a crisis, he would take the lead, relieving the pressure on others for whom this was not their realm. On the other side he would fly out to meet me and organise logistics to help me land safely, helping me sort the boat and ship her on. Wind blowing bitterly, our fingers numb, I appreciated Tony's attention to detail and patience as we transferred all the sponsor decals to *Happy Socks*, turning her from white sugar mouse into smartly proud, professional boat. I knew I wouldn't have been quite so patient on my own.

This is one of my favourite things about my team: while we were all focused on the same goal, our real strength lay in our differences in approach and appreciation of them. George was all about detail, pragmatism and solutions. Sean and Caroline were both practical, soothing and experienced in expeditions. Mel was calm, organised and full of common sense. Rebecca always tried to make things bigger and better and had a heart of gold. Jenny was realistic, straightforward, perceptive and empathetic. Lee was a numbers and possibilities man, level-headed and clear. Briony was pre-emptive, unflappable and appeared at all the right moments. Thank goodness everyone had a good sense of humour. Others satellited in and out of my team according to what was needed, but for the Pacific this was the core. Lucy threw herself into expedition life with all the energy and zest of someone who had been there from the start, joining in seamlessly with whatever needed doing from kit sorting, mailing thank-yous to local helpers, posting blogs, arranging logistics and more.

Japan's springtime weather was fickle and skittish, presenting nothing stable enough for departure, and so Kelly and Kaz invited me back to theirs near Tokyo. It felt like a treat to be seeing them for so long this time, and I enjoyed helping out with chores and babysitting in between training and admin. I made up circuits around the living room, doing pull-ups from tables, step-ups on chairs and press-ups and more on the floor. Being away from *Happy Socks* made the ocean feel like quite an abstract concept.

And then suddenly it was time to go. After shopping for as much fruit and veg as we could get on the boat, Tari and I headed to the cliff-top *onsen*. Being back in Japan with friends had felt like a homecoming of sorts and I knew that rowing again would, too. I gazed across the white-horsed sea to the far curve of the horizon, knowing that *Happy Socks* and I would be more minuscule, by scale, than the full stop at the end of this sentence is amongst the letters in this book. Images of *Gulliver* and Mawar hovered quietly at the sidelines, but for now I was focused and calm.

Lines clattered against masts and flagpoles whistled in the stiff south-westerly breeze as *Happy Socks* bobbed against her pontoon mooring. Gusts sent hurried ruffles scurrying across the water and outside rollers tumbled towards shore. Once I had cleared the pontoon and turned for the entrance I would be blasted by a headwind which, if only I could get out and around the corner of the marina, would let me fly. Climbing into *Happy Socks* after hugs and goodbyes, I was actually certain I would be back on the pontoon very quickly – for weighing about three-quarters of a tonne, she was a slow-moving beast and too heavy to row out into the wind. It took thirty minutes of all-out effort to row to the marina entrance, where waves pinned us face to face with starfish stuck like pictures on a wall. Crabs tiptoed sideways to crouch under shiny seaweed and sea anenomes huddled in squidgy blobs waiting for the tide. I, too, headed back to wait for the wind to drop, leaving again in the warmth and relative quiet of the afternoon. Kelly, Kaz, Tari and Mike waved from the marina wall as I rounded it and finally headed out to sea, pushed by the south-westerly wind.

'*Appy Socks, Appy Socks, Appy Socks* zis is *Lodbro*. Do you read me?' said a French voice on the end of the radio. Stuffing my oars into their stowage tubes, I unhooked my feet from the webbing strap of my footplate and hung half in, half out of the hatch to reply. '*Lodbro*, this is *Happy Socks.*' 'Ow are you? Is everything okay? Over.' Apart from feeding the fish with Tari's home-made cookies, I was OK, with thirty-six hours out from land clocked already. The *Lodbro* must have been surprised to see my sugar-mouse boat amongst the usual traffic of fishing and merchant boats and I was grateful for the call. There is a unique kinship amongst seafarers, borne, I think, of our shared under-standing of our frailty at sea, whether we are 3 or 300 metres long. A couple of weeks into my Indian Ocean journey I woke up to my boat alarm bleeping loudly and stepped outside to see the *Prince of the Netherlands* half a mile away and on a direct course. No one answered my VHF calls for a couple of minutes as I frantically calculated the angles between us, imagining colli-sion. Finally, an Australian voice called and I relaxed. 'Do you need any assistance, or are you just one of those mad adventurers?'

Millpond seas under the soft and growing starriness of the recent sundown welcomed me into my second night afloat and I thanked it by vomiting over the side, seasickness getting the better of me. My rowing was powered by pot after pot of fruit cocktail (gentle on the way down and the way up), and I was glad of the added push from the east-flowing Kuroshio current. Noticing a tricolor of lights snailing towards me, I jumped on the radio. 'Cargo ship at position blah blah blah, do you read me? Over,' I called, again and again, wondering why my AIS unit wasn't receiving their transmission and whether they were picking up mine. '*Happy Socks, Happy Socks*, this is USS *Sealander*, go ahead.' Aha. A military boat, of course they had seen me. 'If you don't mind me asking, ma'am, is everything OK? You're 70 miles offshore.' Queasiness aside I was, but I knew I would be even better once I had added a zero and more to that distance.

Following the Pacific's syncopated, disjointed rhythm, I rowed when she let me and I sat tight on the sea anchor when she didn't, waiting out the headwinds or unsafe seas. In the first week I spent two days strapped to my bunk while a gale yowled over and by day 21 I had only rowed on seven days – the rest had been walled with headwinds. Fortunately, the Kuroshio current was still well defined and carried us with it, snaking usefully eastwards while I slept or read inside. Unsurprisingly, perhaps, the rough seas felt rougher than I remembered from the year before and I was frightened of capsizing. I talked to Chimpy, reassuring him that *Happy Socks* knew what she was doing, and tried visualising her capsizing and self-righting. Shoved into the reach of my harness as the boat slammed onto her side, before being suspended upside down, hands and toes resting on the roof. Water frothing at the hatches. Then I visualised everything being the right way up again. Rocking. Safe. When we really did capsize for the first time, on day 22, I swore loudly at the abrupt wake-up as I was thrown from gentle snoozing to upside down in a flash, and then I relaxed into the idea that all was well. It was satisfying to see that things had stayed in their places, tied down by the extra lashing points, and I was glad to see that the new aerials didn't seem phased. Mostly thanks to the Kuroshio's pull, after two weeks we passed 700 miles out from land, which marked the point where I had been rescued from Mawar. I celebrated with a miniature bottle of bubbles once the weather allowed.

In the first thousand miles the spring weather took me through almost the full range of my onboard wardrobe, sometimes all in one day as flat seas morphed into 20 knots of breeze with the sun rolling in and out of the clouds. Since it focuses on the major radiators of legs and glutes, rowing is generally warm work, but a crisp wind, flying waves or the seeping damp of a misty morning could chill me quickly if the sun wasn't out. So I kept my bag of woollen, fleece and waterproof hats, Buffs, thermal layers and neoprene gloves to hand.

I'd defy anyone not to fall for the ocean rower's life on those days when the conditions meant a day's surfing, pushed by the waves and pulled by the allure of a decent day's progress, trying to keep the boat pointing down the waves to avoid broaching. Sometimes *Happy Socks* was rushed forwards and I was bopped off my seat as waves slopped into the boat and over me, trickling ocean down my neck and flooding the deck for a moment as it all rushed out through the scupper flaps down the side of the boat. Sometimes I bailed it out, and at others I just accepted that it was going to be a wet day and that my feet would be a soggy mess.

I also enjoyed the calm and quiet of flat days, as high-pressure systems sat high overhead, when the splash of breaching whales boomed across the emptiness and even the quietest fluttering of storm petrels' wings at dusk sounded loud. On those days when the horizon was at its furthest away I often broke the ocean rower's code of keeping cabin hatches closed to let the air in and dry out my damp cabin. I rinsed clothes and myself in the bucket and hung them out to dry, enjoying the beating warmth of the sun on my bare skin as I rowed and sorted. Eating was always much more enjoyable on those days, too, compared to the wet days when waves often slapped over my head and into my food.

Along with his daily forecast and outlook of winds, from time to time Lee emailed snapshots of the telemetry-measured satellite depictions of the currents, different colours relating to different sea surface temperatures and, therefore, speeds. He plotted my position and added arrows to show my most likely path or ideal target to row for. Sometimes I had to talk myself into opening his messages, knowing that whatever was within might send my mood skywards or downwards. Sometimes it was impossible and I got frustrated at not being able to make his targets, sending Chimpy chattering at not being good enough or strong enough. *Frustrating, slow, sore day, like rowing through setting concrete. Rowed across SSE winds fighting for NE/E. In one hour I rowed 0.5 miles!* I wrote in my journal on day 77. On other days, I rowed hours for the same or just to try and hold ground, collapsing into my cabin and the comfort of food and a sleeping mat at day's end. But compared to the bike, I enjoyed the fact that my bed was ready and waiting and I didn't have to find anywhere to stop.

Just as we knew it would, after a swift first thousand miles, the Kuroshio petered out into confused knots and twirls and my track tangled accordingly. In my logbook, over ten days in early June, the column for heading shows little arrows pointing around all points of the compass with six days showing that I went backwards, either blown by winds or pushed by currents, whether I could row or not. The mileage column confirms that this was not a good week for progress: −20, −10, −1, +4, +6, +10, −10, −27, −13. The satellite track from that period shows loops and squiggles. On day 76 I just wrote *ZIGZAG!* after being pushed backwards every time I had stopped rowing, making two miles progress forward overall. On those days I would have loved to be a two-person team, with another rower onboard to push us forward when I was resting, although normally I wouldn't have wanted to share my small world with anyone else. I talked to myself and *Happy Socks* and each day I emailed Mel to let her know I was OK, tweeted or blogged and called Lucy.

Now that I was journeying with Lucy, alone took on a new meaning, for both of us. I missed her deeply and wrangled to reconcile the fact that I was the reason for our separation. And yet from that separation we were also finding strength in our relationship, valuing our daily chats and the delay on the satellite phone which forced us to pause and really listen to each other. I heard somewhere that, on average, most couples spend just fifteen minutes a week talking to one another, so for us the irony of a solo ocean row was that we probably spent more time talking to each other than we would have done had we both been on land. When I was worried about incoming rough weather, Lucy cheered me up, and if I was worried about my lack of progress, she would listen to me rant and then distract me with news of home. 'Don't you worry about how far you have left. I'm right there with you, every step of the way. Going nowhere.'

Once a week she sent through tweets and blog comments from my website, which gave me a boost if I was in a slump, to know that others were pushing and pulling for me, too. It helped me feel connected to them, and to her. As I sat in *Happy Socks* out on the ocean, Lucy might be in her tractor – both of us in worlds of our own and worlds which were quite new to the other, meaning that we each gave the other a crash course in spraying fields or surviving the waves. *Spend so many hours dreaming of future, imagining us together – grinning and singing,* I wrote in my diary one day. We talked about marrying one day, and over time this evolved to wanting to propose to each other when I eventually reached the other side. I secretly shifted my goal to the International Date Line, which fell about halfway across, and then, when that still showed no signs of getting any closer, I decided that I could wait no longer. I always rang Lucy at 6 a.m. UK time to wake her up for work, but on day 66 I called her again at lunchtime and asked her to marry me. I had to do it twice as she didn't hear me properly the first time, and with a whoop and a holler and lots of shrieking she said yes. Skylark light, I drew an engagement ring on my finger with a marker pen and, while Lucy celebrated with friends and family at home, I shouted to the school of tuna beneath my boat. 'I'm getting marrieeeeeeeeed!'

Expeditions can often feel selfish in the pursuit of single-minded goals, disappearing from home life for months or years at a time, and that side of it often takes some internal negotiation. I need two hands to count the weddings of friends I have missed while I have been away on my London2London expedition, but somehow the pull of the journey has always won and I have kept on going. But now the focus of not just my journey, but my whole life, had shifted and I knew that finding the balance between expeditions and my life with Lucy would be a journey in itself.

10

Changing Course

The Pacific Ocean | Row | Summer 2013 | 1,500 miles

On days when the storms outside whipped up storms in my head or the lethargy of no progress pulled me under, I did whatever it took to calm things again or re-energise them. I sang. I recited poems. I looked for good things about the day. I rootled about in lockers for a treat of tinned peaches or, if the weather allowed me to cook, a supper treat of pancakes. I called home to hear news that could distract me. If it was calm enough, I hung upside down over the cabin to stretch and ponder the sounds from in and around the boat. A glug of the waterline at the side of the boat. Something tapping. Sometimes a change in activity or a break to stop and listen was all it took to press Refresh and get back on the seat and pull. If the batteries were charged and there was sunshine to top it up again via the solar panels, I ran the water-maker and poured a bucket of refreshingly cold water over my head.

And so it was on day 83, after a morning on the oars in sweltering heat, that I lay back from my seat over the deck, trying to decide what to do next. It would be too hot inside for a midday snooze and, given that the conditions satisfied my wimpy rules for swimming (i.e. a bright, flat day so that I could see down into the water a little way), I sat up to look over the edge, knowing that I would probably stand nakedly on the side of the boat for half an hour before I could do it. Looking over the side, I saw the sleek, neat form of a shark, close enough to touch. It slid under the boat as I grabbed my GoPro camera on a pole, switched it on and slipped it under the surface. I watched the fin track to the back of the boat and saw the grey forms of my fish followers swim hurriedly to the front. The fin cruised casually behind. My fish swam around to the back of the boat and moments later the shark glided back past my camera and dissolved into the blue. I often wondered at the countless creatures which came to check out my boat without my noticing. Given that shark numbers have declined rapidly in recent years, I wondered, too, if ocean rowers in twenty years' time will be lucky enough to be able to see sharks, or if overfishing and the Asian appetite for shark fin soup would have claimed them from our seas. But finally, I could answer the question that schoolchildren always asked – 'Do you see sharks out there?' – with a yes.

My time at sea can be described in contrasts: from the basic night and day rhythms with their colours and light displays, through weathers and sea states and my associated progress or lack of it, to the wildlife spectrum of microscopic to massive. I lived by the sun and the moon, rowed by the weather changes, and lived day to day for the wildlife encounters. The most numerous of my neighbours were the tiniest – the drifting and floating planktic masses, their jellied bodies and trilling featherlite arms an array of colours and shapes. In picking up chunks of driftwood or plastic which floated by, I could literally pull up a whole ecosystem of barnacles, weed, mites and the odd crab. Holding them up for a closer look, their fringed arms writhed in the novelty of space and their shells sucked and squelched. If any of the crabs fell off into the water they swam frantically for the nearest drifting island, my boat or something else. Fish congregated in schools beneath and around my boat in multicoloured hordes, each species disappearing when their invisible limit in latitude or longitude was reached. Dolphins bounced past in playful groups, spinning and leaping, and swimming out to check out my boat. Above the water, occasional birds also used *Happy Socks* as an island, stopping to rest or sleep overnight, either by choice or by accident. I often had to launch tiny petrels back into the air after they had ricocheted into the light on my cabin. Peering out through the hatch one dull morning, I saw a large white bird, its head tucked under one wing, rocking on the forward cabin roof against the motion of the waves. It was a pink-footed booby, sitting above the quote over my cabin door, which said: 'Being scared of something is never a good reason not to do it.'

Setting out to sea as a soloist, you always know that you are going to spend a lot of time being blown backwards or pulled this way and that by currents which obviously lie out of your control. With the North Pacific we knew this would be the case, more so than it had been on the Indian Ocean, as this part of the world is a volatile place known for its changeability. For context, only two soloists had ever made it across to the USA from Japan and only one double, out of many failed attempts. This year the weather was relentless and kept me pinned amid the confusion of the knotted ends of the Kuroshio, as the winds and currents played ping-pong with me. On one stretch I criss-crossed the same 100-mile sea area seven times in five weeks and, having finally broken out of the Kuroshio's grasp, I was blown backwards for ten days by steady south-easterly winds. At the same time, cloud cover and fog meant that my solar panels weren't charging the boat batteries.

My diary entries for two of those days read:

Day 113: East wind continues and cloud cover too. Running out of power and water.

Day 118: Last eight days – weather bound and cloud covered both physically and metaphorically, being pushed backwards and unable to row.

The longer the headwinds prevailed, the less time I had to get safely ashore. Increased frequency and strength of storms through the late autumn and a drop in water and air tempera-tures and daylight hours would mean that everything would get more difficult and dangerous. In turn this meant that the risk of needing assistance or rescue also increased unacceptably. Multiple times during the day I would run through calculations of distance left to run and timings that could make it likely. My hopes for tailwinds rose and then fell as Lee's emails arrived saying that the system had changed and I had yet more head-winds on the way.

Amid the frustrations and angst of going round and round in circles, there were moments of beauty and awe which reminded me why I had chosen to go to sea. One day I watched the moon set in the morning as I got to the oars and the sun set in the evening as a giant moon rose on the opposite horizon. I rowed late into the night under its sweeping glow, listening to dolphins huff-puffing through calm seas and watching the torpid bodies of tuna glide alongside us. Napping for a couple of hours in the middle of the night, I then got up before the dawn, welcoming in the day with the new sunrise and the moonset. It was a reminder that everything happens on nature's terms.

On my 102nd day at sea Justine sent me an email, jokingly suggesting that if I turned north and headed for the Aleutian Islands she could meet me there with my kayak so that I could continue on. Looking up to the map above my head I traced my finger from my position northwards to the chain of islands stretching westwards from the Alaskan peninsula and along to the mainland. At this point we still thought there was a chance of landing on the mainland, so I put Justine's idea on hold for another day.

As month three turned in to month four I called a team powwow on progress and landing options, saying out loud what it seemed everyone else was thinking: Vancouver Island was not looking like a feasible landing option any more. We all looked at charts and maps of the Pacific in our respective parts of the world and brainstormed. Hawaii and Midway were too far away. Anywhere on the mainland seemed like a different version of the risk and impossibility of pushing on to Vancouver Island. Justine's idea of the Aleutian Islands now did seem like a viable option – not just for landing safely now and keeping *Happy Socks,* but also for continuing my journey by kayak in 2014. I called Justine and waited for her to pick up the phone. 'So, JC, are you really serious about the Aleutians?' I said and waited while she paused. 'I'm not saying no, but . . . It will be the most challenging paddling either of us has ever done,' she said.

Justine had paddled all over the world on some very impressive and technical journeys, so if she was worried, then this would be a massive step up for me. Another adventuring friend in Canada who had also been monitoring my progress and roughing out options suggested that Adak Island, an ex–US naval base near the western end of the chain, would be a good place for me to land safely. 'Wikipedia even says it has a McDonald's!' he wrote. The fact that it had working docks for servicing the fishing fleet and a resident population was more important to us and a quick calculation put me at about one month out. My track was already going that way as I tried to minimise westwards mileage loss, so turning north deliberately seemed to make sense on all fronts.

Day 121: After 48 hrs discussions, ideas and angst of waiting for the delay of time zones to chat with people made decision to change course for Adak Island on Aleutians – 550 nm to NNE. Mind racing. Adrenaline. Perfect winds for 7 days ahead – 20–25kts of SSW winds.

I pulled up the sea anchor and let the boat run north – sprinting nearly 250 miles in the first week, which was further in the right direction than I had travelled in weeks. It was a massive relief to feel that we had a feasible option, although the unknowns of arriving in a new place at this changeable time of the year made it rather daunting. Given that winter was around the corner and the upcoming Aleutians journey would only be possible in the summer, I would head home again for a winter and spring of training and planning. It was exciting to think that I would soon be seeing Lucy. But the quick changes in plan were also rather discombobulating and Chimpy ramped up to full volume. This meant that I got no sleep for a few days while he chattered and chuntered and my team were bombarded with all my brain dumps of thoughts and feelings, given that I had no one to talk to in real time.

When we announced on the blog that I had changed course for the north the comments and offers of support were kind and encouraging, especially from those who knew the ocean:

Janice, Pacific North-West native: *I've been saying for a week now 'Why doesn't she go to the Aleutians?' And now you heard me.*

Sean Morley: *The North Pacific is no place to be come fall/winter. In my youth I used to be an oceanographer and while on expedition in the North Pacific our 350 ft ship hit waves that were the height of city blocks and at least 50 ft in height, maybe more, gigantic. No place for you and* Happy Socks.

Patrick: *Please contact me if you need somewhere to stay in Anchorage or Talkeetna.*

A chap called Michael Livingston, an Alaska native from Sand Point, had been emailing for some time with calls to divert north to the Aleutians, so he said that he now looked forward to us passing through the following year. Justine had already mentioned that the Aleutians was one birthplace of the precursor to the modern kayak, the local version being an *iqyax*, so it felt ironic to be diverting here, as though coming full circle to the roots of this sport.

Day 122: Sea has changed colour – more green. More shipping. Medi Antwerp – just 5 days to Kashima, Japan. Foggy today.

Our increasing latitude meant more regular and faster-clocking low-pressure systems, which meant more rough water, and damper, shorter days. At night the temperature started dropping to 10 degrees and I pulled out my fleece sleeping liner, which I had been saving for this point.

Day 124: 411 nm to Adak. Cold and damp rowing – added thermals, balaclava, dinghy top. Cold toes.

I even broke all my rules about cooking inside and, for a few meals of mashed potato, I rigged up my camping stove across the top of a locker hatch. I positioned it by the door so that I didn't kill myself with carbon monoxide, and holding the stove steady, I kept a hand on the hatch ready to close it if a wave hit us. The stove only took a couple of minutes to boil a litre of water. Then it was a quick manoeuvre to turn it off, pour the water over the plate of powdered potato and reposition everything so that it wasn't in danger of colliding or spilling. Inevitably it did, though, and I added to the trail of food down my tops. Even though I knew the steam would add to the damp of the mouldy cabin, which was now making me cough and my nose itch, I still ate inside. The sea changed colour from bright blues to deep greens as the depth changed and with it came a change in the local wildlife.

Day 133: FAMILY TUNA ARE GONE!

It may sound daft to anyone who hasn't spent months alone on a boat, but I missed those fish when they left – as something to talk to and something beautiful to watch as they followed my boat, chased after food or swam out to investigate other drifting things. Some weeks before, the hundred or so yellow fin tuna had left and been replaced by about a dozen or so even bigger tuna, each about a metre long of pure muscle, sheathed in brilliant blues and silvers with a striking crescent tail. I started seeing bird species which tended to stay closer to land. At 289 miles to go, a kittiwake circled the boat again and again, its yellow feet and black tights distinct against the grey morning.

Further north also meant more shipping as we crossed the main routes between North America and Japan. It was eerie to notice that I could hear their engines through the fog from a few miles away, and I was glad for the reassurance of the AIS. By now the fog was thick and wet which meant that a rowing session soon had me covered in tiny droplets. Overcast skies were less good for the batteries, however, as the solar panels struggled to charge with the lack of sunlight. In turn the voltage struggled to stay anywhere near 12 volts as the system gradually got drawn down. Given that the water-maker draws a lot of power as it pumps in seawater through membranes at high pressure to produce fresh water, it needed careful managing to keep it happy and me fed and watered. On day 123 I smelled burning and, tracing it back to the electricals box, realised that the fuse to the water-maker was melting from the extra power it was drawing. I could replace it for the short term, but it was a reminder that things were getting critical. I carried a manual water-maker on board and had even tried using it earlier on in the journey to see what it would feel like and how long it would take. Two hours of pumping for 5 litres of water was not appealing. I often find that my moods align with the sun and so during the grey days of those final weeks I often felt grey inside, too, even if I didn't notice it until the sun appeared.

Day 132: What a few days! Even just 36 hrs. Feels good not to be strapped in – warm food inside, smiling and to have my sense of humour intact. It's cold today and Adak feels a million miles away or as good as. Drifting SE on anchor in storm so angle to island decreases. Before we were even through this storm Lee sent a note saying 'Next storm due in a couple of days.' I wonder how many more we can take. Today, in calmness, I have tried to rationalise the fears, talked to Chimpy and joked with Luce. She is amazing. I cried yesterday – it all felt a bit much.

In the next storm the sea anchor lines got tangled around the rudder and, through the weight and heave of the boat against the sea, ripped it away after a prolonged and noisy few hours of banging itself on the back of the boat. I cursed myself for not having removed it and for not having brought a spare on the grounds of weight and space. I cursed the fact I had added to the floating rubbish of the sea. And I worried about steering without it. Tony and Lee cheered me up; Tony commenting that 'rudders were so last season', and Lee flapping more than I did – 'Holy crap! Holy crap!' At least it was quieter once it had gone, except for the waves. Sleep was almost impossible for thirty-six hours as the boat was slammed and slapped over, so I filled the hours as best I could and tried zoning out. In reading Kerouac's *On the Road*, I took comfort in reading about a journey crazier than mine.

Day 138: This week certainly looks better than the last. Doesn't take much: 2 big storms and a day of light variable.

Mostly, storms and rough weather on my journeys merge into each other in my memory and I am left only with the sense of what it felt like to be lying on my bunk for a few days at a time. Sticky, hot, damp, uncomfortable, painful for my lower back and legs and sometimes scary. The storm of 7 September was one of the most memorable I have been in. It was a big one, with winds gusting at 60 knots through its peak, creating spray and towers of water as wind ran at 90 degrees to the waves, and I was amazed that we didn't capsize. As a goal, I set myself the challenge of sucking a sherbet lemon for as long as possible every hour. It was also the day of my brother Michael's wedding. I rang home regularly for updates. 'Bride appeared – looks amazing. Your mum's in bright pink, had her hair done, looks great,' whispered George as she sat near the front of the church trying to hide her illicit phone action. I heard the bagpipes (slightly garbled through the sat phone) play the entrance music and joined in the hymn as roughly as I could, belting it out in the cabin, crying as I heard the cheer go up, not needing George's explanation, 'The Vicar just said he could . . .'

The final two weeks into Adak were cold, wet and rough. While sorting the sea anchor over the side of the boat in 30 knots of wind, I realised halfway through that I had clipped my line back to itself rather than to the safety rail as I had thought I had done. It was scary how easily I had missed it and so, back inside my cabin, I wrote *Clip and pull* on the wall above the hatch and drilled myself to go through the motions an extra time before heading out on deck. Tiny mistakes could have massive and irreparable consequences.

Day 147: Storm, capsizes, UTI, yeast infection, hallucinations . . . milestones and progress.

I was redlining it: batteries of both rower and boat were flat. A urinary tract infection didn't clear with the first round of antibiotics and gave way to thrush and my waterworks went into overdrive, so much so that Caroline was worried I might have diabetes. With no dipsticks on board to test for glucose, she made me taste my urine to check that it wasn't sugary. Day and night for a few days she got me to count my pulse and breathing rate every six hours so that she could monitor what was going on. Poor Caroline, she said she stayed up through the night worrying that I might drift off into a ketotic coma. Though reassured that I hadn't tasted sugar in my wee, she got me to ration my sugar intake for the final days to land nonetheless. I was energised by the steady progress of 20–35-mile days, though without a rudder, steering *Happy Socks* was hard in high winds. Even though it caused drag I trailed lines out the back of the boat to help her tracking. *THINK STRAIGHT, OUTEN!* I ordered myself in my logbook after losing my food bowl overboard while rinsing it into the water. I just had to keep it together.

My logbook entry for day 148 says: *NEARLY GOT RUN OVER BY* DENSA PUMA *AT 0630 – Thank goodness for bow waves.* At first I woke up to rumbling at close range. Bizarre – there was nothing on my AIS screen. Peeping out through the hatch, it was thickly white outside so I leaned back in to try the AIS again. Louder and louder, I first thought it might be a plane and believed it for a tiny split second when I saw a light coming towards us. In the next split second a black triangle followed, quickly becoming a wall and a ship. SHIT! It felt like 100 metres away but maybe it was a few more, heading straight for us. I remembered reading of Jim Shekhdar on the Pacific going under the bows of a container ship and being pushed out of the way by its bow wave, hoping the same would happen here. With no time to pull the oars out from their stowed position to row out of the way, I dived inside and slammed the hatch shut, steadying myself on the cabin walls as the bow wave pushed us away and rolled us down the side of the red-and-white ship, rocking on its waves. I craned to see its metal form slug past out of the main hatch and, as we were shunted out by the stern wave, I read its name across the transom. Breathing hard and fast, I flicked on the VHF and called up the captain. 'Densa Puma, this is Happy Socks . . .' The voice on the other end sounded calm and was surprised by my question about whether he could see me:

'Happy Socks, this is Densa Puma. No, I don't see you. Where are you?'

'Nearly 200 metres off your stern!' I said as he was swallowed up by the mist. My AIS must not be working properly. I switched the batteries on and off a couple of times and realised that although the green status light was on, the transmit/receive light was not. This meant that it wasn't sending or receiving information and explained why I hadn't seen any other boats since waking up. We were now a sitting duck in an area busy with shipping. 'There is a blow due tonight and a low pressure coming in two days,' said the captain before we wrapped up our call. Turning everything off to allow the solar panels to eke out any tiny amount of light to feed into the batteries was my only option. While rowing for the next few hours this felt manageably tense, as at least in the fog I could hear ships within a few miles. The low battery level had meant that I couldn't run my water-maker for five days either, and I was now down to a single litre. I started on my emergency water. When the seas picked up later that afternoon I returned to my cabin again, peering out through the hatch over the rolling green seas, trying to bat away imagined images of ships looming up over the waves towards me. From time to time I called out on the VHF to say that my AIS was faulty but no one ever responded.

A few days out and I was exhausted, writing in my diary: *Just about keeping it together. Sometimes feel fine, often I know I am only half with it.*

Tony and a photographer arrived in Adak a few days ahead of me to make final preparations for landing. Given the fierce currents in the straits between Adak and Kagalaska to the east, the goal was for them to hire a boat and meet me at the southern end of the island to tow me back around to the north, where I would officially come ashore in the small boat harbour at Adak port. Finding a seaworthy boat and captain was not quite as easy as they had hoped, given the lateness in the season and the increasingly rough weather it promised. Fishing boats had either left or would charge exorbitant prices and have restrictive rules and regulations, so Tony eventually plumped for a small Boston whaler and a seasick captain who could only go a few miles offshore by law.

In the final thirty-six hours I rowed with and for everyone that I could imagine in my invisible peloton. The goal was to stay awake and on my rowing seat as long as possible to make it safely to shore before the storm blew in. Sometimes stroke followed stroke and everything flowed. And other times each stroke took every shred of energy I thought I had and so I promised myself just one more. Just one more. I sang to the night and I battled with myself in the quietness, goading myself to stay rowing. I hallucinated and imagined shapes and colours which could not have been there. From time to time I flopped on my bed in soggy stillness, to gee myself up for another round. I cooked platefuls of mashed potato slathered in tinned butter and steaming mugs of tea to bring feeling back to my crinkled hands. I cried when I read the message on the back of Tari's photograph of us jumping in front of the sunset in Japan: *Think of us when you feel sad, happy or demotivated. Those who love you and believe in you every step of the way. You can do it.*

Taping it on the door in front of my rowing position I rowed on, trying to remember the warmth of that night when we had barbecued by the sea after a day of riding around the Miura peninsula. Instead, here I was on the southern shores of Adak being pulled westwards by the tide and being blown back out to sea by gentle headwinds rolling off mountains which I couldn't see. I had hoped for views of the islands punching out of the skyline in all their volcanic prowess, but instead Camel Island emerged shyly and greyly out of the white when I was half a mile away. 'Land Ahoooooooooy!' I shouted and laughed as I cheersed *Happy Socks* with the news. 'It's OK Chimpy, we're nearly there, mate. Let's just get to shore.' I radioed Tony's boat with my whereabouts, but the VHF signal was poor and we couldn't hear each other properly. Thankfully, there was a fishing boat nearby who received enough of both messages to relay the detail and we agreed that they would leave the cove where they had anchored out of the chop and head west a few miles to find me. Working off the basic map of my handheld GPS, I rowed hard into the wind and the ebbing tide. An engine noise droned on nearby and I kept looking over my shoulder for the Boston whaler. About the same time that dark grey cliffs emerged on one side, a buzzing boat grew out of the mist on the other. I waved madly at Tony and James, excited that these were not only the first people I had seen in five months, but also people I recognised. It was incongruous and yet totally normal to me and I drank in the details as they approached, filming them as they filmed me. Tony was driving under the wheelhouse and James was perched at the back of the boat with a camera over his shoulder and another pulled up to his face. He appeared from behind it and pulled down his big parka hood, grinning at me. Our boats pulled alongside, both rocking, and we leaned over the edges to hug. 'Stand down now, Chimpy; stand down, mate.' I opened a bottle of champagne that I had carried from Japan and glugged a sweet, bubbling mouthful, which ran down my chin. Even though I had made 153 marks on the tally chart on my cabin wall, Tony assured me that I had only been away for 150 days. The timing didn't matter to me and nor did the fact that I was the first person to row between Japan and Alaska – for me the journey was about getting back out after Mawar, of having survived both storms, and of achieving it for everyone who had helped make that happen.

Happy Socks was tied to the back of their boat and they suggested I lay down to sleep in my cabin for the four-hour ride north through the boiling Kagalaska Strait. I shivered in my wet clothes until it occurred to me to change into some dry ones and called home before falling asleep on my bunk. They had been some of the hardest expedition days of my life. A couple of thuds on the hatch roused me from damp sleep into the still air of a lush, green cove, the engine noise now changed. It was calm and quiet and close. The hills felt near. Gently drizzling and soft skied, it reminded me of Scotland or Wales, something like home.

We undid the lines and Tony turned their boat for the low jetty a few hundred metres away where a small crowd of people waited, some of them honking car horns. As I rowed *Happy Socks* those last few strokes to shore, I was a mix of tears and smiles, quietly thanking her and Chimpy for keeping me safe.

Adak's gentle, peaceful welcome and the space and quiet granted by a community who know what it is to live on the fringes was perfect. So, too, was the low-pressure system (which I had been racing to avoid on my way in), which arrived that night and rattled the satellite dishes, disrupting my link to the outside world. For, even though I was glad to be ashore and longed to hold Lucy again soon, there was a part of me, as with every coming ashore, that still wanted to be out there. A part of me which will always be.

II

Crashed: North America and UK

Alaska – New York City – UK |
Autumn 2013 – Spring 2014

'So you've just been diving, have you?' asked yet another A & E doctor as he plunged a needle into my wrist to check my blood gases. I was just focused on trying to breathe.

'No. She's been in a mouldy rowing boat for five months and just flown home from America,' explained Lucy, again.

'A rowing boat? Wow. And how many other people were with you?' Eventually they gave me oxygen and admitted me for fear of pulmonary embolism, a risk factor after long-haul flights and more so for me as my dad had died from them. After a chest X-ray the next morning they said that although a pulmonary embolism *could* be lurking they couldn't see it, and that they definitely could see a patch of pneumonia. I was treated for both before being let out four days later, with the lung capacity of a grape. Just walking to the car felt like a triumph and I apologised to my body for not having done better in my boat cleaning out on the Pacific. The germs that I must have picked up en route home from Adak via Anchorage and a week in New York can't have helped much, either. Normally there's a lot to be said for the sterility of time at sea, effectively in isolation.

I spent that first night out of hospital at my mum's house tearing my skin to shreds and struggling to breathe as everything swelled up.

'It's a good job you came in now,' said my doctor the next morning, as he watched the dial register a low blood pressure reading. Looking at the oximeter on my finger he continued: 'I don't think you'd have lasted much longer.' Diagnosing me with a severe allergic reaction on top of the pneumonia, he sent me away with inhalers, steroids and strong antihistamines, and said I was to see him again that evening and call if I got worse. 'And whatever you do, stay away from dogs. You can't go back to your mum's.' For the next few days it felt like an army of ants was marching all over my skin and I wheezed as I struggled to fill my rattling lungs. The steroids took the reaction down but my face puffed up again in response, marking the start of a year-long Outen vs Outen battle. Repeated allergic reactions meant I took steroids, which in turn knocked out my immune response, meaning an open door for germs and infections. Justine and I were due in the Aleutians in six months' time, but for now anything much more physical than climbing the stairs or going for short walks was put on hold.

After a few weeks staying with a friend of my mum's who didn't have dogs, I moved down to Oxfordshire to live with Lucy in her new house. Once tests had shown up all the risky allergens: dogs, cats, mould, dust mites and pollens – I did my best to avoid them, although that wasn't always easy, given that both of our families have dogs. It meant that I just couldn't go into their houses. Even now, three years later, I have not been back to my mum's. Making our first home together was the exciting, fun, reassuring island amid the sea of frustration at my ill health and the challenges of readying to go again. We made plans and dreamed dreams together, made each other laugh and supported the other through wobbles and wiggles. We celebrated our first Christmas together with our families and planted our first trees in our garden. In February we started our own little family with a collection of fluffy, scruffy orphan lambs from the farm, which we bottle-fed in the kitchen until the morning clean-up and 5 a.m. bleating meant that they graduated to the garden. Lucy cried often at the idea of my going away again and I questioned whether it was worth it for the pain of our separation. It felt selfish in a way that it hadn't done when I was single and yet we both believed in the journey and in our strength together. So we both worked hard to make my return a reality.

Coming off the back of a solo 150-day ocean row and readying for another unplanned leg of the journey in just six months' time would be challenging for anyone in physical, logistical and

emotional terms. Pneumonia and my allergies made it feel insur-
mountable at times. Pushing on through exhaustion and mental
mountains, I thought I knew what running on empty felt like,
but this was different: no mental tricks could help my immune
system. Weight piled on from the steroids, I sounded like I had
been on fifty a day since I was twelve and my skin was red and
angry, scratched raw in places. I felt about as far from being an
athlete as we were from the Aleutians. One thing I could do was
sleep and rest, letting my body repair and recover. Even so, I
looked and felt the poorliest I had ever done.

When people ask me about the most dangerous points of my
journey, it is fair to say that the biggest threats were probably my
own mind and body in this total fail of my immune system and
the mental crash from the year before. That winter the question
of whether I could physically carry on in the spring marched up
and down loudly. First of all, would I be fit enough to fly? Even
if I was, could I then paddle a loaded boat for 1,500 miles at the
pace required by the changeable weather systems and short season?
And if I could, was it even safe to do so, given my allergies and
our impending remoteness? I already had to carry an EpiPen and
steroids just in case of anaphylaxis. The idea of that happening
far from help and in limited communication range was sobering,
to say the least. However, my immunologist assured us that he
was happy for us to go, provided we found a daily dosage of
antihistamines and inhaler that could maintain a decent baseline.
In the spring Justine and I went up to the Lakes for a weekend
of training and preparing our medical kits with Sean and Caroline.
As we practised CPR on the kitchen floor, stitched up a chicken
leg and learnt what to do with a nasopharyngeal tube it dawned
on me how being in a pair brought not only great support but
also great responsibility. Up to now my first aid had focused on
self-fixing and had skipped the really brutal stuff because you
can't give yourself mouth to mouth. I knew that I couldn't have
a more level-headed, skilled team mate than Justine and was
grateful for that, but I also wished that I wasn't bringing such
medical baggage along with me.

'Hopefully, with all that fresh air, away from dust and dogs, you'll be fine and not need anything more than a steroid course or two,' said Caroline. She made up anaphylaxis kits for us to carry in both boats, just in case. 'An adrenaline shot into the thigh and another ten minutes later if no improvement,' she drilled us. And if it happened on the water? 'Anywhere – just anywhere you can get it in.' Call for help, but it could be hours away or days if the weather was poor. Steroid and antihistamine injections straight away. 'You just break the glass ampule like this . . . and then draw up the fluid . . . give it a couple of taps to remove the bubbles and inject at 90 degrees,' she said, pulling out the needle from an orange she had just injected. As Justine took her turn and tapped the syringe, I realised that this was the first time I had ever seen her scared. I drove home hoping that we wouldn't have to use anything more exciting than ibuprofen and paracetamol, not least any sharps. This was one activity where I could safely say that I was braver than her.

Once I was able to do more than just walking, Lucy and I bought a weights rack and various bits of kit for our makeshift garage gym. Through frosty winter nights we bench-pressed and squatted and threw medicine balls at each other, in an attempt to rebuild my strength. I got out biking on the Ridgeway behind our house and paddled on the Thames when I could, empty and flooded in springtime but for the iridescent flash of commuting kingfishers and stately swans proudly ushering their cygnets. Each month I drove out to the north Welsh coast for a week of coaching with Justine and Barry Shaw, the twisting roads through Snowdonia always my favourite as mountainous arms scooped me into and out of valleys and on to the sea. With their tireless coaching my confidence, awareness and boat-handling skills improved in the tide races around Anglesey, though even after multiple pool sessions one skill continued to elude me: I still couldn't roll my kayak. Having never enjoyed being upside down in any boat, especially after crash-landing onto a coral reef in Mauritius at the end of my Indian Ocean row, my confidence had capsized in January when I went over in the surf and struggled to get out of the boat. The idea of capsizing in the Aleutians, nearly 20 miles out from land, terrified me and no doubt didn't fill Justine with joy either. She had an even bigger responsibility than me in being the most experienced, and some people questioned her decision to team up with me.

It all came together when I met a man called John Perrott on a weekend's paddling and we got talking about my rolling block. 'It's all about relaxing,' he assured me. 'And the knee lift.' The first time I tried it, I rolled back up so effortlessly that it felt like I couldn't remember not being able to do it. On my next trip to Wales, after emerging through the formidable tide race at Penrhyn Mawr with a grin on my face at not having capsized, Justine said 'I'm impressed that you didn't go in. But I kind of wish that you had! It would have been good practice for you.' So instead, I rolled in the waves beyond, both Justine and I jubilant at finally having cracked it. Next we practised deep-water rescues, honing our routine for boat emptying and re-entry if one of us went over. 'Whatever you do, keep hold of your paddle. If you don't, we're screwed,' said Justine. The Aleutians are famed for their feisty, unpredictable tide races and so we spent as much time as we could in rough water, given my ill health.

As well as being physically prepared we spent time poring over maps and charts, emailing locals and boat skippers as we planned logistics for the trip. New kit was researched and ordered and my sponsors Rockpool made me a three-piece kayak to match Justine's, so that we could transport them easily out west. Where possible, sponsors sent food and kit directly out to Anchorage where we would base ourselves before flying out to Adak, and the rest we planned to fly out with us or buy in situ. Kit piled up around the house and Lucy came home with boxes from the farm where deliveries were welcomed by her parents with astonishment — how could one person need so much kit? But the arriving kit and logistics plans were not purely for the Aleutians — this was also for cycling across North America the following winter and rowing home across the Atlantic in 2015. I didn't plan to come home again in between, which meant shipping out gear for everything. For *Happy Socks* it meant time in the workshop for updating and tinkering. A new rudder, new batteries, various paint jobs, installation of a life raft and wind turbine. Logistically, financially and emotionally, it was so overwhelming that for a while in February it all felt a bit much and I questioned the journey's worth. Although it might not always be very comfortable, I think doubts and questions are all part of a journey. Only in countering plans and quizzing our belief in projects do we ensure that we are led by passion and purpose rather than blindly following past intentions. Just as mine and Lucy's separation made us stronger and affirmed our commitment to each other, I think the tough parts of the expedition and the times when I was tested to the point of questioning its future cemented my commitment and belief in it. The ongoing efforts and support of so many people helped translate that belief into more progress. Mel's steady calmness helped drive things forward while Rebecca's bouncing enthusiasm and business head helped secure financial support. Once again, sponsors and supporters old and new rallied behind the new plans and needs, backing my plans to continue. I was adamant that it happened now and not some other time, for I knew that if the journey went on even longer, it would be even harder to maintain momentum.

'So, are you disappointed that you didn't make it to Canada?' asked someone at a talk. The very mention of Alaska has always made the back of my neck tingle at visions of its wilderness and wildlife, stories of its native people and history of pioneering settlers. I had to bite my lip with a smile. A few months with Lucy and the chance to journey through the western reaches of North America was an alluring cherry on the cake of missing my original goal.

12

Aang: Aleutian Islands

Aleutian Islands | Kayak |
Spring – Summer 2014 | 900 miles

To say that Scott and Debbie Cameron live 'in' Anchorage is to use the Alaskan sense of the word *in*. Their bold log cabin home is an out of town, edge of the mountains job, peering over the sweep of the city's modest sprawl, overlooking the Cook Inlet way below. When we arrived in April the mountains on all sides still wore snowy skirts but, we were told regularly by locals, compared to normal this was a warm spring. On the way home from the airport Scott had warned us that the garden was open access to local wildlife. He told us we needed to look out for bears and how one day he had answered a knock on the basement door to find a six-foot-tall moose, rather than his diminutive wife, waiting to come in. I flashed a glance at Lucy, who had travelled out with us: she was already paranoid I would meet my end at the jaws and claws of a grizzly.

It didn't take us long to cover the floor of their living room with stacks of snacks and half-filled boxes, piles of medications and gear for us to fly out to Adak or send ahead for resupplies. A retired long-distance dog musher and Scout leader, Scott understood the energy, focus and part chaos of readying for a wilderness trip and so did Debbie, waving off our apologies. 'It's fine! We're used to it and we're just excited to be a part of it. What you girls are doing is awesome.' Scott proudly talked us through faded photos, flags and posters signed by fellow competitors, and snowshoes and sleds on the wall which had seen thousands of wintry miles. After a crammed few days of packing and mailing boxes, visits to equally jammed supermarkets, outdoor stores and local high schools, we were ready to fly out west.

'You could have bought your husbands seats!' said the lady at the Alaska Airlines counter, chuckling at her own joke. 'What have you got in there, girls?' she asked as as we hefted the four kayak bags, each 2 metres long and wide enough to hold a person, onto the belt. 'Just holler if you need anything,' said Scott as we hugged him each in turn. 'Be safe and watch out for the bears once you get to the mainland!'

The peninsula led us west, its folded mountain ranges sliced by rocky valleys like cake in a tin. Blue glaciers crimped and crumpled towards the sea and virgin snowfields glinted in the bright light. Forests thinned, disappearing completely once we started hopscotching over the necklace of islands, tracing the curving boundary of Pacific Ocean to the south and Bering Sea to the north. These are the upper reaches of the Pacific Ring of Fire, an ancient and active tectonic landscape. Peering through the window, names of islands danced in my head and I wondered who was who: Umnak, Chuginadak, Unalaska, Tigalda, Akutan, Uliaga, Unalga, Seguam, Amukta, Herbert and Carlisle. The tallest peeped through duvet clouds, with or without gaping craters. Lava flows had painted some in reds and blacks while others crouched grey and squat, like giant, lonely limpets ringed by surf. Even from up here we could see that they were bluff and isolated, rocky outcrops guarding tiny beaches. On our return journey by kayak we would lace our way between and along them for 700 miles or so before arriving at the fingers of the Alaskan Peninsula, which we would panhandle ever eastwards towards the first road to somewhere in Homer. Justine reckoned it would take us eighty-one days and I imagined more; I was still not well and, though miles on from my winter state, I wasn't sure that I was healthy enough.

Our plane taxied between snow-capped mountains towards the terminal and I spotted some children holding banners against the glass. Finn, who had been besotted with *Happy Socks* in the autumn, was with his mum Lisa; Augie was with his older sister Dasha and their aunt and our local fixer Elaine Smiloff. *Welcome to Adak – Birthplace of the Winds* said the tired sign across the front of the building, a nod to the fierce low-pressure systems which, born here by cool air from the Bering side mixing with warm

air from the Pacific, track eastwards to the mainland, driving their
weather. This is the most westerly inhabited place in America;
the first people to our west were in Russia, a thousand odd miles
away along the remnants of this land bridge between the two
continents.

The flattened space and crumbling infrastructure on that east
side of the island is incongruous in such a ruggedly wild, unkempt
place. Runways, docks, tracks, massive sheds and slowly crumbling
houses mark the landscape above ground, with buildings and areas
marked off limits by barbed wire fences and blunt signs. A
McDonald's, a bowling alley, a swimming pool, and hundreds of
houses all sit empty, their sides torn off by wind and time, no
owners to look after them. Below ground, bunkers and subter-
ranean hospitals are carved and concreted into the earth. Following
the Japanese bombing Dutch Harbor on Unalaska in June 1942,
the fear of further strikes and invasion of western coast America
drove military efforts out west, launching Adak into its key role
during the little known Aleutian Campaign. The Japanese had
taken the islands of Attu and Kiska, some few hundred miles
west, and so within a staggering ten days of arriving on Adak,
US troops had drained the tidal flats and built a temporary runway.
It took thousands of troops three bloody weeks to storm and
retake Attu in the summer of 1943. By the time a second phase
deployed to Kiska, the Japanese had already left. After 1945 Adak
became a key listening post for the submarine fleet during the
Second World War and, at one time, the most important US
naval base in the Pacific, housing thousands of service personnel.

Decommissioned in 1996, the Navy sold Adak to the Aleut
Corporation – one of thirteen regional bodies set up in the 1970s
to represent land and financial claims of the native peoples of
Alaska. Houses were sold off cheap so long as you bought four
at a time and now a hundred or so people live in Adak City –
some native, imagining the rest of their days here, others seeking
an adventure, others still temporary contractors working on the
long-term ordnance clean-up. Having served here twenty years
before, Mike loved Adak so much that he returned with his
Filipino wife. Besides dividends for Aleut Corp shareholders,

seasonal tourism and passing fishing boats brought in the money. Cruise ships and yachts, and historical and bird-watching tours. There's a fish processing plant, and hunters fly in from across the United States to shoot the introduced caribou herd.

'What sort of an adventure is this?' said Lucy, grinning uneasily, having just slid down the last hundred feet of sheer snow slope to where Justine and I were waiting. Ten minutes before and I had been quietly swearing as I came down the gully hand over hand, feeling for the holds Justine had made as she broke trail. Thank goodness for JC – neither Lucy nor I had experience of snow climbing and we're not too keen on heights either. Over the last two days our route had taken us over wintry passes, leaping over rushing streams which chiselled underground caves through the snow, past lakes named after wartime loves: Lake Alice, Lake Mandy Lynn, Lake Debbie, Lake Donna, Lake Susan, Lake Betty. We had tramped through sodden marshes and farting bogs where lazy brooks forgot their destination in watery cul-de-sacs. Brown grass promised lush valleys crowded with wild flowers in the summer, but for now caribou trekked the snow-scattered landscape in search of lichen and the first spring shoots.

Our trek was in order to join up the GPS dots of where I had arrived in *Happy Socks* the previous year at the south of the island and where we would kayak from in a few days' time on the east. Along with the border crossing between China and Russia in 2011, the two miles between the beach that we now hiked to and the point just off the end of the headland where I had rowed to, are unlinked by human power. In another world, with more time to have sorted a pack raft to hike over the mountains with and paddle out to the official point, I could have done so, but for now it had been mission enough just to get back out to Alaska. Life, love and the expedition's evolution had put it into perspective, and I was happy to let go and move on. Similarly, moving away from my original aims of purely human-powered travel, Justine and I had also decided to use small, collapsible sails for this leg, due to the long and treacherous passes ahead. Without them the distances might prove untenable within changeable weather windows and the short summer season. We would still have to paddle, but in suitable conditions we envisaged the sails would add extra power and miles. Justine said that the Aleuts had used sails too.

After the hike, our days were as long as they needed to be, as we split up kit and worked on our kayaks, setting up the sails or adding reflective tape. I fixed a solar panel on the back of my kayak and Justine set up the new satellite phone system. Lucy trimmed packaging from dehydrated meals in a bid to save every millimetre of space that we could. We sent our float plan to the coastguard base in Kodiak and Anchorage and emergency details to everyone who needed to know.

In search of the internet we spent odd hours in the 'End of the Chain Mercantile Store', where religious soap operas invariably blared out from the TV, whether or not it had an audience. On the occasional opening times of the Aleut Corp-owned store in the now defunct gym, we popped in to chat to Elaine or scour the aisles beneath the redundant basketball hoops. It was expensive to fly things out a thousand miles down the chain and the prices reflected this.

Elaine often sat with us at the house while we worked on our kit, keen to see what we were taking with us or to share advice or help set up our fishing rigs. A native of Unga island, further east up the chain, her dark eyes belied a calm spirit at home in the wild and a turbulent, emotional past life. Wood carver, maker, doer, hunter, connector, Elaine's house was more workshop than home, filled with tools, guns and half-carved boats and many stories. A smoke house out the back would, by the end of the summer, be filled with salmon and caribou sausages. Antlers, four-wheelers, a boat and tyres sat about amongst tussocky grass like elderly friends sitting quietly in the sun, just waiting and listening. One night she lit the banya for us and we lay on the wooden benches sweating out whatever thoughts and emotions wandered inside our heads, rinsing them away with bucketloads of spring water. Afterwards she smudged us, burning wood and scent in a shell and wafting it around us with an eagle feather, bringing all the elements of Alaska to us and welcoming us to them. Afterwards, we sat on the floor drinking beer and eating salmon dipped in seal oil, wincing at the putrid taste of seal flesh when she handed around a rib to try. One side of the small room shouted at us with military signs and instructions, while on the other pictures and trinkets of Alaskan wilderness and Aleut history sat more gently.

A carved wooden hand with a hole in it caught my eye. 'It's an Aleut hand,' Elaine said softly. 'You hold up your hands and meet the experience. Then you let it pass through you. Our ancestors teach us to let go.' She believed that if the new fish plant failed so would Adak, and so, too, would the Aleut people. Torn between leaving the island for personal reasons and yet wanting to stay in the wilderness and space of it, Elaine cried with us one night at the chasm between the two visions: 'Is one person's happiness more important than the survival of the Aleut people?' That effort to reconcile holding on with letting go was one we would see time and again along the islands.

While I enjoyed getting ready to go, my head was in two places as expedition team mate and fiancée. Lucy was reassured at spending time with Justine and getting to know her and we made a good team as a threesome, but my time alone with Lucy felt precious and too swift. I could have done with another month of tying up admin and getting some rest before leaving the UK, but that's often the way – there is always more to do. One golden evening we borrowed a quad bike from Elaine and wound through the hills, silhouettes of other mountains to our south fading into shades of sunset. There and yet far away, much like we would be over the next year, until I reached the Atlantic coast. Lucy promised that she would keep pulling hard on the rope we imagined connected us, reeling me home.

A few days later Lucy was settling into farm life again in Oxfordshire and Justine and I were being waved off by the children from Adak school. Jammed with a month's worth of food and all our kit, the kayaks sat low in the water. A few children took turns paddling or being pulled about in the shallows before we hugged our goodbyes. 'Have you got your bear claws?' asked Elaine and I patted the pocket of my buoyancy aid where three claws – one from each of the different bears of Alaska – were wrapped in a plastic bag. 'They'll keep you safe.' She gave Lucy a bear claw necklace for strength.

Our send-off party tracked us down the bay with banners and cameras, winding back up the hill until we had disappeared around the corner and out of sight, behind the sheer, steep cliffs. Justine looked relaxed, but I felt nervous as incoming swell knocked at us, knowing that my comfort zone was about to be destroyed. For the next three months or so I anticipated I would expend a lot of energy just trying to corral my nerves, keep upright, keep up with Justine the Machine and prove myself a useful member of our team. Mount Moffett's snowy slopes glowed pink and orange in the afternoon sun behind us as Great Sitkin beckoned us onwards.

Our aim was to start with a few shorter days to get settled, build my confidence in tide races and sharpen our camp- and boat-packing routines now that we were a duo. Already exhausted before we set off, my stiff muscles and racing brain were glad when strong winds brought us ashore early on our fourth day in a cosy bay, pinning us on our fifth as gusts funnelled down the valley behind us and ruffled the water in front. Our navigation charts warned of tide rips in multiple places across the short passes between us and Atka and we had heard of standing waves being visible through binoculars in the upcoming Fenimore Pass from over 10 miles away, so we were cautious about timings. The goal was to skirt the rips completely or pass through at slack water when the flow was weakest, but the problem was that we had already been told that the current patterns are complex and unpredictable. Even if a chart says the ebb kicks in at three o'clock, you might find yourself out in the pass at one o'clock with it already in full flow. Thankfully, this time Justine's timings and plottings worked in our favour and we made it across to Atka's southern shores without too much trouble or, for my part, angst. With every mile I was growing more confident with the sail and dynamic conditions, and feeling less like my boat was an alien form that I had never seen before. Packing wasn't quite so stressful in the mornings and didn't take quite so long, much to Justine's relief.

In planning we had split up our journey by the sparse chain

of communities we would pass through along the way: Atka, Nikolski, Unalaska Dutch Harbor, Akutan, Sand Point, King Cove, Perryville. We had sent (or Scott would send on) our resupply boxes out to some and we had made contact with locals. Even if we didn't, we soon learned that everyone knew 'the kayakers' were coming, thanks to the bush telephone. Weaving our way through tiny islets which guarded the sheltered Nazan Bay, we scoured hillsides and corners for the first signs of people. Satellite dishes appeared on the skyline in a cluster. Vehicle tracks squelched into the hillside and a nest of colourful buildings, including a Russian Orthodox church, declared itself as Atka City. We were drummed ashore to the community of seventy with traditional singing and dancing, teenagers beating time on skin drums while elders down to four-year-olds joined in. The rhythmic chanting echoed the timing of our paddle strokes, just as it would have done centuries ago as their ancestors beat time across long passes or welcomed hunters home from days away to this very beach, chosen for being tucked into the armpit of the bay, sheltered by offshore islands. Two lads held a sign saying *Aang Sarah and Justine*, 'Welcome' in the local and rapidly disappearing Unangax dialect.

We spent a few wet and windy days here, welcomed into the Dushkin and Swetzoff family home for mealtimes of sea lion soup, reindeer stew and halibut pie, which we all stood to bless under the icon on the wall. We asked questions about each others' lives – grandmother Sally told us how they used to go school on Adak via boat and how now as head teacher of the school here there had been times when children had been borrowed from other islands to keep it in quorum above ten pupils. When I asked about the evacuation of Atka during the Second World War, she told me how all the islanders had been taken to camps on the mainland. 'They burned it all to the ground when they left, for fear the Japanese would use the buildings.' She spoke with her daughter Crystal in their local Unangax dialect, which reminded me of a soft Welsh accent, lilting and gentle, encouraging the little ones to speak it, too, in a bid to save it from extinction.

'Who are we if our culture, our foods and our language is lost?

If that happens, then they've won, the colonisers,' said Crystal tearily one night, as we talked of the challenges of island life and maintaining identity within a homogenising, modernising world where traditional skills and stories are being lost. Curious about why the children spend more time inside in front of a TV than outside, Crystal explained her fears of injury and how it takes nearly a day and costs nearly $1,000 to get to Anchorage and back for healthcare. It seemed as if no one walked anywhere – one teenager told us how she saved up her earnings from her cleaning jobs to buy fuel for the quad bike, at eight dollars a gallon, even though everything needed day to day was set within walking distance. The gathering of one-storey multicoloured homes was not far from the store, the school, the fish plant, the city hall.

Our visit coincided with a tour by the priest, Father Ivan, of his 1,000-mile parish and at his invitation our kayaks were included in his annual Blessing of the Fleet to mark the start of the fishing season. Later, while foraging for spiky sea urchins and vitamin-rich kelp with Crystal and her uncle Danny, we also picked Danny's brains for his knowledge of the passes and islands from his days on fishing boats. He pointed to good water spots, sheltered bays or remembered hunting cabins on our charts. 'Amukta Pass – you've got to watch out for ships out there. That's where they cross from one side to the other and it can get pretty busy. How long will it take you to get to Nikolski?' he said, surprised at our answer of three to four weeks, given that he and a friend had motored it in a day once before. This tiny community of 17 was over 250 miles away, guarded by some of the most exposed and longest crossings of our entire journey with no one for miles around. We just hoped that we had enough food to get there. Plenty of locals doubted our ability to make it all the way to the end, their lives shaped by the weather which they knew (either from experience or stories) turned passes into boiling, seething messes with churning whirlpools and standing waves. 'If you make it halfway,' said Elaine, 'then I think you have a chance.'

For now, Nikolski was our target. From Atka we crossed to Amlia with its jagged, ragged rocky shore, pinnacle rocks of all shapes and sizes marking the towering cliff-line like turrets. Some rock faces were swirled with greens and turquoise and I gazed up as we paddled, tracing shapes and rock lines, looking on ledges for birds. The islands and their edges teemed – whole cliff-sides flying away if we got too close – and rafts of puffins or murrelets on the water. If I were to choose a collective noun for a group of sea lions I think it would be a *honk*. When not bellowing with the rest of the group, rejected lone males often pulled out onto quieter beaches to snooze and posture at each other, no doubt for show and to reminisce about times gone by when they were fit enough to win the ladies. We had a 4 a.m. wake-up call from one group dragging themselves up our gravel beach to grunt and roar into the pre-dawn, hustling and jostling with each other. We hoped they knew that our tent was benign, given that we reckoned they weighed about the same as a fat cow. Paddling along the south side of the island we passed caves blasted into the rock, allowing ourselves the luxury of exploring them if time allowed, threading through arches and rock gardens as I learned which waves to let lie and which to paddle for or away from. I was learning daily how to manoeuvre my boat in close confines and, wanting me to go faster for both our sakes, on every long crossing Justine encouraged me to surf the boat for an extra inch here or there, even into headwinds. I tried and sometimes it worked and sometimes it didn't – invariably Justine took the racing line and I wiggled along behind. In the tent at night, as Justine calculated our strategy for the next day, she would explain her thinking to me. As the days ticked on I did the same, for Justine to feed back on, explaining why such and such an angle was better or pointing out that I had read the wrong line of the chart. She taught me by letting me have a go and showing me how she was doing it. Eager to improve and not to mess up, I stacked each snippet away and enjoyed feeling more confident in the boat or in my decision-making, though I was still nervous. On top of the effort of pulling a laden boat for long hours, the mental effort of learning and being so often out of my comfort zone was tiring and sometimes overwhelming. Pulling ashore at the end of a day was a relief – to have made it a little further along the way, to have stayed upright and to be headed for rest and food.

We generally aimed to paddle 20 to 30 miles a day, breaking the next few days' route up into sensible sections that would match with launch and landing points between islands, bearing in mind that sandy beaches were few and far between and often guarded by surf or rocks. Justine taught me how to choose the best place to land before we even reached the beach – choosing river mouths or the corners of bays and sheltered nooks. I learned to consider forecasts ahead and what that would do to the water the next day for launching, and whether in a few days we might be stuck on a beach which faced the direction of the blow. Steep-shingled get-outs provided happy moments of absorbed foraging for pebbles of different colours, worn smooth by their journeys and time. As we ate our way through rations we each filled the space with a growing collection of pebbles and flotsam whose stories we could never know. On Seguam I found a Japanese glass float on the hard sand, its blueish mottled surface polished clear along the trace of the fishing net which once held it. It made a welcome change from the ubiquitous plastic floats and buoys.

After a 28-mile slog from Amlia into headwinds and shunted by the tides, I was glad of a forecast for strong winds, which kept us from attempting the biggest pass of the entire journey – Amukta. Since setting out into the opaque fog first thing in the morning, feeling grungy with a cold and my arms as heavy as the rocky coast which we were leaving behind, I had been waiting for the stiffness to disperse as it always did and for the painkillers to kick in. I tend to go into myself when I am having a hard time and dealing with doubt, and so I spent much of the day in uneasy silence with myself as I plodded on. I had already learned that when Justine asked how I was doing or whether I needed food, it generally meant she thought I should be paddling faster, which generally sent me even further inwards, worrying that I wasn't good enough. I wished that she would paddle beside me rather than go off ahead and wait, only for me to catch up again and the cycle repeat itself. Eventually Seguam announced herself through the clouds, like someone pushing their head through the neck of a tight woolly jumper. She danced coyly in and out of the fog before gracing us with her full self. Hours edged on and the sun climbed overhead as we crawled to within a few miles of the lava-strewn island, dark red and black sheets of it hanging down from the snowline, some of it fine and other parts looking like tumbled building blocks. And then, we were suddenly running parallel to shore, next to grasses and patches of tundra, picking our way through tangled kelp beds, pushing off the walls of it and trying not to be caught by it. Swell rolled in from the south and I was glad of the kelp breaking it up, wary of getting too close to the rocky catacombs and undercut arches where waves slapped and thundered. Justine went in closer to film. We turned left around the final corner to Lava Cove, where we had been aiming, and were immediately blasted by a screeching headwind which scuffed at the surface waves and felt like it would snatch my paddle clean away if I let go.

'Bit blowy, isn't it?' shouted Justine, grinning, head down as she pulled into it. As we sat in the waves considering the best landing spot, incoming rollers lifted us to see the lower sections of the steeply shelving beach and then hid it from view. Nervous at our biggest surf landing so far and feeling like I had been steamrollered, I asked if I should go in on the back of a wave, wishing that I could magically avoid it.

'Yeah – try that or just surf it in. I'll go in first and give you the sign,' Justine said, starting for shore, leaving me sitting in the waves. My heart thumping, I pulled my video camera out of my top pocket to film her, lifting my hips in tiny movements to balance. A wave knocked into me, sweeping me towards the rocks, and I decided it was time to put the camera away. I back-paddled and turned myself head on to the beach once more. Justine disappeared in the dip between the surf and the beach for a moment and then she was out, pulling her kayak up the sand as the strong backwash clawed at it. 'Paddle in the air. Time to go, Oots!' Each cobalt wave curled to a transparent turquoise peak and I paddled backwards into them, timing my strokes forward to come in on their back side, aiming to avoid the biggest of them. In a flash, one was behind me, rearing up to crash into a foaming wall, rushing me forwards. I leant into my paddle with all my bodyweight, willing *Krissy* to stay upright as we slid towards the beach amid the foaming front of the wave. Fizzing out under me, I heaved a few sharp strokes on my right to spin the nose round to where Justine splashed forwards to catch the toggle and start pulling upwards as I leapt out. I threw my paddle up the beach and the wind took it for me, while we carried both boats far enough up the sand to be safe from the sea while we changed.

I got to work on the tent while Justine set up the stove, waiting for that comforting roar of blue flame which promised warmth and refuelling. After fourteen hours of what felt like dragging an elephant and feeling unwell, I questioned whether I had it in me for the crossing to Amukta, our next island. With 37 miles of open water and a few miles of island on either side, we imagined we would have to kayak nearly 50 miles, almost twice as far as we had done that day. But for now I was relieved and happy to be here, looking forward to sleep and a day off tomorrow. Appearing out of the tent I found Justine cursing and looking for a tiny metal piece of the stove. Of course, the spare was in Anchorage and none of our bodges – foil, a twopence piece or a spoon – seemed to cut it as a replacement part. Trying to cheer her up while also being secretly glad that it wasn't me who had lost it, I proffered that the Aleuts had paddled around here for thousands of years without a stove, and they had done all right.

Two days going nowhere while offshore winds sent the tops of surf lines cutting back out to sea was bliss. Rolling over to a bright morning and the red tent sheets flapping, I checked my watch before disappearing back into my dreams, to wake up when my lower back could no longer take lying still. I slid out of the tent to wander barefoot down the beach, busying myself with collecting driftwood from the tidelines and splitting it with my machete. While filling water from the wide stream after a ribboning solitary run down the mountainside, now gathered at the bottom in multiple nattering channels and eddies, I wondered at the winter storms which had shunted giant driftwood logs this far inland. Justine got the fire going with her flint steel, while I sawed a plastic barrel to make a washtub to clean everything – us, our clothes and cooking gear. Lying in the sun to dry off, tired muscles soothed by the stillness and warmth, I listened to the roar of the surf, glad of the rest and satisfied with progress so far, two weeks in. The dunes behind us were turning green, dotted with yellows, pinks and blues of buttercups, orchids and lillies, all racing to cram growth and reproduction into a few short weeks of summer.

After a pancake feast from the fire we strolled along the beach to explore waterfalls we had seen falling off the cliffs on our way in, passing small birds as they tottered up and down the sand in time with the swish and swash of waves, pecking for canapes. A fine pink tideline of dried shrimp had been left at the top of the water's reach, edged by foam and strands of weed. Later I took my firewood-splitting role very seriously and spent hours batoning and drying wood for the fire with my machete and saw, leaving spares under the upturned barrel when we left for any other paddler who found themselves here in need of a fire. We cooked feasts of curried lentil stews, pizzas and potato cakes, melting chocolate into milk for evening drinks and making popcorn over the fire. And then we stared into its embers or out to sea in that space of together that a fire creates, no conversation needed.

On the third morning we were up early to get ready for our crossing to Amukta, but not until we had been ferried out into the bay for a breakfast date aboard the MV *Tiglax*. For twenty years Billy Pepper has spent his summers captaining this US Fish and Wildlife Service ship up and down the Aleutians and Alaskan Peninsula, running long-term boat-based surveys and transects as well as dropping scientists on different islands to set up camps, picking them up on the return run at the end of the season. As soon as I climbed aboard from the rib they had buzzed out to pick us up with, I knew that I should have taken a seasickness tablet, and I was a bit annoyed that my queasiness precluded a second round of cooked breakfast from the ship's kitchen. The warm-hearted Billy loved that I could row oceans and yet get sick on his boat in no swell at all.

'I've never known anyone to attempt this. You girls are crazy!' said Billy as we leaned over charts with him in the wheelhouse, annotating sheltered anchorages, beaches where we could land or pretty things to look out for. 'Kagamil, out in the Islands of Four Mountains – that's where I want to be buried. It is something else. And you should be there in a few days now. There's a blow coming in the day after tomorrow so you might get pinned on Amukta but then you should be good again for a spell. The good thing is that the easterlies never blow for long out here.' The difference between Billy and everyone else who gave us local advice seemed to be that he understood the capabilities of our kayaks and trusted that we would make sound decisions about when to go or when to stay put, knowing that we wouldn't go out at any time of the tide, as fishing captains might. An hour on board and we were both away: the *Tiglax* was expected in Adak, nearly 200 miles away, for breakfast the following day, and we hoped to make Amukta before dark.

A honk of sea lions bellowed at us as we passed their rocky home on the southern shore of Amukta, sixteen hours after we had set off from our beach. Diving in to rear up out of the water at us in noisy chorus before slapping beneath the surface to reform behind us and carry on, they were clearly not expecting visitors. I often find them intimidating by day, let alone in the dark, so was glad to leave them behind as we turned into the still water of Traders Cove. Changing tides had pulled us away from the island in the final few hours of the crossing, slowing progress and letting night arrive before we did. The sky, the sand, the pebbles – everything was thickly black, lit only by our head torches. Having been in our little boats for sixteen hours our legs and toes were numb and cold, and our bladders full, forcing the obligatory hurried crouch and unzip to wee wherever we stood. We stuffed down a snack before getting the tent up, swapping damp drysuits and thermals for the feathery cocoon of our sleeping bags, where we lay in bed scoffing cold pancakes from breakfast and tepid tea from our flasks.

A low-pressure system blew for the next three days, smashing surf onshore from a grey sea, hemming us in with fog. The island's volcano had the same idea as us – to stay hidden until the worst had passed or, in our case, until the tent had become too claustrophobic. The sky sheeted down at times, and wetted us by something more like osmosis at others – that sort of dampening that happens by degrees and without you really noticing. Cooking pans under the tent poles and edges caught water far more effectively than my efforts to find it elsewhere. All I'd found was a bog and a grossly coloured and slimed pool we called the 'poo pond'. The bog yielded enough muddy water to filter through my Buff and boil, but I wasn't too keen on the worms I had seen coiling along in there. Ironically, on an island chain famed for its poor weather and high levels of precipitation, it wouldn't be the first time we struggled for water. On the third day, my 29th birthday, we cracked open a tiny bottle of bubbles that I had packed as a treat. Justine brought me pancakes with a candle into the tent for my breakfast and, on going out to brush my teeth and stretch, I noticed her birthday card on the sand – a modest six metres wide and made out of driftwood, buoys and old rope. It was the first birthday I had spent on shore and with another person in a while, having spent the last two out on the Pacific in *Gulliver* and *Happy Socks*.

From the lava-strewn beaches of Amukta we paddled some of the most challenging crossings of the journey and some of the most difficult expedition days of my life, as currents pulled us away from land, headwinds ground down my energy and tide races roughed the water into large and messy waves. It started with a surf launch from the beach where dumping waves tried pushing me sideways. Justine held my boat perpendicular while I got in and worked the spray deck on around the cockpit rim. 'Right, go!' she shouted, heaving my boat past her as I pulled myself into the waves, which slapped me cold in the face. Paddling out past the breakers to wait in the chop, I felt energised and glad to have remained upright. By the time Justine made it out to me, her boat full of water from being swamped by waves as she paddled out with her spray deck off for a speedy getaway, I was feeling seasick from the rocking.

'You're going to have to empty it,' she said, climbing into the water to hold on to the front of my boat while I eased hers up over my deck to roll and empty it as best I could. We reckoned each boat weighed in excess of sixty kilograms or more and it certainly felt it. Justine shimmied between the two boats to hook her heels up and slide back into her cockpit, before we pumped out the remaining water by hand. To Yunaska and on to the Islands of Four Mountains the tides mixed with residual southerly swells left over from the storm made for long, messy crossings as we tracked back and forth across the passes, reacting to changes in the currents as we neared or left land and the ebb or flow kicked in, whisking us away from where we wanted to go. My shoulder clicked and crunched continuously now and was always painful, making ibuprofen and paracetamol a daily part of my breakfast routines for maintenance. Each night when I checked the snacks and reservoir supply in my buoyancy aid for the next day I also checked that I had painkillers. Terrified of capsizing and often pushed out of my comfort zone in tidal races where waves snatched at my boat or disappeared from underneath me to send my boat thudding down, it sometimes felt like I spent more time bracing onto my paddle for support than pulling myself forward.

Even if we hadn't known that the Islands of Four Mountains held such spiritual significance for the Aleuts, as the seat of their people, the sense of the place was full and mysterious, not least because local weather and currents made us work hard for the rewards of landing safely. Off shore, surf lines frothed and fizzed and vast kelp blooms broke up swells, offering miles of nursery to otter mums and their cubs. In the tent we were reading Corey Ford's book *Where the Sea Breaks its Back*, learning of the Russian fur rush of the eighteenth century when otters were in the unfortunate situation of being both valuable to fashion in Europe and unafraid of the native Aleuts subjugated to kill them. Georg Steller's diaries depicted mother otters defending their cubs to death and now, two hundred years on, we were glad to see that they had become wary and, thanks to statutory protection, abundant, too. Curving beneath the water in a sleek flash of fur, having spotted us 50 metres away, mums would pull their cub down with them in an embrace much like a human mother would a young toddler, no matter how much fun they had been having playing and chattering to each other. Still, sometimes they were so engrossed in washing, munching kelp or sea urchins or even snoozing on their backs that they didn't notice us until we were a boat length away, letting us see their golden faces and whiskers up close.

Thirty miles away, tucked into the Bering coast of Umnak island, sits the ancient settlement of Nikolski, purportedly one of the oldest continuously habited areas in the world with remains on Rabbit Island dating back some nine thousand odd years. To get there from Skiff Cove on Chuginadak, where we had spent a day exploring the dramatic, sheeting waterfalls and roasting freshly caught black bass over beach fires, we had to cross Samalga Pass. With a forecast for that Alaskan non-committal sweep prediction of 'Variable 10', we aimed to sleep early only to have an uneasy night before the alarm shook us awake before dawn. Justine was out of the tent and lighting the stove before I had so much as climbed out of my sleeping bag and soon we were crouched on our haunches force-feeding ourselves thick, sticky porridge, knowing that the next hot food would be over twelve hours away. A new sun peeped over a clear horizon, underlining the majestic Mount Vsevidof in the distance with an orange streak of cloud beckoning us eastwards.

Paddling away from our campsite on charmed, glassy waters, it felt good to see our goal already and I split up the distance into five-mile chunks in my head, using my imaginary weighing scales to count them down. Every so often I looked behind to watch the peaks of the Islands of Four Mountains change shape or position as we paddled out into the pass, shoulders and elbow creaking and aching before settling in to the day. After a few hours the easterly wind arrived, shortly after the ebbing tide started pulling us south and away from land too quickly for us to paddle across it. Plodding on behind Justine, working hard but never fast enough, I lived for the snatched stops for a snack and a wee, a quick chat and a moment of feeling like a pair again. For sometimes when she was many hundreds of metres ahead, it felt like we were two soloists. And yet as Justine had the main GPS for tracking our course, I was following her, tracking as she played with our angle to see if we could make progress across the current or at least limit the collateral. As the hours ticked on and the flood kicked in, now pulling us north, our target islands which had been getting ever closer, started receding into the distance. We worried that we might not reach any land at all, never mind the bit we were aiming for. Meanwhile, the headwind was ramping up such that at one point where I caught Justine up she said she might even need to tow me. 'Please just paddle beside me; I know I paddle faster when we are together,' I said. I understood why she thought that she needed to paddle faster to encourage an increase in pace, but being left chipped away at my confidence and energy.

After twelve hours on the water the mist socked in and the headwind increased to 20 knots, gusting more, and my muscles screeched in protest at the effort I was demanding. And yet there was something strangely satisfying about pulling into it, perhaps because by now we were confident that we were out of the worst of the tides in the pass and would at least make it somewhere that night. People ask how I keep going in tough conditions and on that day, like many others, the main motivator is that you have no choice, that if you don't keep going then you are a goner. Simple. In terms of *how* I kept going, I used everything I had: my invisible peloton, Lucy pulling me ashore on the rope or literally sitting behind me in a boat where I chatted away to her. Anything to make me feel stronger. Nosing between the kelp beds, I nudged on to the beach, which lay thick with stinking rotting seaweed, falling out of my kayak onto wobbly legs, nothing left to give except a hug and air high five to Justine. Soggy, clawed hands. Arms too heavy to do anything very useful, all I wanted was to be horizontal. We were safe and that was all that mattered.

More headwinds slowed us the next day on our final miles to Nikolski as we tracked up the coast, picking our way between forests of kelp, watching scruffy foxes who watched us from the shore. A quiet church looked out across the final bay and a couple of rows of little houses brightly painted into the landscape drew us in as we absorbed details of people after three weeks on our own. Quad bikes appeared on the beach and over half of the island's registered population of seventeen gathered to welcome us to their village. Olive skin and thick dark hair, open faces and kind eyes. We had been in touch with Scott Ker, a gregarious incomer who never left after marrying local woman Agrafina Dushkin, after arriving on a fishing boat from Dutch Harbor over twenty years before. We were treated to a stay in the luxurious APICDA hunting lodge, which is more used to high-paying parties flying in from all over the world to fish salmon and hunt reindeer around the island, guided by Scott and other locals. We washed our stinking clothes, lounged in deep baths and slept in marshmallowy beds until we couldn't sleep any more, scattering our gear as we dried and sorted it, charging cameras, phones, spare batteries and trackers via just about every spare socket in the house. Display cabinets in the lounge told Nikolski's history: from bone and wood hooks and pictures of the *chaluka* – the four-thousand-year-old midden mound at the bottom of the village – alongside pictures of archaeolgocial digs to photos of bygone ranching by the Harris Livestock Company, and the Reeve Aleutian plane sitting above the village where it crashed many years ago.

Collecting our mail from what might be the tiniest post office in the world, eager to see what was in the resupply box (including our spare stove), we were excited to find another package with Lucy's chicken scrawl on it, packed with treats and letters for us both. I missed her a lot but we generally managed to chat every day or other from the tent, depending on time, signal and battery.

Agrafina and her eighteen-year-old nephew Eric, home for the summer from his boarding school on the mainland, spent a lot of time with us, too. 'I reckon I'm related to everyone up the chain,' she said as we talked of her relatives on Atka, not long before the phone rang with Crystal and Danny wanting to say hello. Remembering a community of 70 in her youth, when I asked about the future of Nikolski she simply said, 'Not good. It depends on whether the youngsters come back and have children.' Eric was more optimistic – there was a new baby and a few children currently off island. For high school he boarded in Galena, deep in the Alaskan interior, flying home for the summer vacation. He had moved south with his parents to Tennessee a few years before, but had returned to live with Scott and Agrafina. 'I couldn't take the heat down there and besides, this is my home. I have to live here. It's where my ancestors have lived for thousands of years. I will probably work away but I want to retire here with my family one day.' When we asked him what it was like living out here we both understood when he said: 'I fish. I hunt. I play. It's pretty good.' The simplicity of journeying is one of my favourite things about it so I could see the fullness and reward of a life out here, driven by the elements and bound by the community.

Eric addressed all the elders as uncle or aunt, whether or not they were his blood relatives, although given the handful of surnames, they most probably all were. Each morning everyone congregated in the store for coffee and chat, putting purchases on credit until dividend cheques arrived or the next flutter of work. On one evening of our five there, Scott invited us into his man cave where we sat on upturned crates and stools amongst the fishing floats and nets, the wall decorated with colourful fishing lures and posters of big-busted women. Overhead hung an inflatable kayak left behind by a Japanese paddler who had returned home early after being overwhelmed by the distance he had taken on, promising to return but never doing so. Eric and Agrafina were both on soft drinks on account of family trouble with alcohol and so I suggested we go out for a paddle.

'Looking good over there!' I shouted to Eric as he cut through the water in *Krissy*.

'Well, my family does have a pretty good history of kayaking,' he said with brilliant understatement.

'Pretty good? You guys invented the kayak!' If it weren't for him needing to travel away for work he would have come with us up the coast to the end of the island when we left, waved onwards by the village once more. I looked out for Sergey, the elderly man who had told me with a wide grin how he would have probably done it when he was younger, but someone pointed out that he would still be in bed. Time felt different in Nikolski and, as I sang 'We'll Meet Again' from the kayak as we pushed off from shore, I wondered about the future of this tiny community and its traditions.

13

Evolution: Pacific Ocean and North America

Aleutian Islands & Alaskan Peninsula |
Kayak | Summer 2014 | 600 miles

I am really glad I was not born a guillemot. Just imagine hatching out of your egg and tottering over to the nest edge to find that your parents have set up camp in a teeny crevice a few hundred feet up on sheer rock faces. It didn't look like a gentle start to life. Justine and I paddled through dank arches clattering with raucous hordes of the nesting birds, parents zipping in and out to deliver food, making us dizzy as we looked up at the terraces. Mottled seal pups flopped into the water in wide-eyed panic as we passed their sheltered pull-outs and on shore we saw the first fox cubs of the season, not yet as bold as their parents, who tried to steal fish heads as we cleaned them and who chewed through Justine's map case and the lid of her cockpit hatch to get at snacks.

Deep-fingered bays reached back into cragged mountains streaked with snow and green grass, promising endless exploration for someone with endless time. At Hot Springs Cove we trekked inland across sodden bogged valleys looking for the funnel of steam we had spied drifting lazily from upper slopes. Herds of keen-eyed and sharp-eared caribou poured over hill crests to hide themselves while broody eagles swooped to warn us away. Like Goldilocks' porridge, the first pools we found bubbled like cauldrons, and the next were too cold, before a bit of ad hoc engineering to divert and combine two created something of shower-tray depth which, with constant swishings of water, was enjoyable. I wanted to stay for ever in Makushin Bay, its turquoise seas so calm and the peace of the space so deep that it was hard to imagine a stormy, fog-wrapped version. There were more beaches than there had been out west and vegetation was slowly growing bigger and more bushlike, though we wouldn't see trees until we were way up onto the peninsula. After two months of relative quiet and no other traffic on the water but for rusting shipwrecks, and just two tiny communities, the relative metropolis of Dutch Harbor was a bit of a shock. Over ten thousand people live there during the summer months, half of them seasonal migrant workers for the fish processing plant, with a provenance so vast that the door of the public library had instructions in English, Spanish and native dialects of Unangax and Tigalik. Famous for its role in TV's *Deadliest Catch*, the port set-up of warehousing, docks and fleet was impressive, and the juicy scallops and buttery king crab which someone had dived for the day we ate them, were among the best food I have ever eaten.

Once again, kind locals hosted us, as keen to hear about our world as we were to find out about theirs. They toured us around the bunkers and tunnels on Ballyhoo Mountain and took us to the Museum of the Aleutians to see replica boats and outfits of paddlers past. *Kamleikas* made of fish skin, rimmed with fur and sewn with guts, and elaborate wooden visors decorated with feathers and walrus whiskers representing the wearer's skill as a hunter. Until we were met by a raft of local paddlers on our way in to Dutch Harbor we hadn't seen another paddler on our journey, which felt ironic given the region's history, and yet perhaps it shouldn't be – after all, at home horses and carts have become relics only enjoyed by hobbyists. I wondered what early paddlers would have made of our journey and gear now. The equipment and the overall goals might be different but the essence was still the same – reading water and weather, manoeuvring boats with paddles and sails, threading together safe landing to safe landing.

As we stuffed marshmallows into our hot chocolate one night and poked at the glowing remains of a fire, Justine asked me how I thought I was getting on. I rumbled through some criticisms of what I thought I could do better, waiting for her to confirm my insecurities that I was still a liability. Instead she said, 'I think you're too harsh on yourself. I think you could go solo now.' Tears sprang to my eyes and my tummy squeezed with pride. 'You might be a bit slower than we would be together because you might be more conservative about days when I would take us out there, but you don't need me any more. You're doing great.' We hugged and I thanked her for the compliment, as well as for bringing me to this point in my learning. It was a huge confidence boost to hear her say that out aloud, for I often read – or imagined – that she was frustrated by my lack of speed and skill compared to hers. Being together 24/7 it wasn't always an easy relationship, especially as I improved and had useful things to offer about decision-making and planning, but the strength of it lay in our being forgiving of each other, open about frustrations and niggles and, above all else, friends. 'I'll still come with you though, don't worry!' she said and we carried on with our night-time fire.

The only time we didn't talk to each other on the trip was for four hours after a big tidal section where Justine hadn't realised the extent of my fear and I didn't trust her judgement call about a particular route. With hindsight it is hardly surprising that in remote and stressful situations we should have had the odd fallout, and I am glad that we were able to overcome. Even if they were uncomfortable at the time and led to tears or emotional comments which otherwise wouldn't have even been thought, they were always resolved with hugs, chat and a surprise present or kind gesture. We are sisters, after all.

One thing we noticed as we tracked eastwards was the increase in plane traffic, tiny bush planes buzzing this way and that. Paddling out of Akutan, where we had spent a day running around with local children up and down the wooden boardwalks and eating seagull egg pie and halibut stew, we spotted a red plane heading in to Akun island just across the water. Its passengers would be taxied back across to Akutan by helicopter. Seemingly out of nowhere, the little red plane headed for us, swooping low over our heads. A repeat run at thirty feet above us, sent me ducking and Justine laughing her trademark cackle, reminding me of the pilot who landed his float plane on the beach where we were camped one morning to come and say hello, saying, 'I guess we do things a little differently out here in bush Alaska.'

It was our second attempt to cross Unimak Pass, having been

forced back by strong winds the day before. We had just spent two days on the teeny, bluff-sided island of Aiktak with two field workers from the Fish and Wildlife Service, who enjoyed us being their first visitors in five weeks since they had been dropped off by Billy. If we were having a full-on time in our world of two with various, albeit infrequent, injections of people, Stacie and Amanda had an even more intense set-up. Living in an 8 foot by 12 foot cabin consisting of an office on one side, a kitchen down the other, a bunkbed which served as both sleeping and living quarters and some storage shelves, they shared everything. Through scopes zoomed in on cliff-top perches they spied on courting cormorants dancing and bowing on perilous ledges and monitored the comically suave tufted puffins waddling out of their burrows to take off and barrel out to sea. To check on petrel chicks they reached into burrows, faces to the mud and grass, pulling out tiny bundles of fluff. Up on the hill top they dodged dive-bombing gulls and wandered the beaches to check on oyster-catcher nests, alerted to the presence of a nest by the parents faking wing injuries as they ran in squawking circles away from their dark eggs. Set against this dramatic backdrop of sea, sky and cliffs, it was a study of life in all its action, potential and fragility, a spike of activity through the summer before a winter of storms and migrations south.

They radioed in nightly to the other research stations, their nearest neighbours just a couple of miles across the water above the sea lion rookery on Ugamak although as yet unseen, busied with their own world and studies. Standing high upon the cliffs, we first saw the shadowy forms of ships rounding Unimak Island to cross from Bering to the Pacific side or vice versa, the halfway point in our journey to Homer 600 miles away and reputedly the most dangerous pass for shipping traffic. It also marked the point at which we would be sharing our beaches with grizzly bears, from where we would make more noise than normal and stoke roaring fires long into the night. We quipped that between us we didn't stand much chance against the keen noses of bears, given that Justine got food all over her face and I generally ended up with mine all down my front. Having been bombarded by bear tales or questions of what we would do in bear country since setting foot in Alaska, we had given it a lot of thought. I had a small plastic air horn which blared like a tanker, making us laugh when I pretended that only bears could hear it. With no trees to hang food bags from, we settled for cooking downwind of camp and keeping food and anything that smelled in our kayaks away from the tents but close enough for us to hear if a bear was investigating them. At least then we could charge outside to startle and hopefully ward them off. Or that is what we thought. As all of our bear encounters would show us, they were more curious than scared. It is unsurprising really, given that they see so few people out on that coastline and have no reason to fear humans.

We saw footprints and scat on the very first beach we set foot on and had our first bear sighting the next night as a huge specimen ambled along the scrubland behind our camp, moving in to investigate when he heard us rather than running away as everyone had said they would. We stood by our nascent fire and clanged saucepans, shouting at it, the video of us looking quite ridiculous. When people asked if we carried guns and were surprised when we said no, we told them of Tina's story while out with a girl-friend on a hiking trip. Her friend blew her own sides out when the gun misfired. As an opener question, we asked people whether they had any good bear stories, as much to scare us as to inform. One artist from Anchorage told us how a black bear had found its way into his studio one day and how, just three days before, a friend of his had been mauled and was now in hospital. In the native community of King Cove, I asked Della what it was like to share the local area with bears, while we drove out of town to look for signs of them, passing the creek beneath the school where bears feed on salmon and the yellow warning sign with a picture of children and bears.

'Do most bears run from people?' I asked.

'No,' she said, lowering her voice to a whisper to protect her niece in the back of the car to tell me how her nephew had been killed by a bear some years before. 'My daughter and her children were out walking one day when they met a mother and cubs. They ran and that was it – the sow chased them.'

The next morning she took us to see a young bear, perhaps two years old, that had been shot and injured after climbing into a garden after the dog – or its food. A fluffy coat suggested why they had become such icons of sweetness in the time of Teddy Roosevelt, but the claws longer than my fingers reminded me of their power. 'I know I shouldn't say this,' said Justine, 'but it's really cute,' and we headed away sobered and hopeful about keeping our bear encounters to a minimum and at greater range than this.

In one community we saw signs advertising a dollar reward for getting your immunisations, while back on the mainland children were dying from measles for the first time in years. Dental hygiene wasn't much better, damage wrought by tobacco, chew and too much sugar. One mother told us how her seven-year-old had lost all her front teeth at the dentist because they were rotten, 'probably because she drank so much milk' when she was younger. Having seen her knock back a couple of cans of fizzy drinks just at lunch and munch through a bag of sweets, we were pretty certain it wasn't the milk.

The pink salmon had started running as we passed through Nikolski and, as we moved eastwards, so, too, did the migrating fish, slogging homewards from the oceans to spawn in their native rivers and streams. We came away from every community loaded with jars of rich potted fish and succulent whole sides of smoked salmon, enjoying trying the different species. Fishing boats looked like donkeys loaded high with saddle bags, their brightly coloured buoys tied down the sides in rows. In the canneries we watched tenders taking delivery of smaller boats' catches to transfer to the huge canneries and processing plants, even seeing inside the plant at King Cove. Fish were hoovered up in their thousands, sliding through the chutes to be washed, filleted, cooked and canned at mind-boggling speed and volumes, at all hours of the day and night when the fish was in. It was in stark contrast to the subsistence fishing we had seen along the way.

If the islands had been impressive, then the peninsula was even more striking, more dramatic and all of it on a bigger scale. There was more land for one thing, and even on our longest crossings we could generally see something of the rugged shoreline, even if hazy or socked in by mist, which it invariably was. We picked our way between the mainland and its offshore islands based on the shortest distances or most sheltered options, the risk of being blasted out to sea by williwaw winds shooting down off peaks a real threat. Clear days were rare and savoured for the fully revealed peaks and the range of blues and turquoise hues which painted the bays, licking up onto yellow sand. We tried to kayak early to make the most of the lower winds in the morning before the land heated up to send offshore winds careering into the bays. I wished that I was less nervous, even though my skills and confidence were a million miles on from where I had been in Adak. Finally I could take film and photos of Justine in the rough stuff – up to now anyone looking at pictures or films would only see me in the waves, for I had always been too wobbly or nervous to take my hands off the paddle.

Where we could, we camped on islands on the premise that there would be more bears on the mainland. That was true, but it didn't stop them swimming offshore. The morning we were due to paddle to the community at Perryville, Justine was packing her boat while I was getting into my drysuit. I noticed amid the dappled patches of glare a dark lump powering low through the water towards our beach. It was bigger and faster than an otter and pulsing in a way that sea lions and seals do not. I was sure it was a bear. 'JC – can you see that thing swimming over there?' 'Where?' she said. 'I'll get my binoculars.' Wriggling into my drysuit while Justine confirmed it was a bear through the lenses of her binoculars, moments later a young one splashed out of the water as though in transition at a triathlon, bounding up the beach, apparently not in the least bit interested in us.

The next bear that we saw up close was definitely more curious. I was naked in a stream, bent double rinsing my hair and enjoying the crunch of gravel underfoot and the tickling nibble of tiny Dolly Varden on my toes, basking in the cool. Leaves rustling overhead and a soft breeze in gentle contrast to the gurgle of water. Movement downstream. Justine? Looking up, hair dripping, I saw a bear padding towards me with the same curiosity and intent as a Labrador trotting in to investigate a small moving thing. In the same moment I started shouting. 'HEY BEAR! GO AWAY BEAR!' Turning on my heel to run out of the river in exactly the way everyone tells you not to, I tripped with a splash. As I scrabbled up out of the water I heard Justine shouting to ask if there really was a bear, just as the bear started running. 'YESSSS!' I yelled, pulling myself up over the fallen logs and through the reeds and grass to our camp, meeting Justine at the brow of the bank, camera rolling. Some choice swear words, shrieking and lobbing of rocks into the river eventually sent the bear on his way, standing on his legs to look one last time as he retreated. More curious than dangerous, the bear had displayed no fear at all and I had displayed none of the calmness I had always imagined would happen in a bear (and bare) encounter.

Further up the coast we spent a few days at Hallo Bay Bear Camp, a wilderness outfit flying clients in to watch the local bears, who, over a couple of decades, have been habituated to people. 'They think of us as quiet things that make cute clicking noises,' said our guide. The guides have learned to read the bear's body language – if a bear gets too close the guide stands up by degrees, rustling a pair of waterproof trousers and talking ever more sternly or, in rare and extreme cases of dangerous curiosity, holding a marine flare out front. In nearly thirty years of the camp they have only had to do that a handful of times, meaning that the rest of the time if the bears are out you can sit and watch them with no problem for either party.

'Just remember, when the bear runs at you, he isn't running at you, he's running at the salmon,' said Lance on our first day out. Sitting cross-legged on the grassy bank we watched bears pace up and down the creek stalking weary salmon from the crowds, holding our breath each time one swung its nose or a glance our way for a dash of a second. We were as engrossed in watching them as they were in finding dinner, except when they got too full and fell asleep in scrapes, legs akimbo. It had never occurred to me that each bear would have its own character or fishing style, and the guides had named them as such – Busy Bear, Bellyache Bear. From the old timers who scooped a glistening, wriggling fish with a single easy swipe to the young-sters who were clearly on their first solo season, snorkelling through the deep water or bounding with more splash than skill in the shallows to try and pin the returning salmon as they hauled themselves along the bottom, bright red and green bodies showing above the surface. Feasting only on the rich fatty flesh, often the bears would just bite out the belly and discard the half-eaten fish, to be picked at by waiting gulls. The efforts of the fish were humbling – their motors powered by instinct to twist every last sinew of its strength. All in the name of reproduction. And there we were, too, nearing the end of our 1,500-mile journey of endurance, driven by the journey and the goal, pushing hard when tired and trying again and again if our path was blocked.

Young cubs play-fighting on the beach, rolling into the water to cuff and jaw each other, oblivious to their spectators, reminded me of playing with my brothers as a child. One night there was a knock on the door at 4 a.m. to tell us that the wolves were howling. Another time there were recounted tales over breakfast from the film crew who were capturing footage for their BBC wildlife documentary, telling us how they watched a wolf swim out to an island at low tide to bring home a dead otter from the beach. Besides bear watching, I spent some time working on my boat, trying to fix the aluminium plate which had recently sheared, meaning that I had no working footplate to push off as I paddled. Para cord, cable ties and epoxy would have to do for now. Earlier in the week I had literally glued my boat together when a couple of the metal lever clips which held the back section of *Krissy* to the middle had bent out of shape until they were all but useless, meaning that only the solar panel fixed across the top deck now held it in place. It was only then, after sliding the boat over boulders and launching and landing on bluff beaches, that we saw the true value of Justine's bolted set-up, which had had us cursing at the start of the journey for its tricky-to-reach and time-consuming fixings.

Before we left, the camp crew told us of a Frenchman's kayak and gear lately found on a beach nearby, its paddler still missing. By all accounts he had been a bit of a wild one, travelling with no passport and bodging together his kayak from various bits of others he had found at the local dump in Homer. Whatever his motives or set-up, he had done well to get this far, navigating his way across and around the Cook Inlet and Shelikof Strait, both famed for their massive tide races. Elaine had described the latter to us as a 'river', such was the flow and force. She had followed our trip closely online and we had spoken to her often, making an effort to call from our camp on her native Unga where we had explored the petrified forests on the western edge of the island. Trees had been few and far between at that point still, stunted by the wind and poor soils. But now, as we approached our final 100 miles of the journey after our crossing of the Shelikof Strait, deep forests began where deep water ended. Thick, dark crowds of spruce stood tall against the skyline and driftwood logs lay stacked like pick-up sticks. Having crept up the coast against headwinds, we were relieved to pull into the quiet of Blue Fox Bay, threading our way between the islands looking for our first sign of Jerry and Colleen's homestead, tucked into the trees on Hogg Island. Here we spent two mad days, drinking mojitos and enjoying the steamy warmth of the banya followed by the shrilling cold of the sea, while Jerry chainsmoked pot and Colleen fussed around us and a fishing party out for a weekend of whiskey and halibut fishing. Outside the wind howled and the trees hushed and cracked as they swayed and we contemplated the final run to Homer.

Pushing north up the coast of Shuyak Island we came across a lone boater sheltering inside her little motor-cruiser with her dog while the rain poured, flattening the sea. At one point we paddled with the outgoing tide through a forested narrows, as though navigating a stream inland, before heading out into the full force of the tide as it turned. Edging up the side from eddy to eddy, we worked our way up to the sea proper where winds chopped and roughed it, eventually finding refuge on a little beach, tucked out of the wind as best we could while a low blew over. *So close and yet so stuck* read Billy's email message after two nights trapped there and another two further up the coast at another camp spot. Justine had a flight to catch and so we pushed out before 5 a.m. on one dark morning, mizzly rain dampening the air and looking like flying pencils in the beams of our head-lights. Along with the pitching sea shapes and shadows of rocks and luminescent waves, it felt like I was in an uneasy monochrome kaleidoscope as we rounded the corner of our sheltered cove, picking our way through safe water. Looking down at my map I felt queasy and so instead I focused on the high-glow strips of Justine's boat and clothing, keeping as close to her as I could.

As dawn happened and grey became day we rafted up to discuss our options – I didn't feel good in the waves and the forecast was for increasing winds, which, given the notorious tide races off the Barren Islands, would mean a tough and possibly dangerous run if it showed. If. The forecast didn't always materialise. Not wanting to go but also aware that Justine was worried about missing her flight in a few days' time, I agreed to have a go, with the caveat of turning back if I didn't feel safe. Off we went into the chop, sails up with the crosswind pushing us forwards. Not enjoying it from the start, I chatted to myself and tried relaxing my legs from their braced position on the bottom of the boat, struggling to hold course as I surfed down waves at the wrong angle. As we bounced and rolled in a race with wind over tide, I felt less comfortable than I had done in the Aleutians all those miles ago and shouted to Justine that I wasn't enjoying it. Long ago she learned this was my code for 'I don't feel safe'. Glad that we had tried and even gladder that we were team enough to make that call together and not push on in spite of it, I was proud of us that day. Of evolving with each other and for each other, forgetting the niggles and picking the other up when they were down. Having started the journey feeling like a liability and not really knowing what I could contribute to Justine's sure set-up and confident routines, I now felt like a useful member of our team, proud of how far we had come and how we had navigated and endured the rough stuff on and off the water. We had laughed a lot, shared hurts and hopes and cabin farts, and looked after each other in different ways. Now we were poised for the final miles, if only the low-pressure system would roll on and let us off our beach.

Two days after our first attempt we pushed afloat into a whiteout, bound for the Barren Islands 16 miles away, pulling ourselves over the pulsating blanket of ocean towards a fuzzy white horizon. Pouring with rain as it had done for the last week, I pumped my legs below deck to stay warm, flexing my toes and shaking my head to shower the drips from my hood, which was cinched close around my face. Feeling comfortable in the flattening seas, it was more about grind than anything technical, encouraging tired muscles to keep on working. With 10 miles to go the crepuscular peaks of the Barrens emerged from their foggy curtain, magnetising us somehow now that we could see them, even though the ebbing tide was dragging us eastwards. As slack water turned through the flood, our course looked healthier and eight hours after leaving our beach we were feasting on salami and cheese as we drifted between the two islands, enjoying the help of the tide. While part of me dreamed of an afternoon finish and an early night, the weather window was too good to ignore and so we pushed on north towards the Kenai Peninsula, another 30 miles away. If we could make it there, then we would be within shouting distance of Homer and Justine's flight home.

The first few miles were swift and useful, bouncing through tide races and away from the Barrens. And then things went less well as the flooding tide started pulling us out into the Shelikof Strait faster than we could paddle across it, northwards. 'We need to turn around, Sarah. I don't think we're going to make it,' shouted Justine and we spun around to face the Barrens again, some five miles away. For ten minutes we paddled hard into the waves, only for Justine to say, rather deflatedly, that this wasn't working either. 'We're just going to have to go for it and hope that something changes,' she said as she turned around again to our original goal of the Kenai Peninsula. For the next seven hours we plodded on into headwinds as rain clouds waltzed over us in different shades of grey and sheeting rain, tide races slapping and rocking, snatching and surfing. I remember the sky clearing a few miles out, a golden sun painting the waves with a majestic glow and the mountains in moody vivid definition. I bounced through a tide race feeling more confident than I ever had done, and found myself smiling at the scene outside and inside. Happily, the powerful spring tides sucked us into the Cook Inlet and we finally made it to the safety of a steep cobbled beach at 11 p.m., clocking nearly seventeen hours and 50 miles on the water, our longest of the trip so far. So tired we could barely eat, the emotion of having one final day to paddle kept us awake until 2 a.m., the rain pattering on our tent as we shuffled and turned in our bags waiting for sleep.

Wrapped in our own thoughts, we were silent for the first part of the next day's paddle, resenting the busyness of odd boats motoring past or helicopters and planes criss-crossing the bay after so much quiet and space to ourselves. Picking out buildings along the far shore and then passing the quaint little town of Seldovia made me want to be way out west again. As always happens towards the end of a leg, I recalled the past months in rolling flashes of memories and pictures, of mountains and waves, of fires and camps. Of being scared in the surf and challenged by tide races. Of disappearing behind waves while clinging on to glimpses of Justine, part excited, part scared. Of grinding out long miles on tired days. Of singing at the sky on others. Of watching mother bears sunbathe with cubs on the cliff top. And watching albatrosses wander the waves. Of being honked at by sea lions and spied on by eagles. Of catching fish and shooing foxes. Of campsites on tiny ledges and in cosy coves, in sweeping bays and fleeting tombolos, at river mouths and beach tops, in the shingle and on the sand. Most of all, perhaps, the journey could be summed up in spirits and senses. Endurance and identity; evolution and time – both in the places and the people we paddled through and past, and in ourselves.

Grinning our way ashore to a group of well-wishers, Justine and I hugged as sisters and as team mates after the most challenging paddling of our lives, just as Justine had predicted. Before starting and in the early days, plenty of people had bet against us. The locals couldn't conceive of such a journey and other experienced paddlers questioned my ability and Justine's decision to lead me. But we had wagered trust in each other and our boats; in the durability of kit and our energy, in the quality of our skills, and in our respect for each other and for the weather. I had spent many hours on and off the water questioning whether I could do it, physically and mentally feeling way out of my comfort zone for much of the 101 days since leaving Adak. And yet, here I was at this end of things, tentatively happy to call myself a kayaker now. Ironically, in pairing up with me on such a big journey, Justine had taught me to fly solo and I am deeply grateful to her for that. A year and 1,500 miles after that call from *Happy Socks* on the Pacific, I remembered that chap who asked if I was disappointed not to have made it to Canada as I first planned. Alaska was my answer.

PART III

Letting Go

North America, Atlantic Ocean and UK

Bike, row, bike, kayak | August 2014 – November 2015 | Total miles from London: 24,400

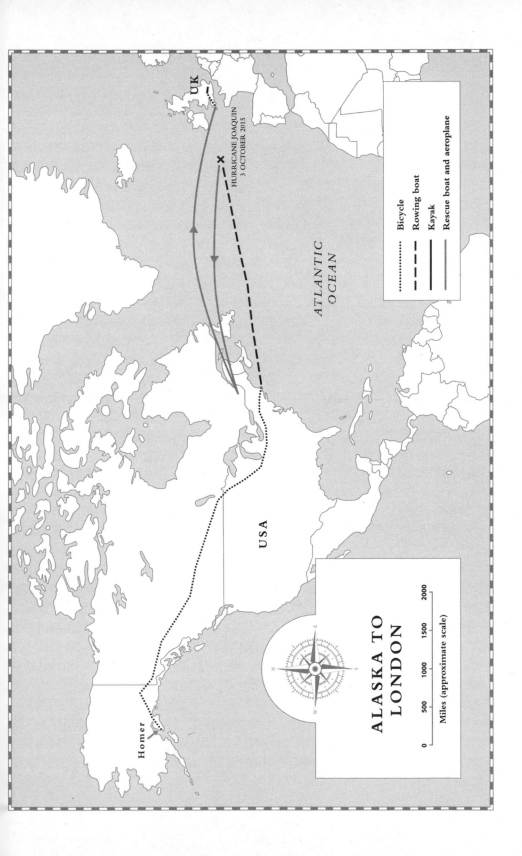

UK

HURRICANE JOAQUIN
3 OCTOBER 2015

ATLANTIC
OCEAN

USA

Homer

Bicycle

Rowing boat

Kayak

Rescue boat and aeroplane

ALASKA TO
LONDON

Miles (approximate scale)

0   500   1000   1500   2000

14

Who Am I?: North America and Canada

Homer, Alaska to Calgary, Canada |
Bike | Autumn 2014 | 2,300 miles

Heathrow, a few days after we had landed in Homer. I spotted Lucy leaning against the rail outside Costa, arms folded across her work clothes. She looked like she would rather be sitting on her combine – it was harvest after all. But we had told her that Justine needed collecting from the airport. I walked through her eye line unnoticed and wandered right up to her. Confusion as she realised that I was standing before her. We burrowed into a hug, gripping each other tightly, and everything in me relaxed.

'Er— I— But— What— What are you doing here?' asked Lucy as she pulled back to check I was real. I wiped tears from her cheeks and from mine.

'Happy birthday, lovely.'

'But you're— You're in Alaska. I spoke to you last night.'

'From Seattle, in transit.'

If someone had told me before the start of this journey that I would fly home to surprise someone, I wouldn't have believed them. But then I probably wouldn't have believed that I would fall in love, get engaged and struggle with the idea of carrying on because of that separation. Lucy and I were doing this expedition together now. Just as I got through the miles away, she was getting through them at home, too. I sometimes think that's harder.

During my week at home Mel left the team as project manager to move on to new things, both of us glad (and for my part very grateful) that she had been part of it. Wondering how to find a replacement with no time to meet anyone and wary of handing over the project at this stage, I flung Sara a quick email asking if she fancied returning to the helm. I was pleasantly surprised by the response: 'How exciting. Let me talk to Howard and the kids and get back to you.'

I flew back to Anchorage after a week at home with Lucy, swapping harvest for mountains. After a phone call with Sara she was back on board, both of us excited about working together again. It felt like things had come full circle. But one thing that hadn't changed was the money headache. George took control of the gnarlier bits of accounting and Lucy's twin Katy took up the day-to-day stuff. Ongoing admin for the ride – which cities I would make major stop-offs at for recovery and talks and where we would have winter gear sent along to – sat alongside planning for the row, so there was plenty to do.

The goal was for me to be on the Atlantic coast by the end of March, seven months and 6,000 miles away, heading through Alaska and down through Canada before turning right across the continent. The final launch point for the row wasn't set yet – it might be Nova Scotia, Canada, or it might be New York or Massachusetts in the USA. Winter would decide whether or not that was possible. The year before had seen record snowfalls and temperatures on the east coast. I joked that I might have to swap to skis, half believing it could end up being true. Everyone I met asked about the winter or assumed I would be taking a break and sitting it out. While wary of its ability to scupper my plans, I was also excited by the idea of it, having never experienced a deep winter like that. I was looking forward to the challenges of living by the lore of the cold.

It took a few days to reverse the spread of kayaking gear in Scott and Debbie's garage, from where we had left it to hang across boats and lines to dry a week before. Local wilderness rower Jill Fredston offered herself to the effort in packing and sorting and running errands about town, getting it all done in her no-nonsense east coast way.

'Fall's a short season out here,' she said and, as an avalanche expert, she gave me lists of fall lines to look out for on the first few days' ride from Homer to Anchorage. Fall lines were the places where avalanches were most likely to happen in winter. 'And watch out for tourists, too; sometimes they just stop right in the middle of the road to look up the mountain at something. And then there's the belugas once you get to Turnagin Arm, if you're lucky.'

Once the kayaks and gear were sorted and ready for homewards or onwards shipping for the Atlantic, I turned my attention to *Hercules.* Scott and Debbie joined in. Scott waterproofed my tent and sewed up some holes. Debbie stitched flags onto *Hercules'* new flagpole, adding the Stars and Stripes. Piecing my trusty black bike together was like reuniting with an old friend; besides *Happy Socks*, I had never spent so long travelling with any other. As I rebuilt him on the garage floor, I was filled with rushes of recognition. Scratches and marks, added bits and changed bits, were all a part of *Hercules* and my journey, much like scars and changes within me are. Even if I don't know their impact yet, I know that when I am too old or weak to journey physically, I shall journey in my mind, guided by these marks and scars to remember the path I took to the me of now.

Debbie drove me the 250 miles down to Homer ready to start the ride ('just down the road', she called it). Bumper stickers in Homer read *Quiet drinking village with a fishing problem* and signs through town declare it *Halibut Capital of the World*. The harbours on the inner side of the four-mile spit for which the town is famed bustled with boats and boaters. A small canvas city housed the casual workers in for a summer of fishing, while a trailer park looked like a motorhome showroom, crammed with vehicles as big as bungalows. Perhaps there's no surprise that the place has a laid-back hippyish feel to it, given that it is the end of the road – or the start of it to somewhere. I had a couple of days here before my ride, staying with Billy Pepper's wife Lizzy in their beautiful log cabin, surrounded by boating paraphernalia and animal skins.

Flying across the bay to Seldovia in a four-seater on the post run, I was transfixed by the waves washing onshore below us, and I imagined how tiny Justine and I must have looked in our kayaks ten days before. Hig and his friend Björn picked me up from the airstrip in a battered old car for the winding run past the gently touristy waterfront up to Hig and Erin's yurt. For a few years I had dipped in and out of their Groundtruth Trekking blog, reading tales of months spent hiking and packrafting all over Alaska to literally groundtruth the effects of mineral extraction, waste and water usage projects, current or proposed. Their six-year-old, Katmai, began his journeying pre-birth, conceived on their honeymoon trek from Seattle a few thousand miles north up the coast and westwards along the Alaskan Peninsula in a brutal and beautiful journey. Now joined by three-year-old Lituya, they trek and adventure as a family on explorations more hard-core than many adults would ever conceive of taking on. Spending a day biking and hiking down to the beach and back, we talked of learning and life while we picked redcurrants, fielded torrents of questions from the children, looked out for marmots and hopscotched on driftwood jams. 'It would be hypocritical if I was having more fun than my kids, so it makes sense for us to take them with us. It's a great chance to learn, at any rate,' said Erin.

'I like to live around zero,' said Hig. 'I don't see the point in keeping money stashed away. I'd rather be working on other projects than earning money, so we live cheaply. Everything can happen for under $1,000 a month.'

Dinner was fresh and fun, home-made and home-grown, and was shared with friends amid lively chat and laughter. The diminutive and always smiling Chunk offered to boat me back across the bay at dusk. First he gave me a tour of his log cabin down the hill with its greenhouse roof garden. Stacks of mountaineering kit waited for the snow and hundreds of jars of salmon and jam were ready to feed him for the year ahead.

'I eat healthy, wild and free out here. It's great,' he said.

'And what about in the winter?' I asked, knowing that for me the lack of light would be difficult. It sounded like for Chunk the darkness was inside and out, and I got the impression he longed for his special someone to share it with.

'Three friends of mine have gone this year,' he told me. 'One in a wilderness race. One on a kayak trip. And one in an avalanche.' He turned away to stare at the sea and way off into the mountains. We pootled out past the other boats and into the bay in a little skiff called the *Pearl*. 'François, did you hear about him?' 'The guy whose kayak was found way down the Peninsula?' 'Yeah. Well, he stayed here in Seldovia for a while before he left on his trip. With his accent it sounded like *Peril*.' 'What do you think happened?' I asked, having read various theories and heard others. 'I reckon he's faked his death and is laughing at us all from some cave somewhere,' laughing, as though he wanted to believe it. And with that he howled into the sky, which was heavy with cloud. 'Lone wolves, Sarah! That's what we are. Lone woooooooolves.'

I wasn't so sure. Maybe I once was – or thought I was – unattached and independent. But now my wholeness depended on my life with Lucy. It was something I was still trying to reconcile within myself, but I was getting more used to the idea.

My final visit before setting off was to Nikolaevsk School a few miles out of town in a community which was set up by a group of Russian 'old believers' in the sixties. It now schools a mix of Russian and American students from kindergarten to school-leaver age and was an interesting fusion of the two languages and cultures in corridor and classroom signage, traditions and dress. Some of the teachers and teenage pupils wore long floral dresses and headscarves as I had seen Russian babushkas doing in eastern Europe. The headmaster had briefed me beforehand to go strong on following dreams and ambition, given that many of the girls, in particular, are not encouraged to have a life beyond staying in the village to marry early and raise a family. Knowing that, I was more pleased than normal when one fifteen-year-old found me afterwards to tell me how my talk had inspired her: 'I want to do something now.' Another girl told me that going around the world was dangerous and that I might die, suggesting I could ask God to help me, just like she did when she was in trouble. Not feeling it was my place to introduce atheism to eight-year-olds, I moved the conversation on, flicking through some pictures of my journey. 'Is that a castle? Do you have castles in England?' asked the same girl, Amelia. 'Yes, we do. This isn't a castle – it's Tower Bridge, in London.' 'Oh, that's where the queen lives, right? Do you still have a queen?' 'Yes we do. Queen Elizabeth.' 'Oh great. I thought she died.' And, half an hour later as we all gathered our bags for home time, she asked if I would say 'Hi to Elizabeth' for her. I said yes, while imagining that, too, was about as likely as me asking for help from God on my journey.

Sea and sky were bright and calm as I loaded up *Hercules* with gear for the road and tapped the hand of the bronze giant at the Seafarer's Memorial, just as I had done two weeks before when Justine and I stepped out of our kayaks. A few people had emailed to say they planned to ride out with me and one lady, Cat, had suggested she might see if she could gather a few friends from the local bike club. We set out with about thirty riders from children to retirees, taking breaks from shopping runs or making this their morning's activity, riding out on racers and mountain bikes and anything else with wheels. There was even a small child in a trailer. *Hercules* was the veritable carthorse, so I felt like a rather slow Pied Piper of Homer. I was touched by their efforts and company, and humbled by gestures of kindness as people gave me snacks to stuff into my panniers, a coffee card charged with ten bucks, a mirror for my helmet, a sticker for my bike. I was already wearing my Alaska cycling jersey, given to me by a local riding company.

Most people turned off at the farmers' market and given the Baycrest Hill out of town, I understood why. 'We're going so slowly!' said seven-year-old Frieda and, smiling inside, I spun my wheels a little faster, grateful nonetheless when someone wanted to stop and talk with me. There's nothing like starting from a low baseline for feeling excited about future improvements, and I settled into the fact I would be slow for a while yet. It had been a couple of years since I had ridden a bike. At any rate, I didn't mind, for this was Frieda's first time riding out of town and up Baycrest Hill and I had thousands of miles of mountains ahead of me. Part of a journey's beauty for me is that you settle into it, growing into your fitness and mode of travel. It is all about starting out and carrying on, for once on the way the rest will happen. For now, I just had to knock down the gears and stand up on those pedals, working my lungs like bellows. When people said to me 'I couldn't do what you are doing' with reference to the endurance, I disagree. Body allowing, I think if anyone wanted to ride a bike across a continent, they could. Some would be faster and fitter and some could take years instead of months (or days), but the most enduring muscle of all is attitude. If you want to get there, you will.

Cat carried on with me all day as we tracked north in parallel to the volcanic skyline on the other side of the Cook Inlet. We passed adverts for boat charters and people posing with their catches of giant halibut, through leafy groves and over creeks invariably lined with fisherfolk. It was salmon season, after all. Roadsides were lined with fireweed, its bright pink flowers and green stalks a colourful contrast to the tarmac. Seed heads drifted in the breeze, collecting here and there in fluffy piles, the end and the start of a journey. 'Out here we say that when the fireweed seeds, it's six weeks till snow.'

Way back in Adak, Lisa Spitler had told me that I would be welcome with her parents-in-law in Ninilchik, a day's ride from Homer. And so it was that I spent my first night on the road inside talking about our different experiences of the Aleutians. Lisa's mother-in-law Sherry's parents had been evacuated from Unalaska in 1941 and, unlike many, had returned. Doug had piloted out west for many years and we both enjoyed remembering mutual friends from Atka and Nikolski. Riding back to Anchorage felt like riding home, knowing that familiar hugs and space waited before I had to push on alone. Sixty miles out of the city, having descended past the glacier and run along Turnagin Arm where, way back when, Captain Cook had turned around after realising he hadn't discovered the Northwest Passage but instead a glacier field, I stopped to visit one of Jill's friends, Lisa Taylor. We had met Lisa in a fish restaurant in Dutch Harbor while she was working for one of the tribes as an accountant. Tucked back into the woods, the spectacular log home she shared with husband Peter Brondz and daughter Iris felt like something from a book of fairy tales, sculpture and art nestled between trees as though it had always grown there. Scarcely five minutes passed between arriving at the front gate at dusk and lying in the sauna in the garden.

After the solitude of our time kayaking way out west, far from people, riding along the only road from Homer to Anchorage at the tail end of summer felt rather social and busy, even though I was pedalling alone. Giant motorhomes whooshed past in convoys of six, seven, eight at a time while timber trucks thundered by on twenty-eight wheels, reminding me that my main aim was not to become roadkill. That was the biggest threat to my safety on the road, though my mum was scared of people doing something nasty to me and Lucy was terrified I would be eaten by bears. To be fair, I was scared of the latter, too, making me cautious by day as I whistled and sang my way down empty roads and turning me into a fire-stoking worrier by night. Within the glow and warmth of my campfire's light, I felt braver.

I often dreamt of waking up in the jaws of a bear as it carried me off up the beach and woke myself trying to scream, so when invited inside or offered a B & B night, I graciously accepted, provided there were no dogs. Some lax house choices had led to a few rounds of steroids early on and I didn't want to continue the trend. It is a wonder I managed to find anywhere that fitted the bill, for in Alaska dogs were like guns – everyone had one. Mostly, though, I slept out, on the roadsides or tucked back into the forest as far as I dared go, freaking myself out with every crack of a branch or rustle of leaves. That said, the only animal I ever saw anywhere near my tent at night was a tiny mouse, as it scurried about in my torchlight trying to find the safest way to run, no doubt more scared of me than I was of it.

Besides bears, my other big fear on the bike was one which I had not anticipated: heights. Barrelling downhill at 30 miles an hour on a road with no hard shoulder and being passed by trucks as long as the logs they carried made my forearms numb from pumping my brakes. Most of the time there was just a tiny barrier to the right with a steep drop-off beyond and more traffic just inches to the left. My raised heart rate was as much to do with fear as it was physical. Out of Anchorage I weaved through one mountain range after another – the Chugach, the Wrangells – all patchworked with autumn. Golden swathes of aspen. Scarlet maples. Dark heathers and berries and the deep year-round green of conifers. Trees as far as I could see.

This was the autumn of my expedition, too, in some ways, the end of it now near enough to contemplate, even if the reality was still thousands of miles away and no more certain than it had ever been, but for the fact I was closer. Perhaps it was more that 'the next leg' was now the Atlantic, the last major one of them all, whereas up to now the legs had always been counted in plurals.

Heading north, lakes reflected their mountain neighbours in glossy waters, cut across by beaver or graced by a passing pair of swans, heading south for the winter. Velvety nights splashed with countless stars made the mountains feel near and all my neighbours, whether man or beast, somehow close. Hunting groups travelling and setting up camp in convoy, all dressed in camouflage, headed out to hunt moose or headed home with their hauls, racks with or without their owners attached bungeed down on top of trailers. I only saw one moose feeding quietly at the roadside, just as I only saw a single black bear, galloping across the road – though I saw plenty of scat from both.

Winding through the Talkeetna Mountains alongside the Matanuska River, where the highly folded contours on the high-res map I had been given looked like the folds of a brain cortex. The highest ridge line peaked at 12,000 feet. I was scared by the sheer slopes that, from time to time, sent chunks of rock skipping and bouncing down to the road. I thought of Jill and her fall lines. Looking down I was scared by the drop-offs and the nothing, the thigh-high barrier feeling inadequate to a biker twice that tall. Sometimes there was no barrier. Caribou Creek was no steeper than the steepest roads I had pedalled so far, but I still froze for ten minutes at the top before talking myself back on the bike. I bartered with Chimpy that I would go really slowly and only walk when I was too scared to pedal, pleading with myself not to as I had just seen a sign saying NO STOPPING, with the symbol for 'rock fall' on it. Either way, it would take for ever as I didn't trust myself or my brakes enough to ride it with my usual commitment to eking out every inch downhill possible. Then came the angular turn at the bottom as it wrapped around the other side of the creek. Never before or since did I consider flagging down a ride out of fear, but now I was. But I didn't. I nearly cried I was so scared, but I managed to go fast enough to still call it cycling. I rode in the centre of the road, keeping my eyes focused on the tarmac, only moving in if a car came. When an oversized load filled the road, its brakes hissing at the downhill, I froze on the tiny shoulder and tried pretending that the edge wasn't really yawning out to my right.

At the very crook of the elbow, I pulled out my video camera to film the post-descent thoughts of a scared biker, hands trembling. Having spied the yellow school bus starting to trek downhill towards me, I was glad I wasn't the driver. The bus stopped and a lady with soft brown curls and chewing gum wound down her window to see if I was OK. Seeing how shaken I was, she asked if she could give me a hug. I generally turn to stone if a stranger hugs me – or asks if they can – but this time I said yes and let my body relax onto hers for a moment.

'My husband has seen you out these last couple of days. He told me to look back at you in my mirror as I passed because he says you're always smiling.' If she'd seen me ten minutes before, I would not have been smiling.

Pedalling on beneath Sheep Mountain, I wondered if the dall sheep for which the craggy peak is named ever felt scared. I was touched by a blog comment from one of the cyclists who had escorted me out of Homer: *Sarah – you departed us here, but you never left us. We ride with you still. Be brave. Be confident. Be true to yourself.* I hadn't imagined I would be scared of the ride, but when I needed to get some brave on, I pulled out my invisible peloton, talking to them to distract myself or imagining us leading each other up and around through the mountains, taking the edge off things.

Fears aside, I also enjoyed the return to soloing once I had settled into it. At first Chimpy goaded me at every break, but not once I had reminded myself that it didn't matter when I rode my miles each day, so long as I was off the road before dark. But I did miss Lucy. If I had never imagined flying home to surprise someone I loved, then I would certainly never have imagined considering packing it all in to go home to her. When I spoke to Lucy, both of us in tears, she told me in no uncertain terms that I wasn't coming home until I had paddled under Tower Bridge. Instead we decided that she would come out and join me in Calgary, 2,000 miles south in southern Canada, and that for now I would just keep pedalling.

I slept late the next day, taking my time to pack away my tent and get going from Sheep Mountain lodge, where I had eaten a piece of every pie flavour on offer the night before, to the surprise of the waitress. My school bus found me again a few miles down the road. 'Will you come home with me and have dinner with my family?' asked Suzie, the driver. I gratefully accepted, enjoying mealtime with the grandchildren and tales of buying a new bus every year or so from somewhere in the Lower 48 and driving it back up here for vacation. There were only nine kids on the route to Glacier View School and not many more on the register itself, but still they ran a normal capacity bus. I visited the children the next morning and asked, 'So, what's it like living out here?' 'Awesome!' was the unanimous verdict, and the list of favourite things to do was largely based outdoors. 'We middle school boys live for our snow machining,' said one lad, while another enjoyed mountain unicycling and another again told me that he was a keen trapper. If only all children had as much access to the outdoors and enthusiasm for it as they did, I am sure we would have a healthier school age population than we currently do.

Turning off the Glenn Highway to join the Alaska–Canada Highway (or AlCan) at Tok felt like a big moment, for it was also a turn southwards, away from my beloved north, towards Lucy. A strip of land, denuded of trees, swept up the mountainside and beyond, marking the unfortified border and leaving me to pedal 30 miles through open marshland and forest before I came to a checkpoint at Beaver Creek.

'Why are you here in Canada?' asked the officer.

'I'm cycling across the country.'

'When do you plan to leave?'

'Well, it depends on the weather, but probably sometime this winter.'

'Well in that case we had better give you six months, then. Where are you staying tonight?'

'In my tent.'

'You do know there are bears out here?'

'Yes, officer, thank you. I haven't been eaten so far, so I think I shall be fine.'

'Do you have bear spray?'

'Yes, thank you, I do.'

'And when will you be back in the UK?'

'Next year. I'll be rowing home across the Atlantic.'

Gathering up my passport to hand back to me, he realised that in his excitement about bears and rowing, he hadn't stamped me into Canada yet.

Communities along the AlCan are a bit like islands in a chain, connected but scattered and getting even more so as services dwindle. No one needed to sleep on the road; people would just strap a spare can of gas on the roof of their car and drive three, four hundred miles at a time. As such, giant billboards started conjuring up punters for thirty miles or more outside each tiny strip of commerce – the gas station, RV park, diner. Many old places stood empty, vehicles and farm or prospecting gear rusting. Most of the traffic I saw was for construction, often through dust clouds as trucks rolled past at speed.

'There's two seasons out here in the Yukon: construction and winter,' said the fellow waiting at the traffic lights in his truck as I pulled up to wait, a couple of miles out of Snag Creek, where I had just packed up my tent. He was waiting for an escort through several miles of roadworks.

'No bikes through there, ma'am – I'll have to get you a lift,' said the lady overseeing the lights. I explained my human-powered aims, declining the lift and asked if I could walk my bike alongside the road margin instead. 'There's work vehicles out there until 5 p.m., so you'll have to wait until then. Are you sure you don't want a lift?'

As it happened, they let me through on their lunch break, and I rode through rocky mountains and marshes, alongside striking lakes whipped with white caps. Over gurgling creeks and wide, glacial rivers, their flows a fraction of the gushing snakes they would have been in the springtime. Some were still impressive, as much for their flow as for their valleys. Mini tornadoes whisked along the edges of the Donjek, swirling up sand from its flanks. The White River, so named after the volcanic eruption which had spewed white ash into it, hurried on over an albino river bed, wide and rocky. By the Toad River, with its valleys of multicoloured rock, haughty elk trotted off the road into the forest when they saw me coming and called out at night like transistor radios searching for contact.

As with the rest of the ride, I loved the road for its contrasts: the wild and peaceful scenery and the solitude and the interactions with people. There was the gold panner who taught me how to sift and search. The guy driving to Anchorage to go shopping, twelve hours away, because it was cheaper up there. The lady who cooked me pancakes in a greasy diner at Muncho Lake who told me: 'I thought we'd had the last biker through a coupla weeks back.' I spent a couple of days cycling with the smiling Iohan as he meandered towards South America on his bike *Dead Horse*, teaching him to light a fire in the rain, surprised he had never toasted a marshmallow before. There was the shout-out from a fellow cyclist as she zoomed down the hill I was pedalling up: 'You're a woman too – that's awesome!' A shared campfire with Swiss photographer Claude, who commented that it was 'so British to toast marshmallows'. The hunter who recognised me from a snowy pass a few days before, and the drivers who escorted me past the shaggy herds of buffalo which roamed the roadsides in Northern BC. The native guy who declared he was a 'self-prescribing First Nations doctor' as he lit up his first joint, telling me how his girlfriend had kicked him out again for drinking too much.

Just down the road I cycled off my route to the tiny native village of Champagne, to see the place behind the name. A wall of shiny hub caps nailed onto tall wooden poles was my first view of the village; not exactly what I was expecting. Information boards told me that the Southern Tutchone clan had lived here thousands of years ago and that the arrival of the Alaska Highway in 1942 had changed the face of the village and its people for ever. Men went away to work and trade and disease came in. Presumably new genes did, too. There was a mix of traditional sod-roofed huts, which looked to be storage sheds now, small log homes, and some which were more modern. It was quiet and empty, but for the gophers scampering about in the ruined homes and squirrels who screeched from branches in rustling trees. I found a native man named Glenn sawing wood and stacking it in piles outside his log home. This was his grandmother's house and had been here for about a hundred years. I wanted to photograph him; his face was wizened and weathered by years of hard work outside, hunting and beer. I held off asking him until we had been chatting for ten minutes. It was almost as long as he held off suggesting that I could come and live with him one day, offering to pay for my family, too.

As I sat eating a snack on the edge of the village I noticed an elderly man on a quad bike coming round some upturned Quonset huts. I waved in greeting and he came over and, on introductions, I realised I had just cycled past his house – the one with the little sign reading *Ray and Dorothy* over the door. He told me that she had just died 'in ninety seven' and that he had too many grandchildren to count. Pointing to the mountains behind us, he told me of packing 40 miles into the hills with his horses to hunt, of fishing and trapping. 'I like this life, living from the land. I like it here. Though I came from Alberta in forty eight. It took three days to get here back then.' We chatted for a while, and Ray wished me a joyful journey as he turned for home to cook moose for dinner. I pedalled onwards, silently thoughtful, memories of home evoked by this gentle grandfather, a link to my own, long gone.

Hector Mackenzie found me at the side of the road three weeks in, squeezing a tube of jam into my mouth. 'Well, well, well, Sarah! Why waste time with bread, eh?' he said in his cheerful Scottish brogue, bristling me with whiskers as he kissed both cheeks. I was already looking forward to staying with him and his wife Miche Genest in Whitehorse not only for the promise of good company but for the cookies which they had surprised me with at my roadside camp two days earlier. We had been connected via Jill as Hector was also an avalanche maestro. I arrived at their house in the colourful suburbs of Whitehorse, the territory capital, anticipating a couple of days to rest, sort and repair kit, get a massage for my knotted muscles and a fix for *Hercules'* brakes. But there was something about the house as soon as I walked in that made me hope I had got my timings wrong. In the end I stayed for a week, enjoying the warmth and energy of Hector and Miche, their cavernous bath and the artistry that came out of their kitchen (Miche is a gourmet chef). Hector took it upon himself to be in charge of bike improvements, making me a pair of pogies and fitting an extra bike rack so I could carry more winter gear.

Thick flakes had already laid down a couple of inches of snow and were still falling heavily when I woke up. A week before I had been excited by thick frosts turning my tent solid in the morning and flurries of snow on the highest passes, so to have this much snow now was quite novel. Chimpy was hammering on inside somewhere, too, tut-tutting about riding through winter and all the white stuff ahead, worrying over whether we would make it.

'Sarah, dear, it's white outside. Are you sure you want to go today?' said Hector as I emerged from my basement bedroom. Ignoring Chimpy I said yes and regathered my gear into bags, packing away the shop-bought food and the home-made treats before setting out into the white. Hector and Claude, the Swiss photographer, escorted me out of town to take photos and asked me again if I wanted to carry on. Yes, I did. Things might change in a few days but for now, all miles were good miles, as I was bound to be held up by blizzards more regularly later on. The mountain snow was thick and wet, soaking my bike shoes and their felt liners to sodden within an hour of being out. But it wasn't freezing yet; ice would be a different story and I didn't want that until I had my spiked tyres. It was quiet but for the sound of my waterproofs shushing and the light-footed snow tiptoeing on my clothes. Slush caught in my forks, built and built and then either fell off or I kicked it away. Cars belted past chucking wheelfuls at me. The wind picked up as the afternoon wore on, blowing snow horizontally as the road ploughed on east. I stopped in a mail shelter and ate my snacks with the post boxes, turning down my first offer of a lift. Many more drivers stopped, asking if I was OK and whether I needed a ride somewhere. I was intent on getting to Jake's Corner and was happy to do so in the dark, around 8 p.m., the orange glow of a few solitary street lights making the snowy forecourt look warmer than it really was. Snow still fell. There was no better night to have been met here by blog followers Dick and Maggie, who had driven 50 miles up the track from end-of-the-road Atlin in their camper van to have dinner with me and bring me inside for the night, undeterred by the conditions. In fact, they appeared to enjoy the adventure of it all as much as I enjoyed their tales of previous lives running mussel farms and doctoring on the west coast, and their current life of rowing and living on Atlin Lake.

The temperature plummeted overnight and the new day was fresh and sharp, snow frozen hard. I hid my nerves as I rode out of the parking lot and slipped on the ice, Dick and Maggie asking if I was sure I wanted to carry on. I quickly learned to handle the bike on the compacted snow and ice, not yet melted by traffic or grit, wondering if I would need my spiked tyres sooner than I was currently scheduled to meet them, 1,000 miles south in Edmonton. Hector had already said that two friends of his whom I had met in Whitehorse would be driving south in a few days and could deliver anything extra that I needed. I called and asked him to buy me a pair of exactly the same fleece-lined neoprene welly boots that Dick had lent me the night before. I knew that my cycling shoes would not be adequate to Edmonton.

Thankfully the snow petered out within 20 miles and I cycled in mostly dry conditions for the next two weeks as the road wound south-eastwards through the Rockies, alternating between unseasonably warm and bitingly cold. My mood rolled, too, in a softened version of the peaked landscape. Sometimes I sat in contented emptiness or gentle awareness as I pedalled, legs spinning in a sort of meditation. Other times I thought of other things actively and busily, my mind whirring along with the bike wheels. I inhaled calories for the mountains and for the cold, cooking deep potfuls of noodles by night and slicing butter onto bread as though it were cheese. In roadhouses or diners I treated myself to hot chocolate and multiple slices of pie, making me glad that these stops were so few and far between for my wallet's sake, at least.

In Watson Lake I spent time with Ann Maje Raider, leader of Liard Aboriginal Women's Society, a local social charity supporting native people. I knew little about Canada's dark history of residential schools and Ann, herself a survivor, told me more. In the early nineteenth century industrial expansion and mineral exploration was bringing First Nations people into conflict with the establishment. Over a 150-year period, thousands of native children were forcibly removed from their families and tribes and taken away to institutions which many describe as more prison than school. Their aim was to aggressively assimilate them into white, modern society.

'I was six. I didn't want to go and so I clung to Dad's leg,' said Ann. 'The agent said he would be put in jail if I didn't go.' Boys separated from girls, heads shaved, identical uniforms and numbers instead of names; it reminded me of the Nazi camps. 'We weren't allowed to talk to our brothers and sisters and they beat us if we did. Or if we talked in our own language. We had to speak English. They made us feel ashamed for who we were — for our heritage and our culture.'

Allowed home for a summer with her family, Ann said she was one of the lucky ones; 'Some kids never went home if it was too far away.' Beaten and abused, many children died or fell into addiction, violence, abuse and even suicide. Those who survived often returned to their communities as strangers, neither part of white society nor their native one, lacking the skills for either. Sadly, the results still cycle through the generations today and native communities have high rates of alcohol and drug abuse and domestic violence.

I was shocked not only that it had happened (and in such recent times, too) but that it wasn't more widely known about.

It happened on the watch of a government set up from Britain, after all. Ann tried telling me that I was brave for taking on my journey, but for me, hers was the brave one and I was grateful that she had shared it. Just as I had done after meeting native Alaskan communities out west, it made me question my own identity.

One focus for the North American leg was remote assemblies via satellite phone with forty-five schools in Lincolnshire through my role as an ambassador for the youth sports charity Inspire+. At the same time, Daesh were calling for lone-wolf attacks in Europe and North America; a gunman's shooting spree in Ottawa in late October had recently stunned Canada. Juxtaposed with the humbling and generous kindness and openness of people on a personal level, were these examples of collective inhuman or unjust treatment of others.

The sulphurous heat and buoyancy of the milky green water at Liard Hot Springs felt like a version of heaven I could believe in. My muscles did, too, now pulling over 70 kilos of bike and gear. I filled up on food in the lodge at Toad River, its walls and ceiling lined with a sea of signed baseball caps which have been left by travellers. I chatted with other punters, generally prompted by them seeing *Hercules* standing outside. One guy was putting out posters for his son's pony, lost recently on a hunting trip with four others. Another couple were teachers from nearby Fort Nelson. I duly signed my Buff and planned to pedal on after a night camped in the silence of the grounds. The next day, I woke feeling poorly, but to find that my first nephew had arrived safely in the world.

After a couple of days' rest but still feeling rough, I rode up and over Steamboat Mountain on hairpin bends cutting sheer escarpments, enjoying the silver trees and lakes not yet fully iced. Elk on the roadside pronked majestically out of sight. Flying down out of the most rugged of the Rockies, I hunched down over the handlebars for speed, and in an attempt to convince myself that I was not cold. Brain freeze. In Fort Nelson a doctor prescribed antibiotics for bronchitis and reminded me that I had asthma, which I generally forgot, explaining that this was contributing to my tight chest. I spent a week sleeping and resting in a hotel, visited by strangers I met in the supermarket while looking for a cashpoint. Wendy brought home-made chicken and ginger soup and Sonja took me for dinner with her family and to meet friends and colleagues. When I came to pay the bill, I found that half had already been covered by donations from friends and strangers after I tweeted about being poorly.

Sonja also took me to a school on the local tribal reservation and talked to me about some of the complexities and challenges faced by tribal bands in managing their ancestral lands and resources in the context of a government which is keen to develop and prospect. An ex-rower, she had hoped to make the Olympic team but a back injury had forced her out of the race. She now ran her own environmental consultancy, one of her roles being, in her own words, 'hanging out of helicopters and setting fire to shit!' in the controlled burning of land for soil regeneration and species management, with a particular interest in the restoration of bison populations.

The road turned south from Fort Nelson, down into Southern BC through the dense forest and pockets of pastoral land. The oil and gas industry was becoming more and more conspicuous and, I think it would be fair to say, obnoxious both in terms of the landscape and the driving styles of the trucks. Sometimes I spent more time off my bike than on, walking for miles on snowpack too slippy to ride on. Like convoys of metallic ants, the oil and gas trucks were being driven by young guys being paid far too much to be on time to worry about anyone else on the roads – $150,000 a year – many from Mexico who had never seen snow before, let alone driven on it. I steered off the road at what felt like the last moment on too many occasions to count, wishing the miles away for the promised hard shoulder of Alberta's roads. And yet I knew I would miss the mountains. I loved the thick wetness of mountain snow, if not for what it did to the road, but for the way it made feathery igloos around my tent and the way that, in falling overnight and smoothing over the foot-prints I had left behind, it created a whole new day to walk into, a Refresh button, of sorts. I took a childish pleasure in crunching new paths. The soft non-thud of snow sloping off heavy branches. Snowfall while I was still riding was fun to a point, irritating to another, and eventually it became dangerous because I couldn't be seen and nor could I see. So it was a case of pushing hard for miles when possible and waiting out the snow when it was not.

From BC the road sank into Alberta, where oil and gas companies were busy sinking pumps and drills into the landscape and trucking it all over, expanding towns and cities that would otherwise have been much less developed and, probably, much less diverse. There were pros and cons to being around more people and traffic: a higher risk of RTA but more chance of a ride if I broke down; more bike shops and opportunities for a decent sports massage; less expensive groceries and, generally, better roads. Mostly, though, I was excited by the fact that further south meant closer to my winter tyres and clothing in Edmonton, and closer to Lucy. For now, I borrowed some ski goggles and winter gloves from a couple of different families who had invited me to stay and kept plugging on, excited by the novelty of each drop in temperature. Once it dropped below −10 degrees it was new territory for me, and I learned quickly that the cold is a swift and severe teacher, requiring speed of thought and action, but also method and logic. Reminded by coldness or numbness to be quicker next time or do something slightly differently, routines and rituals soon became second nature. A snack: stop, straddle bike, open bar bag, take off gloves, unwrap and stuff into mouth, then reglove, begoggle and get pedalling again as you chew. A wee: stop, get off bike and turn away from the wind (which you have already sussed), deglove and stuff into jacket or bike, pull trousers down – crouch – wee – wipe – pulling trousers up needs to be almost instantaneous, then bag paper, reglove and go, all happen within seconds. Lingering might mean chilblains, chapping or frostbite.

Doing mechanical work on the bike in those conditions quickly meant numb fingers, which then ached as warm blood returned. Colder temperatures knocked out all pressure in my hydraulic brakes, meaning I spent a lot of time trying to adjust them at the roadside, and that, over the entire continent I patronised many a bike shop. Unfortunately they were a design of brakes that isn't really used in North America and so proved difficult to replace, sometimes just because the mechanics themselves hadn't seen them or more often than not, didn't want to deal with them. But *Hercules* was holding up pretty well in the cold so far, except for shot front bearings, a few broken spokes in the back wheel and a couple of flats. I was confident that we would be OK, even if it meant riding ridiculously long miles once winter was over to make up time.

It was other people who seemed to be more worried about me, leading me to write *Don't Worry I'm OK* on the back of my high-vis vest to let people know that I had chosen to be here. Still, cars often stopped to ask if I wanted or lift or needed food or water – although when I say cars, mostly they were 4×4 SUVs with bonnets as high as my shoulders. I always accepted food and water, as melting snow for the latter required fuel and time and there were sometimes long distances between places where I could buy the former. Serendipitously, I accepted a lift from Dave the trucker when he stopped his artic lorry to talk to me on a fast road in northern Alberta, himself a winter biker. I had just been pulled over by a police car who had received reports of a cyclist. 'May I ask what you are doing, ma'am?' the officer said, brow furrowed. 'I'm cycling.' She wasn't pleased and took my details, advising me to stay off the road. 'Drivers aren't expecting to see a cyclist out here and right now the sun's in their eyes so they can't see you until they're on you.' I reassured her I would be careful. After a while chatting with Dave and deflecting his suggestions that I drive with him to Edmonton, I saw sense and we loaded *Hercules* and associated panniers and rack bags into his cab. It felt strange to be sitting up so high, miles slipping by quickly. I could now see the police officer's point.

'The best advice for winter camping and biking is to get inside whenever possible, so you can dry everything,' said Dave. Reaching behind his seat he pulled out a winter boot, part mountaineering boot and part cycling shoe, with a cleat on the sole, which Dave suggested gluing around to stop water getting in. 'These will sort you out to minus twenty or more,' he said. 'Expensive, but they'll revolutionise your ride.' Once in Edmonton I bought a pair of the boots, some candles to help burn off the condensation at night and a four-season tent big enough for me and Lucy that we later nicknamed the Orange Dome. Opening the boxes of winter gear that Scott had sent down from Anchorage, it felt reassuring to be reuniting with more heavy-duty gear which would make riding and tenting safer and more comfortable: gaiters, extra thermals, ski goggles, balaclava, winter gloves, thicker socks, neoprene face mask and of course the spiked tyres. Riding on ice with the new tyres felt like riding with normal tyres on dry road – no slipping, sliding or wheels spinning to try and find traction. With gaiters and the new boots, my toes and legs stayed warmer for longer, meaning fewer walks off the bike to bring them back to life, and I actually believed that cycling through winter could be not just possible, but comfortable.

People's kindness continued to humble me as they invited me into their lives to sleep, to eat, to share food and stories and join in. Family Noga-Martin in Grande Prairie, where teenage daughter Katie and her boyfriend Matt serenaded us with the *Les Misérables* songs they were practising for a show and we played silly games around the kitchen table, getting bellyache from laughing so much. Family Keeler in Fort St John, where I experienced my first Halloween on this side of the Atlantic, the kids dressed as a juice box and Abe Lincoln. They shared their plans for their first extended family kayaking trip and took me cross-country skiing in the park. To Whitecourt I cycled with Ray, 'the only winter cyclist around here', and stayed with his family for the night as they prepared for a birthday party for their youngest son the next day. As I pumped *Hercules'* tyres ready to ride, ten-year-old Elijah handed me a painting 'for your tent' and said he was excited that he could tell his friends he had had a celebrity sleep in his bed. I apologised that *Hercules* had spent the night in the garage. Byron, who acted as delivery man and escort about town. The Millars, who let me ping-pong in and out of their home as needed as I transited through and back to Edmonton. One morning I woke to find this note in the kitchen: *Decided to stay home from work to fix your brakes. Popped out to get parts but will be back shortly. John.* This had never just been my journey, and I was humbled by that.

In the wee hours of a late November morning the back roads north of Calgary were quiet but for the occasional howl of coyotes and my bad singing as I tried to stay awake. I had been pedalling since 9 a.m. and still had 80 miles to go to Calgary, where an escort and charity reception had been planned for the next day, postponed from a week earlier. The stress of trying to predict my arrival date in the face of *Hercules'* brakes going crazy in the cold and a dodgy back wheel had got to me in recent weeks. Driving slowly past me twice in the space of twenty minutes, a car seemed to be tracking me. When they stopped in a lay-by with the window down I just carried on pedalling, pretending not to hear, battling with myself for not being braver. Or was I being sensible? It was dark and I was far from people. *Ride on Outen, ride on.* Arriving at some traffic lights on the outskirts of the next town the window of that same car hummed down to talk. 'Is everything OK?' the driver asked, introducing himself as Chris. Feeling at ease now that we were closer to others and lit by street lights, I told him that I was meeting my partner in Crossfield, a couple of hours ahead, and that we were due in Calgary in the morning. Driving off, he wished me luck. A while later he appeared again, telling me that he had found Lucy in the reception area of a motel in Crossfield, snuggled under her down jacket on an armchair. He said he would wait at the outskirts of town to escort me in. I crept inside and kissed her awake.

It was 2 a.m. when we got back on our bikes and more than eight hours of pedalling before we made it to the Olympic Park in Calgary, the day crisp and sunny. Local cyclists and reps from one of my supported charities, WaterAid, greeted us beneath the national flags while children had their Saturday morning ski lessons on the slopes above us. I had been cycling for the best part of twenty-four hours and Lucy had just cracked out over 100 miles of riding through the night on her first ride in Canada. People had asked how Lucy would keep up and I now gave them this as my answer.

To fit with the rest of the team, Lucy named her bike *Olaf,* in salute to the snowman character from the Disney film, *Frozen*, though she couldn't remember how to pronounce it, so it became *Ovlov*. Wanting to jazz up her high-vis jacket to match mine, she daubed in thick black letters *I'm with crazy*.

15

Thirty Below: Canada and America

Calgary to Cape Cod | Bike |
Winter 2014 – Spring 2015 | 3,400 miles

As the door opened a waft of pot smoke drifted out and the house's occupant swayed a bit as he worked out what he was looking at. 'Larry from the Prairie' would have been forgiven for thinking that Lucy and I were some weird branch of the police, dressed as we were in bright yellow jackets, high-vis vests and luminous helmet covers, goggles on top. He looked even more surprised, but a bit reassured, when I introduced us and told him that we had left Calgary yesterday afternoon on our bikes. And, because of the snowstorm which was now making the world look like the inside of one of those little ornaments you hold upside down to shake the snow about, we wondered if we might camp on his land, in the shelter of a building, please?

'Well, sure, you can. Unless you want to sleep in the kennels with the dogs?' he said, pointing to the building we had just tramped past. 'Last year we got snowed in. It drifted twelve feet high and over the top of the house. I had to dig us out.' I sensed that 'we' meant him and the dogs. We opted for the side of Larry's house and dug our Orange Dome into the snow, covering our bikes with the tarp and ferrying all the multicoloured dry bags of gear that we needed into the tent: foam mats, air mats, sleeping bags, down jackets, tent clothes, snacks, dinner and breakfast bags, stove, water, head torches, electronics' bag, wash bag. The blizzard continued on unbothered, blowing over and into anything which stood in its way. The mini-landscape of hills and caves which greeted us the next morning was mesmerising, like diamonds glinting in the sunlight. The orange glow of the tent was the only thing that was warm – the mercury read −30. Sitting up to pull on more clothes and retrieve everything we had put in our sleeping bags to stay warm – batteries, clothes, EpiPens, cycling boots – had to be done as carefully as possible to avoid showering the other still horizontal person with hoar frost from frozen condensation on the inside of the tent walls. Finding the water bag between our sleeping bags fully frozen, we made a mental note to boil flasks of water at night to ensure that we had enough to make porridge and drinks. I chuckled when I remembered Lucy scrambling back into her sleeping bag after the circus of using the en suite facilities (a saucepan) and turning to me and saying with a serious face, 'What on earth are we doing?' We dissolved into giggles, but it was a question we heard from others often and we sometimes asked it ourselves. Winter had to finish at some point – it was just a case of when and how uncomfortable it was going to be in the meantime.

Given that he had dogs, only Lucy could accept 'Larry from the Prairie's' offer of using his stove to cook breakfast, while I hung the sleeping bags to defrost in the sun and started doing the same to the tent. Appearing with steaming porridge and tea half an hour later, Lucy looked a bit pale. 'I feel a bit funny,' she said, 'I think it's the pot.'

It took us four hours between first waking up and heaving our bikes through the knee deep snow out to the track we had come in on the day before, gear all squashed and rolled and pushed back into panniers again. While we were packing, Larry appeared on his doorstep with the accompanying cloud of smoke and watched us intently. Breaking into a smile he shouted: 'You two girls are awesome. Most hardcore people I know,' before wading to the kennels to wish the dogs a good morning.

The jump from my previous record of −20 to now felt huge. Fingers turned cold immediately on exposure and the inside of your nose froze, the skin on your cheeks tightening in a moment. Poor Lucy had only just flown in from a relatively warm and damp British winter – at least I had been acclimatising for the last few weeks. Not wanting anything more than the cold to intimidate her, I was keen that we took things as steadily as the weather allowed for the first week or so. Knowing how mental processes slow sub-zero and how joining someone's well-established routine can be discombobulating, I explained that I might need to take the lead for the first few days, as much for the sake of our safety as her morale. But beyond that, this was our ride and outside of the rough goal of getting as far east as we could before Lucy flew home, we both had equal ownership of it.

On our third night we stopped at a fish farm and asked if we might camp in the yard. The owner, a Chinese lady called Wei-Fung, was incredulous that we would want to be outside in such temperatures. Even though the sun was still above the horizon and painting the sky orange and the distant Rockies a faint purple, it was en route to −30. We put the tent up together and decided I would get the stove going while Lucy started work on making up our nest of mats and sleeping bags. When I looked in ten minutes later, cursing the stove for going out while I was cooking the pasta, Lucy was half in and half out of the tent, flustered about what to do next. I suggested putting some warm clothes on and swapping her boots for down booties and getting a snack down. A few minutes more and I found her crying, still in her cycling gear and faffing with the mats. I gave her a frozen Mars bar and pulled her down jacket out of the bags to help her into it. Warming her toes between my hands while she ate, I made it a rule that we both had to eat something as soon as we finished for the day and that we would swap into our warm gear together, inside the tent if needed, reassuring her that this was a natural reaction to the extreme cold.

Just as we had checked each other's faces for exposed skin amid our jigsaw layers of face mask, balaclava and goggles throughout the day, we now must check that the other was fully dressed and functioning at all times, too. Stamping about in the crackling snow, now freezing solid, I did jumping jacks to warm up, the last light of the day disappearing. My eyelashes were laced with frost and sticking together, so I bent down to the stove to be close to its heat as it roared inside its crinkled metal wind guard. Glad that this was a dry cold rather than a wet slushy one, I wondered just how cold it would feel overnight and through the winter ahead. One child had already told us that it wasn't even officially winter yet. Pasta now soft, I took my big gloves off to mix in soup powder and bits of jerky, which turned pale in the heat. Cheese. A sprinkle of seeds and a squeeze of peanut butter. It was all about the calories. Passing the saucepan in to Lucy while I manoeuvred myself in through the door and zipped us in, I realised that she was in zombie mode again. Undoing the Velcro and lace of my cycling boots and plunging my feet into down booties, I simultaneously shuffled into my sleeping bag, with the result that I looked something like a very fat and puffy mermaid. Steam twirled up from our food and our breath clouded the beam of our head torches as we hugged the bowls and slurped from them. Lucy needed some prodding to eat enough as all she wanted to do was lie quietly.

The cold was a fierce teacher and especially so in that first week of Lucy being on the road; brutal for the conditions rather than the miles, it was a mental game as much as a physical one. If we got lazy or complacent it might mean discomfort at its best and hypothermia, frostbite or death at its worst. None of these appealed and so we constantly tweaked our routines and looked out for each other. Whenever one of us shouted 'How are your toes doing?', we got off to march for a mile, pumping blood and feeling – sometimes painfully – back into our feet. It also warmed our 'cold fat bits' of thighs and bottom, which always chilled quickly in the winds blasting across the plains. Ironic really, as mine is so substantial. Remembering a down skirt that someone had offered me in Anchorage, I ordered two to be sent onwards to Regina, holding high hopes for them. Each morning we made hot drinks for the day, stashing the flasks in the middle of our panniers to prolong their warmth. Lucy quickly became lunch monitor, preparing peanut butter and jam wraps or bagels before we set out, squirrelling them in our pockets to let our body heat keep them soft on the coldest days. If we hadn't remembered to put them in our jackets when we first woke up, they remained stubbornly frozen inside their tube.

After a frustrating and tearful confrontation during porridge duties early on, Lucy declared that she never wanted to see the 'sodding stove' again so I became stove monitor, and we soon found out that there were certain bits of the tent that wound

Lucy up every time she so much as looked at them, making them my parts of the tent construction by default. In return, Lucy was much more sensible than me about when we could stand another night in the tent and when we needed to stop in a motel.

'You seem so much happier with Lucy there,' said Sara one day – and she was right. Lucy tempered the brutality of still being on the road at 3 a.m., pushing on to reach somewhere before the weather turned. Taking it in turns to slipstream into the fiercest headwinds, and doing more minutes in front than our agreed ten to protect the other one. Peering out of the downy hoods of our sleeping bags to watch the other one's chest at night to check they were still alive in the cold, beneath their own mountains of down. Burrowing together to keep warm at night and doing the roadside 'cold toe dance' together by day, laughing at how daft we looked as we did so. Scratching the frost off the other's goggles or pulling a Buff down to cover a sliver of exposed skin.

'Are you guys lost?' asked the lady in the car, rumbling to a halt on the gravel. Her deerstalker hat gave her away as the cattle herder on horseback driving her charges down the road earlier. Surprised that we were not lost, she was even more surprised that we were on bikes, 'No one ever cycles out here, not even in summer.' Asking where we were going, we gave her our goal of Swift Current, a few day's ride away. 'Wow. So in a little way up there,' pointing to the near horizon of miniature hills, 'you'll be going to altitude, then.' We nodded, stifling smiles – the Prairie Rockies. When we asked for the turning to the hamlet of Hatton, a few miles on, she looked confused. 'You do know there's nothing there, don't you?' We weren't bothered – we just needed a smaller goal out of the whole to aim for, breaking up the indistinguish-able back roads which we had opted for over the main Route 1 east, with its traffic and noise. Here we could ride on whichever side of the unmarked gravel road we wanted, or take up all of it. Pee wherever we needed. Stop to sit and have food in the middle of the road. The expansive Prairie skies and the miles of rolling land below held their own stark but understated beauty, made all the more so because, but for a car or two a day, they were all our own.

In Hatton we knocked on the door of the only farmhouse we could find with lights on and, with no answer forthcoming, pitched our tent in the corner of their garden anyway. Revelling in the night's relative warmth and all that it meant – being in our tent without every single layer of clothing on that we owned; not having to share our sleeping bag with all the things we usually needed to protect from freezing – we watched a film on the iPad and fell asleep hoping that we wouldn't wake to find a gun in our faces. Another Chinook day welcomed us out of our unfrosted tent and it felt hard to believe that only a few days before it had been −30, and that once we were far enough east it would return to that. So for now, we relaxed into the reduced effort it took to stay alive and functioning in less hostile temperatures, feeling a bit like naughty children waiting for the teacher to arrive back for more lessons. Packing up was comparatively swift compared to the days when frozen material stiffly refused to comply with our intention of making it small enough to fit in the bag that it normally did. We left a note on the door, thanking the owners for their unknowing hospitality.

Pedalling on unnoticed, we criss-crossed through the grid system of quiet country roads, seeing more birds, deer, coyotes, foxes and cattle than we did people. With little snow on the ground in the driest areas, we struggled to find enough to melt for water. Derelict farmsteads grew out of the landscape here and there, grain stores and barns rising up like volcanoes out of the flats. We rode out of the way to get to them, hoping for water, only to find them empty on arrival, but for tiny songbirds raucously reminding us that they were still here, nesting in machinery. Footprints in old snow said that rats and foxes still dropped by. Cars, trucks and tractors stood silent and empty of people if not of rubbish. Farmhouses looked run down and abandoned, and yet in some yards there was a sense of working machinery just being on winter routines. In the hamlets it was the same. Knocking on doors and peeping through windows to see if anyone was home, I half expected Miss Havisham to loom out of the half-light within. Eventually, finding a house with children's toys outside, a car in the drive and lights on inside, we took our opportunity to fill up with water and asked the young mother where everyone had gone. 'There's nothing left out here for people any more. Everyone's moving out to the cities for jobs and school. Farmers leave for the winter and come back in the summer or have just sold up completely,' she said.

One night we turned off the road into the village of Hussar. Knocking on a house door to ask for water, the owner told us to head to the ice rink. Surprised that a community this small had its own ice rink, we headed down to watch junior practice with the parents. Pucks flicked this way and that as our chat did. Life on the bikes. Life in Hussar. (It had taken them a decade to fundraise for the ice rink.) The farm chat continued, too. The issue, they said, was in Hutterite communities using their collective wealth and multiple companies to outprice family set-ups. 'Paint, construction, chemicals . . . They're just bigger than all of us,' said one farmer. I had first heard of the Hutterites up in Northern BC when someone asked what I knew about them. 'Do you mean like squatter rights?' Recognisable by their home-made dress of skirts, blouses and scarfs, or braces and shirts, men always had beards and women always had men with them. I regretted not having a chance to meet any of them beyond glimpses in Tim Horton's, the doughnut joints.

We spent a lot of time riding by night, not just because it was winter and the daylight hours were so short, but also for the general lack of headwinds. With headlights reflecting off our high-vis and reflective strips, an array of lights across our tail ends, we were like mobile Christmas trees at night. Many cars slowed down, thinking that we were the police. The only downside to night riding was the drop in temperatures, meaning that once we were out of the Chinook range, we generally looked like Mrs and Mrs Christmas, frosted hair sticking out from beneath our helmets like bunches of tiny branches, icicles bearding our face masks. So really we didn't see much of each other on our ride, for being togged up top to toe in layers of fleece, thermal, down, neoprene, goggles and more. The tent rig was a different version of the same, as we each wrapped ourselves into more layers and cinched the hoods of our sleeping bags tightly to expose only enough face to avoid suffocation. And even then we sometimes pulled Buffs over our faces to keep noses warm, leaving only a mouth for breathing. I found that the cold air, heavy with condensing, freezing breath, made my asthma worse and I often sprung upright to gasp. Finding myself too tightly wrapped into my sleeping bag for comfort, I often thrashed my way out enough to breathe again. Calm. Settle. Rewrap and zip into sleeping bag once more. Murmurs from Lucy by my side. Head torch off.

After a night of chilly riding under a climbing moon, we were glad to wheel into a field just off the track, happy that we wouldn't be disturbed, the second and final car of the day having gone through a couple of hours before. Confident that there were no cows in the field, we marched around to flatten a snow patch and rekindle our toes. Tent up, Lucy was nest-making while I fixed dinner when a set of lights turned the corner further down the road. 'Torches off and let's see if anyone notices', hoping that they wouldn't. Lights turning into our field (which turned out to be their field) and now shining at the tent and our bikes. Better say hello. Three women – 60 per cent of the MacNary sisters – returning home from an evening out. 'We always have to stop and check if we see anything. Out here, someone could run off the road and hurt themselves and no one would know.' Not very long later and we had been kidnapped down to the ranch for showers and food around the table while Bess played the piano and Mother MacNary handed out offerings to the girls from her trip to 'the Hat' – Medicine Hat, their nearest big town. Father MacNary teased Lucy for being a farmer: 'You guys just drive tractors! The *real* thing is ranching – we ride horses out here,' and they showed us pictures of swimming cattle across rivers, riders thigh deep in water. 'You'll see us tomorrow on the road. We're moving some cattle.'

And so we did. In between watching herds of antelope pour across the track and talking to the frosty-mouthed cattle who stood steaming and munching hay in the morning air, a truck pulled up, a huge hay bale on the back. After some chat, we both carried on. We rode late into the wee hours, determined to make the most of the relatively easy temperatures before it changed again. Twelve hours later, Lucy and I were thirsty and waterless, no houses for miles around, only the nodding heads of solitary oil pumps, each lit up by a tiny maintenance house at its side.

'Luce, can you see that green thing over there? In the sky,' I asked, yawning, having watched it move about for a while but not yet being sure if it was real. Thank goodness – yes, she could – we were not hallucinating but looking at a rather apathetic show of the Northern Lights, more green smudge than dancing brilliance. We had run out of water and were thirsty, still miles from people. Having already tried eating snow to quench our thirst without the effort of melting it, we knew that we had no option: the sodding stove was needed. Finding enough usable snow was tricky: what was left on roadsides was stained brownish grey with gravel and fumes and tasted of grit. Lucy flagged down a trucker, hoping for water. We sipped at the Pepsi he gave us, wishing it was water. Kneeling over the stove, we were contemplating a further few hours of exhausted, thirsty cycling when an SUV pulled up. Mother McNary got out and, though she didn't have much water, she had oranges and grapes and the hug of a mother which said 'I know you can do this, girls' without needing to say the words out loud. Pedalling on under the moon, we played games or rode in silence as we each battled the fatigue and ache of too long on our bikes. We talked and we sang. We walked to stretch our legs, now wobbly with exertion, and we stopped to eat and to look at how far we had left to go. Determined only to sleep in Swift Current, we pushed on, grateful that between us we have stubbornness in bucketloads. It was 2 a.m. when we arrived, and, of course, we arrived on the wrong side of town for motels. And, of course, the only ones we could find at first were full, red LED signs shouting *No vacancies* before we had even got near enough to ask. On the far side of town we found a bed for the night, our bikes taking up most of the room. Protein shake mixed with mushy banana downed. Tight muscles eased under the hot shower. Chafed skin stinging. Clothes roughly hung up. Boots opened out to dry and air. Tent hung over the shower door and sleeping bags draped over chairs to defrost. Another chunk marked off the road. Another triumph together. Another long ride in just a few short hours. Sleep, sweet sleep.

Opting to get some fast miles down for the second half of Canada, after Swift Current we made for Route 1, which would take us all the way to Winnipeg. We stopped at motels or pulled into towns to find gardens or playing fields to pitch the Orange Dome. In diners and doughnut joints we paused for the heat and charging points as well as the food, and we bought the rest of our calories from petrol stations and supermarkets. Asking for water at one house, an English accent answered our knock at the door and invited us in to sleep, but their newly hatched litter of beagle pups meant that I couldn't. So we pitched the tent and were about to make dinner when the couple, Mike and Mikaela, appeared with a fan heater which they plugged in via a long line back to their house. 'We can't have you going blue on our front lawn,' Mike joked, adding that we weren't to cook anything yet. 'I've just told my mother-in-law about you and she says I'm to go down to her house and bring you back up some food.' Returning half an hour later with a bag of home-made bread, chicken heart stew and cheese, we couldn't believe our good luck. The novelty of being too hot in the tent and of not having to spend an age cooking felt unreal and we were grateful.

The generosity of strangers was a defining feature of this stretch of the journey. When, on another night, we arrived in the small hours at a motel in Brooks after a seventeen-hour day, gruelling for the monotony of the roads as much as for the distance itself, the lady on the front desk insisted on raiding the fridge for snacks with all the attendance of a mother hen clucking and fussing over her brood. And just outside Indian Head, as we sat with *Hercules* upturned on the shoulder trying to sort out a buckled wheel, a local goldsmith stopped to give us his number and invite us home. Sure that we could sort it ourselves and press on, we thanked him for his kindness and declined. An hour later we called his wife to say that we were on our way – the wheel still wasn't right and trying to adjust it in the shelter of a house would be much easier than doing so in the cold. Having had a few spokes break en route to Calgary through the rough and tumble of the mountains, I had so far been unable to find a replacement wheel of the right size, given that we were out of touring season. Now we were firefighting with rethreading the same wheel (it had been relaced with two rounds of new spokes) and tinkering and tightening around broken ones in the meantime. We just had to get to Regina where a bike mechanic called Darryl had offered to take *Hercules* in for an MOT and host us at his house.

The Prairies rolled on and so did we, aiming for around 50 miles a day, though often sitting either side of it depending on where there were settlements. The day before we were due to arrive in Regina, spirits high at the idea of a few days' rest and a proper fix for *Hercules*, we decided to swap bikes for a bit. Just as Lucy was getting off *Hercules* I noticed the familiar hiss of a tyre flattening itself. At the same moment we noticed that the phlange of the Rohloff hub, which houses the gear mechanism, had cracked in a couple of places and would certainly shear off in time. With just 100 miles until Darryl's house we planned to ride on and keep an eye on it, but over the next few hours of pedalling we stopped four times for flats, swearing louder with every one. Eventually we found a piece of wire poking out of the tyre rim, looking exactly like a tyre should not. Within ten minutes we had hitched a ride and were on our way to the city, borrowing a bike from Darryl so that we could retrace the miles the next day. (Interestingly, on another day when Lucy's tyre had gone we waited over an hour trying to flag someone down. Eventually I had to hide so that it looked like there was only one person waiting. Moments later, she had a ride.)

In Regina our days were spent sorting out bike fixes. Darryl rebuilt both of my wheels in his beautiful hand-built basement workshop in a generous and endearing fit of crazed enthusiasm, chattering at ninety miles an hour about how and why he loved bikes, this bit of kit and that one. Train driver by day and night, depending on which way the shifts work, bikes were his *raison d'être* and clearly an outlet for his incredible internal energy. Coming downstairs after the first night, we found that Darryl hadn't been to sleep, consumed as he was by the idea of fixing my wheel. Rubbing his hands on his brown dungarees and pulling us over to look at the bike, he said he had realised at about midnight that he had relaced it incorrectly. 'So I just pulled it apart and started over.' Lucy and I went in search of a temporary weld for the hub, while my bike sponsors Santos ordered a new one to be sent on from Holland to Winnipeg, where we had been invited for Christmas. To reduce the load on my back wheel and therefore hopefully save the hub, Darryl kindly offered to loan me his trailer, which he had used on his own trans-Canada ride. Excited at the novelty of it, though not excited by the extra weight, I took my first pedal strokes away from his house. I hit the brakes before the junction and swore loudly as I slid right across it, dragging my feet to stop me. 'Bloody brakes!' I tinkered with them at the roadside and, second time around I made the junction fine, but stopping at the traffic lights I found that my new and super-warm down skirt got caught on my seat, suspending me mid-straddle. Within days, however, it had asserted itself as a favourite piece of kit, much like wearing a duvet around your middle. We bought a new flagpole, too. Somewhere between arriving in the city and leaving, *Hercules'* flagpole had been left or borrowed and I had to fight to put it to one side in my head: I shouldn't be attached to those flags but I was, for they had been with me all the way since London. Sewn up multiple times, they had been drenched in heavy rains, dried to a crisp in desert heat, snowed on and blown to tatters and signed by drunk Russians without me realising. Darryl's girlfriend crafted us a couple of replacements.

As always seems to happen when you most want to be somewhere else, our final few days to Winnipeg were grindingly slow, as headwinds and side winds buffeted, snow and fog blew in from the north and *Hercules'* brakes demanded constant tweaking to remain vaguely useful. Lucy's bike *Ovlov* was extremely well behaved, but for a ruined tyre en route to Brandon. Hitching a lift to town so that she could get a replacement, it felt ironic that she, a farmer, should be picked up by a farming family.

'Did anyone tell you they call us Winterpeg?' laughed cycling fanatic Currie Gillespie when we met him at the service station in Portage la Prairie, with his gathered group of local cyclists ready to escort us the last 50 miles into the city. Somewhere before my first attempt on the Pacific, Currie had started following my journey and subsequently invited us to stay with them in Winnipeg, but my allergy to cats prevented us from accepting the kind offer, leading him to ask his friends Philip and Kate Evans. It couldn't have been a more unwelcoming weather day, with the side winds whipping across the vast fields, thick fog and freezing rain, so to have company, chat and some extras for slip-streaming was great. That and the chance to unload our gear in the van, which Currie was driving slowly behind us in the shoulder, flashing orange lights on top and a boot full of repair kit and snacks giving it something of the professional touring team feel as we pedalled in our little peloton. It felt like a crowd to Lucy and me. It was only halfway home while talking to a wiry chap with glasses about cyclocross (while not really knowing what it was) that he said I needed to speak to his son, Oli, and I realised that this must be Philip, father of the family who had invited us to stay with them in the city.

Christmas lights had been making streets and homes colourful for weeks, huge inflatable figures of Santa and snowmen billowing in front gardens, but we hadn't really felt festive, focused as we were on staying alive, moving and day-to-day admin. Being welcomed into Philip and Kate's house on Home Street felt like a warm hug, open and easy-going with an energy that was at once gentle and vibrant. Around the dinner table we shared a lot of laughter, chat and games and a fair bit of gin. For Lucy and me it felt like the first time we had properly relaxed in weeks and we felt totally at home. A national champion cyclocross biker, sixteen-year-old Oli spent most of his time in the basement riding miles on rollers or cleaning and tinkering with his bikes, where we joined him to clean and tinker with our own, Oli ribbing Lucy for having a dirty chain and showing us how to clean it properly. It was inspiring and motivating to see his focus and dedication and really moving when he bounced into the dining room with his new Canada kit on one evening, ahead of his debut at the Junior World Championships in Belgium in the new year.

Their daughter Jasper cried on the morning we were due to leave and she cried again that night when she found us back home, after *Hercules'* brakes failed yet again as we tried to leave town. On our second attempt it worked and, with another escort of three bikers, a car and flashing lights, we pedalled south under clear skies along the snaking, frozen Red River to our east. Sun dogs either side of the halo around the sun reminded us that it was bloody cold in case we should forget it. Sometimes we got frustrated at being with others, protective of our own time together, while also being grateful for people's kindness. But this had felt different; this felt like leaving family.

We spent New Year's Eve in a sparse motel outside of Emerson, buying beer from the local pub to toast midnight with, though in reality falling asleep before nine thirty, beers unopened. We were across the border by lunchtime, stamped into the country by guards more interested in our journey than our paperwork. On the one hand it felt like a triumph making it to America; on the other it was a double-edged sword, since Lucy would be flying home in three weeks from Minneapolis, where my weather router Lee Bruce and his wife Sherry had invited us to stay. 'We're going to leave the Christmas decorations up so you can see them,' they promised.

'You know there's a blizzard coming tonight, girls?' said the guy working outside his house and the two cars who stopped to tell us the same as we rode away from our camp beneath the trees in Drayton. The sky promised snowfall, wind picking up as the snow started a few hours down the road. Turning off the main road and following signs for Oslo, we were surprised to find a car showroom making up part of the more likely local businesses in this tiny town of precisely 326 inhabitants. In K's Diner we warmed up and dried our face masks and gloves while we made a plan over egg sandwiches. 'So where are you girls goin', then?' asked Kathy as she came over to clear our plates. 'You're not goin' out again today, are you?' We asked where we could camp, wondering if the park area we had spotted on the way in would work, and she winked at us before heading over to the table of old men by the door, who I was sure had heard our conversation anyway. A smiling man declared that he would take us home if we would like to stay with him and his wife. We gratefully accepted and decamped to one of the basement bedrooms, assuring him that we only needed one bed, much to his bemusement.

After two nights there, we reckoned this gentle-hearted, hunting-mad and henpecked man must have been keen for the company and a break from his rather assertive wife, whom we only met on the last morning as she got ready to go to church. 'What religion are you?' she asked, and Lucy and I looked at each other before proffering: 'None. Well, bikes, for now.' We smiled as she harrumphed and tutted. 'Well, I'm superchurched,' she declared. 'It's the most important thing in the world.' Shortly after the church chat, she spotted my engagement ring around my neck. 'Oh, Lucy gave it to me.' 'And she's got one, too?' she said, pointing at Lucy's hanging around her neck. 'We gave them to each other. We're engaged.' 'Well, I'm off to church, then.' Needless to say, I found religion across the Bible belt of southern Canada and the conservative Midwest a bit full-on at times, and the anti-abortion billboards downright offensive.

It felt as though people were handing us through the country, making sure that we were safe and sorted. Now – as it always had done – that felt humbling and beautiful and it certainly helped make the miles more manageable. Be it spontaneous hospitality or something pre-sought through reciprocal hosting websites like WarmShowers or Couchsurfing, or pre-offered through my website, the essence of it was the same: we want to do good by you. I love journeying for the different lives you encounter, new ideas or different ways of looking at things. I also love it for highlighting the shared things, the sameness and the connectors through our lives. Staying with local teacher and bike fanatic Dave in Grand Forks was the perfect example. A placid soul in a towering man, he only truly opened up when he showed us his bike collection. Twenty or more bikes stood in various states of re-repair in the cellar, spare tyres and old wheels stacked up on tables and hanging off walls. 'I do them up and give them on to folks who need them. I just ask for donations,' he said while proudly showing us his little troupe. 'It's magic when you see someone smile when they take their first pedal strokes.'

'I thought you two were guys when I first drove past,' said the stranger at the petrol station where we were warming up with hot chocolate, 'because I didn't expect to see two ladies riding out here at this time of the year.' My feeling was that most people didn't expect to see anyone riding out of town at this time of the year – we hadn't seen anyone doing so yet, except in our escorts. America was made for drivers and it felt like most people took that very seriously, driving everywhere, if only for a few blocks or around the corner. Whether it was the cold or laziness or something else, I don't know, but the lack of walkers – especially out of town – felt noticeable. So, too, did the lack of women in any sort of outdoor adventure media or advertising in outdoor stores, so that I wasn't wholly surprised when a twelve-year-old boy asked me after an assembly I had just given whether 'anyone had told you this was just a guy thing'.

That we were in a patriarchal part of the Midwest was clear – ads for huge pick-up trucks oozed testosterone and in one outdoor store that I visited the only pictures of women I found were in the camp cooking and personal alarms section. Meanwhile, pictures of square-jawed, bristled men looking into the distance with a steely gaze were being used to sell everything else. At the same time, Justine's film of our Aleutians journey was winning awards all over the world, and Sara told me how her young daughter had enjoyed watching it when every other adventurer she was seeing on TV was a bloke. Over the winter months I followed keenly as, state by state, same-sex marriage became legal, feeling a mix of optimism that things were changing but also frustration at the white conservative majority stalling the process. The idea that something as intangible as a state border could allow or disallow us to marry angered me, all the more so for the fact that we were in the so-called Land of the Free. But six months later, on 26 June 2015, the Supreme Court ruled that marriage rights be granted to same-sex couples nationwide.

Our route curved south-east through Minnesota, 'land of 10,000 lakes', as the mercury continued to hang out at the lower end of the thermometer and we continued to pedal when possible and wait out the blizzardy stuff when we couldn't. Lakes and rivers were freezing or already frozen, turning them into pop-up fishing communities of huts and shacks and trailers. We rolled our bikes onto one lake, its deep greeny-blue surface jigsawed with heave lines and flecked with bubbles, suspended in time and space. Creaks and cracks pushed us towards the nearest trailer, illogically fearful of falling through the ice. Jeff was getting set up, piling snow around the bottom of his home-made insulated 5 foot by 3 foot shack. 'Wanna see inside?' he said as he opened up the door to show us the set-up. A curtain was drawn to make it easier to peer into the pale green-blue of the ice hole and a small heater warmed the space. A small spool of line and simple lure hung above a head-sized hole in the ice, and Jeff ladled out ice to clear the water. He dropped a small fish-shaped camera down on a line and showed us the bottom of the lake, telling us of a '3-foot Northern beauty' which had swum in and out of shot a few times. Two little perch lay in a bucket of ice, hauled out of their icy winter home to become fertiliser for Jeff's garden. As we walked our bikes off the ice, wondering how a 3-foot fish could be hauled up through said ice holes, Jeff went back to his FishTV. It made me think of my brother Matt, for whom just being outside is as important as catching anything. (It seemed that ice fishing for many is a lot about beering, too – 'nothing else to do up here in the cold', apparently.)

Our routines were so natural to us by this stage that we did things the other was thinking of doing without any word, or with just a look or a hand signal, one produced whatever it was the other was looking for. When I got stressed about onwards planning for the expedition or gaps in the finance, Lucy soothed me and helped me see other options going forwards. When I felt nervous ahead of a talk or interview, she calmed me. We had saved two beers for our last night together in the Orange Dome, and in a snowy woodland Lucy brought them out to enjoy around the campfire, its warm glow chasing the shadows of aloneness which stood waiting in the wings for both of us. Lucy put one down her top to keep it warm and opened the other. In the time it took for her to bring it to her lips the amber had frozen up the neck of the bottle into an icy volcano, spewing frozen lava in torrents. We opened the second to watch it again and retired to our tent nest with hot chocolates instead.

Despite the best efforts of our two candle lanterns the air soon felt saturated with frozen breath and we both agreed this felt like it was going to drop to our coldest night yet. With apt timing, my sleeping bag zip had decided to resign from duty and refused to zip up. Lucy's had always been a storage unit for whatever needed stowing, so we jiggled into hers, squashed up against each other, upper halves out of the bag, like unwrapped caterpillar twins sharing a tail. Chuckling at the irony of managing all these miles and it happening only now, we zipped up tightly into our down jackets once more. Silence as we separately wished for morning to hurry up and arrive.

Ten minutes later: 'Are you alive?'

'Yes. Are you?'

'Yes. But —' wriggle, shuffle, wriggle — 'there's something in between —' shuffle, shuffle, wriggle — 'my toes,' said Lucy, now huffing and puffing. 'There must be a hand warmer in there, I put one in earlier.'

By now I also needed to use the saucepan, so I wormed out of the bag to get as close to the porch as possible while Lucy shimmied round to look at her foot.

'Hmm . . . Well, that's weird. There's nothing there. I just can't feel my little toe.'

Weird isn't the word I would have used, I thought, as I spun around to examine it with my head torch. Her little toe was not toe-coloured any more. It was white and slightly bruised-looking at the tip. Lucy couldn't feel my pinching it and so I stuffed it under my armpit, skin on skin, flinching at the coolness and wondering how she hadn't noticed it getting so cold. I massaged her calf while she wiggled her other toes, wondering how we would get to hospital if it didn't resurrect. After thirty minutes blood rushed back in and the pinch test confirmed it was OK.

The day before she had reported frost-nipped nips after taking off a gilet from beneath her waterproof jacket, lulled by the sunshine into thinking it was warmer than it really was.

Everything was waiting until the end to happen, it seemed, for on the very final day into Lee's home town of Wyoming, Lucy's luggage rack snapped off its fixings, forcing us into creative mode with duct tape and cable ties. At the other end of the day's ride, just a few miles from Lee's, we heard a honk from a car behind us and pulled around to be blinded by its headlights. Its blue and red lights flashed through the glare and the smartly behatted state trooper pointed out that we were not allowed on Minnesota's Interstates. Apparently we had missed the *Bicycles Prohibited* signs amid our thoughtful pedalling as we contemplated our final miles of this ride together. A few days before we had cycled over the slowly slugging Mississippi River, rafts of ice heaving into each other, slipstreaming behind each other with our helmets down into the wind. Riding in front of Lucy, I imagined that I was pulling her along and that she was pushing me forwards. In her tailwind, I imagined the reverse. Either way, we were connected and moving forwards.

Some people had worried for us on this trip, fearing that 24/7 in each other's pockets would be relationship suicide, but it had never felt that way to us. We had one bicker while packing up her bike about how best to make this bit of kit fit around that, but that was it. On one of our last nights together, Lucy cried because it was nearly over, but it turned into laughter when she said, 'Make me stop – the tears are freezing to my cheeks!'

After Lucy flew home, I had a final few days at Lee and Sherry's house, immersing myself in onwards admin and talking to Lee about the Atlantic ahead and our experiences of the Pacific. Some people are surprised that an ocean weather router could be land-locked but I bet they would be more surprised to know that from his little office, at all hours of the day and night, Lee knows what weather each of his clients – be they super-yacht or ocean-rowing boat – might be facing. Trained in the US Air Force, his attention to detail and his encyclopaedic knowledge were reassuring. Filming our conversation about the tropical storm of 2012, strong emotions were stirred up for both of us, and Lee recalled having 'never seen conditions like that for a rower' before. We talked about working remotely and the importance of a satellite phone in connecting rowers to the outside world. Often, Lee was one of only a few links to a boat, and he understood just how important that contact was.

I rode on from their house down through Minnesota and towards Iowa, unused to the space and quiet of alone. Critical voices chattered in my head about timings, to-do lists and finance gaps and sadness sat in my chest. Fears about how my allergies might behave also rattled about; the idea of being totally alone out there and having a massive reaction was frightening. I could really have done with a clear rest and ironically some of that came on the bike, if only for the fact that long days of exercise in the cold meant that I slept deeply. I built small fires to cook on most nights, enjoying the dance of flame lighting up the snow.

Once again, the simplicity of spinning pedals was therapeutic and restorative. I followed the Mississippi eastwards for 200 miles beneath high bluff banks, watched by eagles, the roads clearer of snow here and sometimes warm enough to ride without my usual layers. Road names told of immigrants past and missing homelands across the world: Lisbon, Paris, Lima, Chile, New London, North Wales. Later I would ride through Climax, Intercourse, Nectarine, Force and Challenge, but I was glad not to go to Boring or Normal. Turning east through Wisconsin, wheeling past farm after farm of dairy herds with icy beards, past occasional Amish trap drivers trotting in quiet, steady contrast to the usual traffic, the snow arrived once more. A blizzard grounded me in Argyle with a welcoming family, and they invited me in to watch the Superbowl – a national institution, apparently.

As I rode into the flatlands of agricultural Illinois the snow continued to fall, stalling progress and offering me more insight into America by winter. The contractor snowplough drivers who work twenty hours a day. Lines from houses heating car engines overnight. The vicar running a soup kitchen for the local needy a few days a week. A firefighter in the deprived city of Rockford told me stories of families losing everything in house fires as they struggled to heat their homes with open-doored ovens or over-loaded electric heaters.

In Chicago I stayed with kayaking friends of Justine's, Sharon and Alec Bloyd-Peshkin, recharged by the space of their home and energy, hugged by their laughter and warmth and the connection of knowing Justine. It was reassuring to chat expedition niggles with people who understood it and got that sometimes I needed my own space. *Hercules* and I got maintenance fixes to keep us both going until the next big stop, in New York – me for my lower back and he for a new bottom bracket and, of course, a rebleed of those bloody brakes.

Off the bike, time and head-space were full of the normal social media, sponsor connections and route admin, as well as onwards preparations for the Atlantic. *Happy Socks* was due to be shipped out to Chatham in Cape Cod to arrive in early April, along with food and kit, which itself needed to be ordered and gathered. Spreadsheets and lists calculated what was needed and Lucy, Katy and Sara worked to get it ready. In equal measure, the expedition was being pushed forward not just by my pedalling but by the efforts of the team, all of them working on it alongside full-time jobs and lives. Another spreadsheet told us how much more money we needed to the end. With a projected shortfall of tens of thousands still, it was an ongoing project to secure the rest of it. The extended timescale and budget of the project meant that it wasn't an easy task for sponsors to commit more money, for their personnel, marketing aims and budget controllers might have changed since first committing. Sponsors and supporters rallied again where they could, Natracare and the Transglobe Trust coming to the rescue with a cash injection once again. Blog followers pitched in here and there. Lucy took on lodgers to raise some extra cash; I pushed out my overdrafts and borrowed the rest.

Now that I was south of the Great Lakes the frequency of the blizzards increased and I found myself spending more time off the bike waiting for useful – or at least non-lethal – conditions. In Warsaw, Indiana, a kind lady called Wendy, who had heard about my journey, contacted me to say that she wanted to buy me breakfast; she invited all her friends and we had pancakes before troubleshooting my to-do list. She was one of those people who grinned from the inside out, mothering me as if I were her own daughter. Her partner Rick asked to take a portrait of me: 'With your eyes closed, Sarah. Your closed eyes tell a story.' I wondered what stories involuntarily told themselves from my face, eyelids wrinkled and skin chapped and irritated from the jump of hot to cold.

Through the flatlands of Indiana and Ohio I tracked eastwards, balancing going too far south for the extra mileage against the extra snow risk of staying too far north. One obtuse email had arrived through the website declaring that the *only* way to New York was to take an old railway route through the south of Pennsylvania, emailing with repeat instructions that I should heed his advice because it was the *only* route to take. I stayed north instead. Trucks nearly squashed me and on windy days cold winds chased spindrift down the roads as I chased miles and daylight, pushing and pushing. My lower back was screaming by now and my hip flexors were like steel rods, stiff with too long spent in one position. I was pushing for New York and for Cape Cod. At times I found it hard to balance the logistical need to be on the coast in good time to transition and prepare with enjoying the moments of the ride, which, once ridden, were gone for ever. My nights in the tent were my favourite because there was more time to just be. That said, a stomach bug keeping me off the bike for six days was a perfect reminder that there were more things than the weather which I couldn't control.

'You know it's getting colder tonight?' said the chap filling his car at the petrol station. 'Really cold,' he said, frowning as though I might not understand what that meant. The snow concerned me more, as I knew it would keep me off the bike. I thanked the lady who had just let me use the petrol station toilet under oath that I wouldn't tell her boss and swung my leg over *Hercules*' frame to start hauling up the hill. 'Be safe, friend!' she shouted and I grinned and waved back, trying not to wobble off my bike. It hadn't taken me long to realise that the North American greeting of 'Hi, how are you' doesn't have a question mark at the end of it and that people didn't actually want an update on how cold my toes were. Gestures outside of the robotic norms of 'Have a nice day' felt charged with good-will. Maybe more so because it was cold, strangers continued to go out of their way to be kind to me. Kathy, who drove for an hour to bring me medicinal gin. Shelagh, a long-serving blog follower, who rang up the hotel where I was staying in Massilon while waiting for a viral bug to pass and paid for a couple of nights. The Scheurich family, who invited me in for dinner, egging me on to pretend to their daughter that I was their long-lost friend from a party years ago and letting me sleep in the gardens of their employer. The lady who gave me an orange. Ralph, who mixed silence and easy chat over a lunch break while he washed floors at a service station, whistling as he worked. One day in a comical giggling sort of ping-pong, playing up to my video camera, a guy called Isaiah wished me everything under the sun to keep me warm and safe, suggesting extra coats, his own blazer, a scarf. An escort van with tea supply to my very own bus. 'Hell, Sarah! I'm more worried for you than you are!' 'Hey look – she must be OK – because it says on her jacket *Don't worry I'm OK!*' Rower Glenn and his wife who drove twelve hours from Canada to have home-made chilli on the roadside before turning around and driving home again. There are too many people to mention here, so many people who became a part of the journey by their kindness.

In eastern Ohio the landscape started curling in to steep hills with outrageous grades. I soon came to learn that *Scenic Byway* signs promised charming riding and lots of work. I plodded up with steady carthorse efforts, noticing my surroundings in minute detail or a vague, drifting sweep. A red cardinal splashing colour amongst lyre-string hedges. A deer on the pinked snowy ridge. Wild turkeys scrabbling through fields at a trot, heads down, imagining that they couldn't be seen if they couldn't see. Downhills were a mix of survival or joy: either folding myself over the handlebars to be aerodynamic, pedalling hard for every extra fraction of forward; or standing high on my pedals to stretch my calves, wiggling my toes for warmth – chin always tucked into jacket to alter the angle of my goggles ever so slightly, just enough to stop wind whistling through the vents and freezing my forehead.

Just two handspans to the Cape on my map, it dawns on me that my time biking on this continent is dwindling, and that the conversations I have will soon be markedly different. Instead of the mother in the diner telling of how her son made a trap in the forest behind the house and caught the family Chihuahua, I will hear the passing whistles and trills of dolphins.

In Pennsylvania (which could really have been called Pennhillvania on account of its rippling steepness) I pushed through lung-burning days in the Allegheny Mountains. *Hercules'* brakes did not like the gradient, just as they did not like the cold. Sometimes I had to skid my feet on the tarmac, sparks flying off the metal cleat as it ground down. Without brakes, some downhills forced me to get off and walk. Holding the saddle and the handlebars, I countered gravity as it pulled down on the 80 kilos of bike and gear, my back pulling, too, as we walked into deep valleys, making my shins hurt. Streams rushed down roadsides as snow melted, sliding off roofs and dripping off doors. More salted slush gnawing at the bike's metalwork. Having only seen white for months, the appearance of brown grass was exciting, promising spring. The animals were excited at the idea that spring was on its way, birds foraging and chattering in hedgerows. The bike was moving more smoothly now it was warmer, and I was, too. I saw more people walking and children outside playing than I had seen in months. People wearing shorts. Runners. Two female road cyclists, the first I had seen since for ever. The PA45E road through the Penn Valley was swift and sweet, warm westerlies helping me eastwards past reels of wooded peaks and through wide fields of wheat, squeezing through tiny villages and towns. All of the farm buildings were painted a rich maroon and houses were varied and colourful. I remember an elderly couple sitting in their rocking chairs on the porch, and a washing line as tall as a telegraph pole, clothes flying in the wind. I stripped off layers and enjoyed the air on my skin, just as the land was delayering from snow. I didn't freeze when I stopped for a break. I followed the clear waters of the Susquehanna River for a while, then on to road names that made me smile: Carefree Lane, Chillisquaque Creek, Freedom Lane. The excitement of nearing New York drove me to ride some ridiculous days and miles, the pull of people I loved reeling me in. Claire, Rebecca, Krissy and Maren – they had all flown out to see me and I didn't want to miss them.

Feeling rough with a sinus infection which had also arrived, I pedalled 125 miles through the day and night to arrive on the outskirts of the city in Fort Lee at 5 a.m., just as commuters were waking up and traffic was filling the roads. I spent a few hours in a grimy and overpriced motel room, too full of adrenaline to sleep, before being hugged by Claire on the 1.5-mile-long George Washington Bridge. I didn't want to let her go. I had last seen her a year ago. Skyscrapers. Noise. People. So many people. Every colour. Every shape. Every size. Untold languages. Women kissing women. Guys holding hands with guys. It was refreshing to see so much diversity again after what had felt like a very white, conservative ride for the most part. I had a bike escort down the Hudson River Park to Pier 49 where Rebecca and a local WaterAid group waited with banners and cookies next to the Intrepid. There were more hugs and smiles, and photos in Times Square as adverts and screens scrolled. After such solitude, I had to fight to keep my panic in check amid the bustle, glad that others were here to shepherd me. Am I the only one who doesn't know what I am doing? Smartly dressed and well-behaved police horses. Bolshy and loud traffic. Sirens. LED screens and scrolling signs. Selling, selling, selling. Advertising and opulence. Smells. Dirty. Potholes. Steam coming from manhole covers. Police officers directing traffic with whistles. Overwhelmed. Boxed in. Exhausted. Banner welcoming me to the Holiday Inn, which was sponsoring my stay. Clean clothes. Deep baths. Pause. Contrast of busyness and other people stressful in a different way to that of life on the road. A proposal from a stranger on the Tube as he hands me a letter with all the details: *We are going to get married next year on June 18th – the hotel is booked and you will wear this dress . . .*

After a few days I caught a train out to Coney Island to dip my toes in the freezing waters of the Atlantic, remembering the salt water of the Pacific. Spending time with friends and doing school trips and media events was great, but tiring, and my final few days I spent gently alone.

Back on the move, I left New York and headed for Chatham, Cape Cod, 400 miles away. Following quiet roads north and east, I made my way to the coast, through Connecticut and Rhode Island and on to Massachusetts, enjoying the New England scenery and traditional houses. More space. Less concrete. And the sea. Wheeling along the coast, I was transfixed by the vastness of it, as though being pulled towards it. In Hammonasset Beach State Park I rolled out my sleeping bag on a picnic bench and let the sea air drift over me. Memories of the last seven months of riding rolled in and out like the lapping waves. As I wheeled over the roundabout into Chatham, a police car pulled in front of me, lights flashing. I followed it through town past the wooden-clad homes, which reminded me of armadillos. How ironic that the police were going the same way as me, I thought . . . And then I realised they were escorting me in. Rain-jacketed representatives from Pleasant Bay Community Boating held signs and flowers in the mizzly afternoon and applauded. 'Welcome to Chatham, Sarah! Welcome to Cape Cod.' Introductions and thank-yous over, I wandered down the sand to stand in the shallows with the tracker. Looking out east, it was surreal and exciting to know that home was just across the water now, albeit a very long way away.

16

Across the Water: Atlantic Ocean

Cape Cod, Atlantic and beyond | Row |
May – October 2015 | 2,000 miles

Due to the fact that winter had been especially snowy and slow, I was later arriving on the east coast than we had first imagined. This forced me into a super-swift and stressful transition, as Tony and *Happy Socks* arrived just two days after I did. But the hours I spent inside *Happy Socks* felt comforting and reassuring, reminding me that we had been here before and all would settle. Our goal was to be ready by May 1st and to go as soon as there was a clear space in the weather, which in real terms meant offshore westerly breezes for a few days and nothing too rough in the mid-range forecast.

Local couple Roz and Bill Coleman had kindly allowed me the use of their quaint holiday let Ship's Light, the house of a nineteenth-century sea captain. There we had the space to spread out all the boxes and bags of gear and food which needed breaking down and sorting. After my allergy issues on the Pacific and my low immune issues over the winter, we had worked with a nutritionist. So this time we made up precisely calculated day bags for a rotating weekly menu. 'Cabin days' had reduced calories compared to the 'rowing days' and had things which didn't need cooking, like snack bars, jerky and nuts. Finally, on my fourth ocean-rowing voyage, it felt like we had my food nailed, although Lucy was sceptical about whether I would be able to stick to it as history shows that I often go treat-seeking.

Yoga, massage, physio and a gym plan helped still my mind and work stiff muscles and joints back into useful alignment. Release would be a good word for it. Releasing what had been, what was, and allowing myself the space and energy to think about what was about to be. Somewhere in my mind I had stashed away the anxiety of going out to sea again, and the fear of having a major allergic reaction while alone and the sadness and guilt of being away from Lucy. I thanked my body and mind for taking the strain I was asking of it, promising myself that rest would happen in time. Though I was excited that home was just across the water now, it was tempered by the understanding that anything could happen out there, that there were still no guarantees. Chatham knew it, too – for they have a long history of ocean rowers leaving from their shores, of which most had been unsuccessful. John Ridgway and Chay Blyth had famously rowed from there in 1966, and one lady we met remembered helping fill up their water bottles and how her dad had helped build up the sides of their wooden open-top rowing boat. Chatham was affable and welcoming, with local businesses and people getting behind us with support and good energy.

'I still can't fathom it, Sarah,' said Bill, shaking his head as he tucked his reading specs into his shirt pocket. 'That row of yours is quite something. Now tell me about . . .', and he reeled off questions about the expedition. He was sitting on the recumbent bike, my book open on his lap, pedalling his one-hour session because a sore on his leg was keeping him out of the pool. 'Normally I like to pool walk a half-mile forwards, a half-mile backwards and then do 400 bicycle revolutions in the Jacuzzi,' he told me, eyes smiling. At ninety-three, he was Chatham Health Club's most active member, clocking 300 visits in the previous year. 'Bananas! That's the secret,' he said, 'I'm on two a day. I keep away from too much sugar and fat and I haven't had a drink for years.' Bill reminded me of my grandfather and I enjoyed spending time with him, uplifted by his spirit and spark. I was especially interested to hear about his military service, piloting along the Aleutians and as a submarine commander in the Pacific, where he had subbed in the Sea of Japan and the Sea of Okhotsk. 'It was *real* flying back then – in an eight-hour flight we were on instruments for seven, cloud cover at 400 feet. One of our planes went down on Little Tanaga – pulled up too late. Poor guy just didn't see the mountain,' he said, shaking his head. Of his time in submarines, he said: 'A Japanese sub was a juicy target, you understand. They had all but destroyed our entire fleet at Pearl Harbor. There was the time that we sunk one of their subs going ashore, all the men in their whites up on deck. That could have been us.'

In late April Lucy flew in to help with final preparations and everything felt calmer for her being there. We trained together and worked on the final tinkering and testing of *Happy Socks*, modifying the new foot straps which had broken in trials and replacing part of the main hatch, which we had found to be broken. We had a marine electrician come out to troubleshoot the AIS, which didn't appear to be working properly, and after taking it away for testing, he confirmed it was kaput. A new one was shipped in and installed days before I launched. The new wind turbine was nicknamed *Chopper*, and we were hopeful that it would solve power issues once out at sea.

A friend of Lucy's came out to film preparations and as a trio we had a lot of fun, except the time that Lucy overheard an interview that Jen was filming with me, asking me about the dangers at sea and the potential for life-threatening scenarios. At the time, Lucy wrote on my blog: *The essence is that I am scared. I'm terrified. I'm terrified Sarah will be totally alone if anything bad happens, and I'm terrified she won't come home. To let go, not knowing if you'll ever see them again, is mind blowing. It feels like a huge conflict of emotions. I have learned it is not so much about putting barriers up as letting the emotion in, feeling it, accepting it and working with it, that will help us both get through.* I promised Lucy that I would do my best to come home safely.

Originally we had hoped that I would have been able to leave while Lucy was in Chatham, but the weather was making us wait. When Lucy flew home it felt like part of me had done the same, and I felt very flat for a few days. The Chatham sand bar is notorious for the waves it can kick up in certain states of wind and tides, so I kayaked from Lighthouse Beach out over it to put a GPS fix in, just in case it was too rough for me to row it myself on launch day. Then, if I needed a tow, at least I would have been joining the human–powered dots. Being afloat felt like being reborn. We then did yoga on the beach, saluting the sun while being blasted by sand, all of our rough edges being smoothed. On the way home from the beach I had a message from Lucy: 'Coming back out, couldn't not be there when you leave on Thursday. Leave the door open and I'll see you later!' I almost exploded with excitement: now I was ready to row.

The final couple of days before launching were busy and at times flustering. I was glad to have been there before on other launches, to know that this was fleeting and, in its own way, useful. I was also glad and grateful to have Lucy by my side. The night before launching we had beers and pies with the lovely team at Ryders Cove Boatyard who had helped us so much. Mylène drove down from Montreal to be there for the launch, too.

On 14 May, under a cloudless sky and blazing sun, we prepared to launch from the beach, cheered on by a crowd of locals on the sand, escort boats bobbing at the jetty. After a press call and little speech, Lucy and I walked hand in hand to the jetty. *Happy Socks* was bobbing happily in the water, and I said my last bits to the cameras, hugged those who needed hugging, and took some deep breaths. There were lots of smiles, and some tears. A boat came alongside the jetty and offered me a lobster to take with me while escort boats milled to be there for the first strokes. After a final hug with Lucy before I climbed on board, I undid the bow line to let the wind blow her round. I was afloat. Pulling into the waves. Grinning with my whole body. Grateful, calm and energised. Scanning the shore and the boats to take it all in. The escort boats turned around at the bar, which thankfully had turned out to be a non-event with waves no more testing than the ones I had just paddled through. The escort boat Lucy was on stayed with me the longest as I pulled steadily out to sea. A couple of miles out we said our goodbyes.

'Don't forget to tell Sara I've left!'

'Don't forget the houmous in the fridge!' I called, and then rowed in and out of tears as I watched the white mushroom cab of their little boat fade into a line of white wake and morph into an invisible pixel of land.

The only thing I have ever been able to be sure of on the sea is that I will get sick. A doctor I met in Chatham promised me that a drug called Zofran would change this. No seasickness. No side effects. No risk of overdosing. Intrigued and optimistic, I gratefully accepted the prescription. Now, for the first time, my food stayed where it was intended. As a result, I had more energy to row for longer than usual during those early days.

Massachusetts is famed for its seafood and for the first few days sporadic lobster pots provided a useful place for me to tie up to and hold position when the tide or wind was against us. It felt like the settling process was much easier and steadier than it had been on previous journeys. In fact my first week at sea felt so settled that I even questioned whether this meant that I was more suited to solitude. In another first, tides pulled me in ovoid loops when I wasn't rowing, tracing neat squiggles on the chart plotter and kicking up patches of rips and race which felt strange to see this far out.

As it happened, the Atlantic turned out to be the most sociable voyage of the journey, both in terms of wildlife and also in the amount of contact I had with other boats and planes. Given my course, the size of the Atlantic, the surrounding nations and their relationship with the sea, it is perhaps not surprising that it was a busy ocean. I saw boats on a daily basis, either at varying distances from us on the horizon or via the AIS – when it deigned to work properly, which, despite the replacement, it often didn't. Winds pushed me further north than we would have liked, encores of southerly gales eroding my efforts to avoid the notorious Grand Banks which guard the eastern and southern reaches from Nova Scotia. At the same time I didn't want to get tangled up in the Gulf Stream to my south, which was knitting pretty patterns for the satellites but not for my course. Many people assumed I would be getting a free ride home on the Gulf Stream, but the reality was quite different. As on the Pacific, the challenge would be to try and use it to our advantage when possible and avoid it when it wasn't.

At one point Nova Scotia lay just 60 nautical miles north, its coast reaching out on a north-east run beyond. Ironically, this south-westerly wind was what I needed to get home but at this point it was not helping my bid to stay south of those incessantly fogged-in shallow seas. They seemed to be magnetised and my course curved just shy of its most southern reaches for days and days as headwinds and southerly gales pushed me north and currents swirled. Sometimes that meant just a few hours of rowing before putting the sea anchor out and sometimes it meant more rowing than anything else in a day. North-easterly gales of 30 knots nudged us southwards while I lay strapped to the bunk. I noticed that I felt more scared than I thought I should be, given that these were not big conditions. It took me a few of them to realise that maybe it was because I had swapped my sleeping position so that my head was nearest the main hatch onto the deck, meaning that while lying down I couldn't see the waves outside. On every other row I had been head to stern and it seemed this extra visual input made waves less scary.

It took me a few times to get used to ships passing within a half-mile of the boat, and I often radioed them to check they had seen me, sometimes chatting with the operator on the other end and sometimes being a bit disappointed that they didn't care for a chat as much as I would have liked. Other times I saw it as an interruption to have to talk, enjoying my own patch of ocean and quiet. I didn't always keep the radio on during the day and just relied on the AIS alarm to tell me when a ship was within a few miles' radius. If I was rowing when it went, I stashed my oars back into their tubes, unhooked my feet from the foot-plates and popped inside to check where the boat was. The AIS told me the heading, speed and name of the ship, meaning that I could hail it directly on the radio if needed. One afternoon a ship passed within half a mile of us and I enjoyed picking out the various bits of gear on deck and scouring for people. I rowed on singing to myself as I watched it shrink away, wake churning and whiting the sea as it trailed out the stern. I disappeared back into my thoughts about dinner. And then it seemed to be growing bigger. Getting closer. Heading straight for me, bow on this time. Shuffling into the cabin the AIS confirmed it and so I called them up on the radio. 'We wanted to check you were all right – given that you are so far offshore.' I thanked them and reassured them, and part of me wished I could write a note on a high-vis jacket as I had done on the bike, letting people know all was well and that I had chosen to be there.

While on my sea anchor one day, a far-off roar growing closer sent me outside from my bunk to look for a plane. A behemoth military transporter, Canadian Aerial Surveillance Plane 104, rumbled low overheard and I waved enthusiastically as they swooped over me. A wave knocked into the back of the boat and soaked me, so I whipped off my trousers, thinking that they had left. They looped back and got a full view. The next day (my birthday), back at the oars, I heard the familiar sound and got on the radio to hear a plane calling for *Happy Socks*. 'We normally look out for bad people doing bad things but we like to keep an eye out for rowers as well. Is it OK with you if we do a flyover?' It felt like a birthday party and I jokingly invited them down to enjoy the brick of fruitcake from a friend and they returned with a bright red companion plane to criss-cross the sky in tandem for me. Up until I was out of the 200-mile Canadian Exclusive Economic Zone, I was buzzed by multiple surveillance planes, enjoying chats with many of them. I was not surprised when they talked about checking up on my friend Mylène in 2013.

On another evening near the Grand Banks, I was rowing on pink seas when I noticed a trawler, the *Lady Denise*, working a mile or so away, and we drifted closer as they dredged for scallops in zigzag sweeps. We talked on the radio and in soft Newfoundland tones the skipper, Don, rounded it off with an offer that I was to shout if I needed anything, for they would be there all night. Later he called me back to say that he had just looked up the website and told his wife at home. The next day, Sara had an email from his wife. It still baffles me that even in isolation I could be so connected with the world.

Within reach of the Grand Banks there was often a lot of fog. Rowing in it was disorientating, the world shrunk to a close and touchable whiteness, thickly hemmed in and lit by a flat, muted sun. The return of the sun was always uplifting. On those days I cleaned boat and rower, while the solar panels recharged, and my morale with them. If the sea was flat enough I could dry and demould my bedding and clothes, wiping away the general crud of cabin corners – hair, shed skin cells, random shreds of this or that, wet and mould. Everything would go out on the deck to be blitzed by the sun – bedding and a pile of clothes waiting for the laundry. The day would be filled with the anticipation of a fresh – inasmuch as anything can truly be fresh at sea – pillow case for that night.

Emerging from a damp cabin after anchor time or entering a period of warm weather – either still in the centre of a high-pressure system or bouncy with waves – felt liberating; energising for the warmth and the fresh air and the movement. My moods and energy followed the weather like sunflowers bend to the sun. Warmth distracted from discomfort. Sunlight made the windy days less threatening and made dowsings less uncomfortable.

May on the Atlantic was rough, cold, wet and foggy, with occasional sun. June on the Atlantic was rough, cold, wet, foggy, with a bit more sun. Hooray for late July, then, arriving with a balance tipped in favour of sunshine and warmth and a run of the most useful weather yet. Progress in those months was slow and involved a lot of scribbles in my track, including a ten-day loop which couldn't have looked more like Australia if I had traced it. I finally had a break in the weather which allowed me to row east and beyond. August was, by comparison, a dream for weather and progress. A week of 40-mile days in rolling seas with a few fifties thrown in. It felt like England was possible again, though it was also clear that it was going to take longer than we had first thought.

'Another seventy-five to ninety-five days,' said Lee, confirming my own predictions, which I had hoped might not be true. End of October, early November. Not ideal times of the year for a rowing boat to be out on that ocean. Something had to change, with the weather in my favour. With nutritionist Rin's advice, I started rationing food, stockpiling an item or two from each day's bags to make up extra day bags for later on. Counting up all my medication, I found that my inhaler supply wouldn't last all the way to a late finish either. A resupply would be needed if I was to make it back to land under my own power. Tony started looking for resupply options, contacting cruise ships and yachts that might be passing and willing and able to help. We tweeted and messages were posted on forums and noticeboards in sailing clubs. It was getting on in the season for Atlantic crossings and insurance policies were pushing boats out of the Caribbean ahead of the winter, so none was forthcoming.

One morning in July I cried because I couldn't find a bag of couscous for breakfast. Everything tiny felt huge. Having been focused for a day of good mileage with useful winds, it had been demoralising to be screeched back by negative currents when I rested and to not make useful progress when I rowed. I hadn't slept well for a few nights. Body and brain were hanging. As day's end approached and the cabin beckoned, I noticed a tanker three miles away, on course for us but barely moving. I radioed to confirm she was drifting, though I was too tired to ask why. Instead I added a fleece hat and returned to the oars to outrow it. *United Hope*, she was called. For three more hours I rowed into the dark, keeping an eye on her light set. Fog drifted across the boat like a cloud, illuminated by the navigation light. At midnight I gave in to the sleep fairies now hammering on my eyelids, and went inside. Not bothering to undress so that I could wake quickly, I lay back on the bed and dissolved into damp fitful sleep. We drifted and danced with *United Hope*, and I woke sporadically with the AIS alarm. After four hours of crazy dreams about leaving my boat in the ocean by mistake to go to a tea party where I then discovered I had forgotten how to interact with people, I woke up. Back stiff from lying down. Eyelids like lead. Every part of my body rebelled at being back on the oars so soon. I rowed another sprint session as the grey dawn rose, putting my invisible peloton into action. Eventually the tanker drifted far enough away for it to no longer be a collision risk. Annoyingly, it drifted on the track I would have liked to hold. I continued to do the best I could to minimise collateral and row when I could. I found the bag of couscous which had made me cry the day before – things felt OK again.

Certain things need a bit more ranting, talking, crying to put aside and be able to release and regain perspective. Getting outside of my own head was important, and emails, texts or calls with the team and to home helped with that. Calling Lucy was an immediate Refresh button if a day hadn't gone too well; just getting it out and knowing that someone was listening was powerful. She always made me laugh, too. One day I wrote in my logbook after a tough day losing miles: *So it has not been my favourite day. But I listened to* King Lear *and it doesn't sound as bad as it is for them (everyone falling out, killing each other and gouging eyes).* I blogged about the tricky bits and shared my frustrations at the weather and myself and was always buoyed by the spirit sent back my way from blog followers, touched that so many people were pulling for me and offering little (or large) nuggets of advice.

Sign me up for a midnight pull on the oars for you – heck, sign me up for anytime you need to take an imagined break.

Only doing will mend your mind. Good words are good reading, but solid actions talk to the soul. Do, Sarah. We are all with you.

'Doing' was important and often just a simple change of task was enough to ease whatever was going on in my head. Sometimes that was a treat or reading a letter from home, a hair wash or a stretch, a bit of fishing or, if inside the cabin, a change of music or book. I found respite in stillness, too, and took to listening to a Body Scan meditation each night before going to sleep, checking in with each part of my body and aiming to notice what was going on. I generally fell asleep before the end and was surprised one day to wake up and hear the calm voice talking about breathing out of the top of your head like a dolphin.

One day when 'doing' definitely did help settle my mind was after the rudder was torn away during a gale when the sea anchor lines got wrapped underneath it, hammering and slamming it into the back of the boat. Unable to do anything during the gale conditions but curse the fact I hadn't removed it before the conditions came in and curse again the fact that I hadn't brought a spare after also losing one on the Pacific, I tried making one out of the boat hook and a chopping board which I had brought with me. For an afternoon I was in my element with a drill and cable ties, pipe clamps and carabiners. When it came to fitting it to the leftover rudder pintle, it didn't work out, but in certain conditions afterwards I jammed it alongside the hull to act like a skeg in helping the boat track.

On another day I was rudely awoken from a snooze by a wave slamming the back of the boat and sloshing through the slightly open hatch, soaking my feet. Having just had a rough night with scant sleep, I was catching up while the wind backed. I sat up and slid out of my fleece liner, crusty and damp, before scooting out of the hatch on deck to use the bucket. I heard something coming through the water at close range and at the same time noticed a dark grey-black lump coming towards the boat, one of my resident fish swimming out to meet it. A split second to clock the ridges running down its back and huge blunt head, and I realised I was having my very first sighting of a leatherback turtle.

'Leatherback, leatherback, leatherback,' I chirped over and over as I dived inside for the cameras, fumbling to release them. Old Mrs Turtle was on her way, the reflecting sun and cloud turning the sea a metallic mix that made another sighting impossible. Goodness knows how many years old she was. I had always wondered if I'd be lucky enough to see one. Given the predation, poaching, pollution and fishing pressures on sea turtle populations worldwide and their long, slow life cycles and lumbering land time ashore for nesting and laying, they are vulnerable. I hope that there are still leatherbacks in existence for when the next generation are travelling the high seas.

One hot morning, I couldn't work out what the new sound was when I opened the hatch onto the deck. Part splash, part glug – I wondered if there was a big fish in the bilges or something hitting up at the boat from the water. I knew I had petrels as I had heard them scratching about; they flew into the antennas at night, attracted by the light. New moons or foggy nights were the worst, and I winced as I heard the twang of an antenna, followed by the soft thud(s) as the bird(s) bounced down onto the deck or into the footwell. I always popped outside to relaunch them if I was awake, their tiny bodies soft in my hand, feet leathery and thinner-than-matchstick legs. There were three little petrels, one tucked into a corner and the other two in another, sitting on top of each other. But as I launched them into the morning sunshine one by one I could still hear splashing. I looked down into the life raft cubby hole as bird three took flight and saw a stuck and bedraggled petrel struggling to get out. Scooping the little fellow up, his feathers wet and useless, I popped him on a towel where he stood with wings outstretched in the sun, trying to dry. I dabbed gently, blowing on his feathers and then realised this was stressing him, so I moved away and watched quietly. Fifteen minutes later I launched him, only to watch him flap madly and fall straight into the water. There he stayed for half an hour, flapping all his energy in vain as he tried to get airborne. I heaved the sea anchor in and rowed back for him. It took a few loops before I got close enough to scoop him on board in my fishing net and then put him on the towel again. I called him Duracell and was happy that after another half an hour of preening and basking in the sun, flight two worked. I wouldn't normally interfere with the course of nature, but this felt like *Happy Socks* and I were responsible.

My Atlantic swimming tally did not look likely to surpass my Pacific one. Two plunge sessions – with the first on a relatively wavy day and Lucy on the end of the satellite phone for a confidence boost as I leapt in and out and in again. The second swim, later on, in the midst of a double high-pressure system, both keeping the other static, I swam around the boat and under as far as I dared in order to scrape barnacles away. It is one of my favourite feelings in the world, while also being scary, feeling tiny even against the hull of the boat and tinier still in this ultimate infinity pool. On two other days I longed to be brave enough to swim, wishing I wasn't alone as I imagined I would be braver with two. The first was a bright, flat day of dolphins, the water turquoise and so clear that every mottled detail on the dolphins was crisp and sharp. Curious about the boat, they threaded loops and twirls beneath and around. And then I noticed a trail of poo and decided I would wait for another day to try and swim with dolphins. As I sit here at my desk I curse myself for being so daft, promising myself that if I am ever in that situation again, I will swim. Fear or no fear. Poo or no poo.

On the other day I was waiting for the wind to change direction, lying in my cabin with the hatch slightly open. Bobbing with the waves. Everything relaxed. Then there was a knocking somewhere. A hissing. Louder. Quieter. Thinking it might be air escaping from my water bottles I ignored it and carried on reading. Ten minutes later I checked the water bottles and they were all fine. But the noise was still there. Another ten minutes later and, worried that something was amiss outside, I stuck my head out. Noise even louder. I climbed out and something in my wideside vision made me turn my head. Four giant grey-brown sperm whales as long as – and longer than – *Happy Socks* swam on the surface. Rolling, with fins leading and outstretched like playful Labradors on their backs. Spy hopping to look at the boat, their blockish heads a sea around tiny eyes, their narrow jaws open to expose rows of peg-shaped teeth and tongues of pink. The younger whales were wrinkled; the older ones more scarred, leftover marks from squiddings, hunts and fights. I thought perhaps they were mothers and calves, resting and playing. I laughed with excitement at watching this mini herd of giants as they watched *Happy Socks*. The depths they dive to, lungs squashed in enormous pressure squeezes, are unfathomable. The whales swam on and I rowed on, high on joy and wonder, humbled by their closeness and hugeness.

The Atlantic was treating me to a wildlife spectacle. I saw more turtles, whales and dolphins than I had seen on any of my other ocean-rowing trips. One day I even had a songbird land on the boat, looking as out of place on the ocean as I did, and clearly tired. I tried coaxing it to stay and rest for a while, offering a plate of nuts and dried fruit. Twitter twitchers identified it as a Baltimore oriole taking the scenic route between the Americas. As with all my other trips, I also saw countless pieces of litter. From bags to crates to lids to buckets to discarded clothing and lots and lots of bottles. This was the first trip where I had actively sampled for microplastics, on behalf of an organisation called Adventurers and Scientists for Conservation (ASC). This essentially meant sampling along my route, collecting a one-litre sample every couple of hundred miles to be sent back to them for analysis.

Across nine samples there were twenty-one pieces of microplastic, with only one sample with none, microplastic being defined in this as less than 5 millimetres across. That in itself is rather shocking, but looking on the ASC website, there have been samples with many hundreds of pieces of plastic in them. Microplastics have been shown to impact survivability of fish and to concentrate toxicity up the food chain, meaning that humans eat them through seafood consumption, too. The US has recently imposed a ban on the use of microbeads in cosmetics and, at the time of writing, the UK is following suit.

A weather-routing friend of Mylène's had come up trumps with a resupply option: a flotilla of French yachts on the final legs of a year-long Atlantic rally. They were heading from Saint-Pierre in Nova Scotia to the Azores and on home to Toulon, and were keen and able to help. I made a shopping list of extra carbs, protein and gas, with requests for a few treats as well – fresh fruit and cheese and chocolate. A doctor on board prescribed some more inhalers. Lee best guessed my position according to the weather forecasts and, on day 86, I scanned the horizon in eager anticipation. In the late afternoon three matchsticks appeared, metronoming this way and that as puffball clouds headed eastwards. The masts grew cabins and hulls and, all of a sudden, *Diadem*, *Eraunsia* and *Le P'tit Mousse* were circling us. Smiling people, all bronzed and blond from months at sea. Someone playing 'God Save the Queen' on the clarinet.

I grinned and grinned – this would be one of my happiest days afloat ever. The bags of food had been divided between the boats, so I rafted up alongside each yacht in turn to take delivery of them, piling them on deck. 'No bananas in Saint-Pierre!' one said, as he handed down a bag which felt like jars and apples. 'Your inhalers are in here,' said another. 'Are you sure you don't need any other medications?' Each yacht had a gift for me, too – a bag of marshmallows, some Sudoku books, letters which made me cry when I read them that evening and, my favourite of all, a bunch of flowers. They looked like daisies and I stared at them, having not seen flowers or anything green (besides the slime on deck) in months. There were questions in both directions. 'Do you fish?' 'Yes, we caught some dorado yesterday. Do you fish?' 'Yes, but I've caught nothing.' 'How many of you are on board?' 'How long will it take you?' 'And how long will it take *you*?'

I waved and waved when they left, the sinking sun now deeply golden and painting the waves and boats in the same richly soft light. Tears here and there as they sailed away, looking up from time to time as I opened the bags. I was childishly excited to discover loaves of bread, salamis, a 2-kilo vat of peanut butter and bottomless jars of jam. Onions, oranges and carrots. Deep, deep joy. Sweetness and freshness and crunch that I hadn't tasted in a few months. I was humbled by everyone's efforts in working together to make it all happen, the weather routers collaborating, Mylène translating and the French sailors going one step further than home delivery would have done. There was an outsized bottle of Dutch beer from Mylène which made me tipsy. The stress of diminishing supplies was eroded and for the next week my diet was mostly cheese and jam sandwiches as I savoured the taste and texture, racing to eat the bread before it started going mouldy. They were some of my most mindfully eaten meals ever, I think.

September's weather was rough, contrary and full of shifting counter-currents. Lots of anchor time due to more headwinds than were normal for this time of the year and wet days rowing made the cabin swampy, and with no chance to dry anything out. I was close to the Azores now, just a few hundred miles north-west of the most westerly islands, and Lee was surprised that the weather patterns weren't holding as they normally did. After yet another gnarly forecast suggesting that I would need to be on the sea anchor in negative-flowing currents, I questioned whether a UK landfall would still be possible given that my average daily mileage was so low and the forecasts continually pessimistic.

Sarah: Crapness. I stand to lose a lot of miles in that. Anchor will whizz backwards in current. Do you still believe landfall is viable? Something has to change soon in my favour if it's going to let me get back unaided. Average miles made good daily this last wk only 10 and only 13 for whole row. Crazy.

Lee: Agreed miles made good have been dismal, and no big help is in the outlook for now. All I can offer is that it's not your fault. You're where you 'should' be based on weather and rower history. We want a persistent high-pressure center near or south of the Azores. The long-range outlook into October shows that pattern, so don't give up.

Sarah: Current must be pretty strong as even with all this wind and me rowing I am going practically nowhere.

The high-pressure system which normally sits over the Azores had shifted many miles further north, meaning that I got the contrary half of the circulation, something we later found out was due to the North Atlantic Oscillation. A British pair had already made it across ahead of me, having left from New York a week before I had set out. Out on the Pacific the other two boats that Tony was looking after were facing reversed trade winds due to a full-blown El Nino. 'It's not nice when one of your boats is having a hard time,' he said, 'but when all of them are going nowhere, it's really demoralising. I feel for you guys, too. It's like my head is in multiple places at once.' The whole team was feeling the pressure of progress.

My dreams were riddled with anxiety: I was missing French lessons I didn't know I was supposed to be at and not handing in my homework. In reality this meant that I was anxious about whether or not it was going to be possible to row ashore under my own power. Was Falmouth possible? The Scilly Isles would be less distance to row. A diversion to Spain? Everything was down to the weather and whether it would allow sufficient rowing days and enough westerly and south-westerly winds to be useful. In short, would the Azores High re-establish itself in time? We decided that if I wasn't 500 miles closer within a month (that is late October), then we would have to look at chartering a boat to tow me ashore, all of us hoping that wouldn't happen for so many reasons. I was down to my last bottle of gas for the stove, because the additions that the French yachts had brought did not fit, and so I had started rationing hot meals and drinks. I predicted I would run out of my thyroid medication on November 5th.

Towards the end of September two stable high-pressure systems were holding each other in place, flattening the seas to a calm. This meant more regular rowing, twelve- to sixteen-hour days on the oars. At night my brain wanted to row on, loving the star-jammed skies, but my body wanted to sleep. It just wasn't sustainable to push it out even further. Annoyingly, it happened to be in an area of negative current and I lost five miles overnight every night. Jellyfish bloomed in colourful drifts, and, being near to the Azores, I saw a difference in the bird-life. A fulmar followed my boat for an afternoon, paddling hard to keep up and sit nearby, pecking at my GoPro. Dolphins continued to swim by, always uplifting to watch even if they didn't come to investigate the boat, clicking, squeaking and whistling at each other and *Happy Socks*. Other times they porpoised along, as though stitching the sea, in pods of up to a hundred. What looked like blue-jellied Cornish pasties drifted by – pretty beginnings of the infamous Portuguese man o' war. Turtles swam by almost daily, mostly unbothered by *Happy Socks* until I turned to row after them to try and get a better look. And then, heads down, they flippered themselves away at speed. One bumped into my boat while I was on the phone and I poked my head out to see a huge brown shell, half of it carpeted in red weed. Hurrying the phone call on, I spent ten minutes filming it investigate the hull, swimming away before noticing my GoPro underwater and returning to look at that, too. It resulted in a brilliant close-up of its horny beak and prehistoric eyes, its skin knobbled and gnarled. Squadrons of mohawked doradoes often flanked the boat for a few hours, diving away at lightning speeds to investigate anything in their path. Two shining specimens, one blazing blue and one iridescent mantis green, circled *Happy Socks* for a week as if attached to a motor, bright lips on an obtuse head. I had long given up fishing and knew that these beauties were way too savvy to be conned by my hooks. It felt ironic that the first ocean row in which I had really tried to catch fish had resulted in barely a bite. The one dorado that had once dived for the lure had thrown itself out of the water in a jerking dash of silver and then plunged out of sight to lose it, followed by the others, like cruising boy racers.

One hundred and thirty-three days and I was two-thirds of the way in, but there was nearly 1,000 miles to go. Within the space of a few days a key cable in my comms set-up broke in the same way that the spares had done before it, meaning that I could not receive emails on the boat. My charging system for the phone was failing me, too, meaning that comms were in short supply. The AIS hadn't been working properly for some weeks, meaning that I had to wake and check for ships every half an hour at night. I was being drained of power as well. My iPod charger had broken a couple of weeks before, forcing me into my own truncated version of *Desert Island Discs* as I rationed play time. I decided I would listen to five songs a day until the battery ran out, although this quickly changed to just one or two songs on repeat. Dolly Parton's 'Nine to Five' and '*Comptine d'un autre été*' from the film *Amélie* became my daily listens. The first I could belt out to my cabin concert hall or the sky; the other was about absorbing myself into it, pressing the headphones into my ears to block out any other sound, escaping for two and a half minutes. At first it had added to the feeling that everything was going wrong, tiredness making molehills into Everests, but then I accepted it for what it was and just enjoyed the music. Sixty days to go seemed impossible, too, and I said to Lucy on the phone one night, 'I'm getting the distinct feeling I shouldn't be out here.' A rainy day's rowing refocused the mind into the moment rather than the distance to go. If only for a day or hours or a moment, it was all about holding on to each of them and trying to sustain them.

After the double high-pressure system came two looping lows, literally two low-pressure systems within a small sea area looping around each other to become one large cyclonic system, rather than blowing on their normal trajectory across the ocean and, therefore, out of my reach. More rough weather and negative progress, confined to the cabin and unable to do anything about it but wait. Wait, wait, wait. *I don't have time to wait much longer. Winter won't wait.* Chimpy was not enjoying it.

Lee sent over some weather forecasts. He was watching a developing situation which threatened two periods of winds of 40-plus knots and waves of 8-plus metres, within a week of the looping lows. Hurricane Joaquin was causing havoc down in the Caribbean with winds of over 100 knots and forecast to make landfall in North America.

As normal I called Lucy before I went to bed on day 142, anticipating a rowing day and looking forward to getting out on the oars again. 'Have you spoken to Sara?' she asked, and at the same time a message from Sara buzzed through, telling me to call her. 'It's about the weather,' Lucy said. She read me the email from Lee which said that Hurricane Joaquin had changed course and was now forecast to recurve across the Atlantic. It was on track to pass overhead in a few days' time and Lee predicted sustained winds of 55 to 60 knots and waves of 11 metres. Good for the people of North America but not for *Happy Socks*. After speaking to Sara I called Lee and was surprised when I had to think about my decision. Now that I was with Lucy, I had always been so sure that I would evacuate immediately if another potentially row-ending system was forecast. And yet now there was a moment of indecision. What were the chances of it changing course? It was covering a huge sea area meaning that traffic was already clearing out and rerouting. A ship had been lost in the Bahamas with a crew of thirty that day. I asked how it would compare to the Pacific in 2012. 'It's going to be worse,' said Lee's soft voice, distant but close. 'You know I don't like to exaggerate things or tell you what to do, Sarah – I just give you the facts. But in this case I would say it could be life-threatening.' Decision made. No second guesses. 'It will soon be too rough for any pick-up so it needs to happen in the next twenty-four hours.' Lee emailed the team with my decision and I called Tony who called Falmouth Coastguard who issued a request for assistance from any shipping in the area.

It felt right and it felt wrong. Suddenly packing my bags way out at sea, a calming sea, much calmer than it had been for days. 'Oh Socker, my faithful friend. Not even one capsize this year. Thank you for keeping me safe.' Normally the end of a journey is a period of adjustment and mourning, coming to terms with what has been and what will be, but now it was about to be mind-bogglingly swift. More phone calls and updates in both directions. A message from Tony reminding me what to do in making her ready to abandon. A call directly from Falmouth. A ship 20 miles away and there in a couple of hours. Bulk carrier MV *Federal Oshima*. So soon. And then a surge of hope when I had a message saying that they were going to try and lift her on board. Perhaps I wouldn't lose her after all.

I pulled in the sea anchor for the last time, and when the lights of the *Federal Oshima* appeared I talked to them on the VHF before rowing around to their starboard side, which they manoeuvred to be in the lee of the wind, protecting me from the waves. As I rowed into the welcome of their lights I crossed a boundary from my world into theirs. It was intimidating being alongside her red-metal wall, which stretched skywards and in either direction for 100 metres like a giant letterbox. So many faces up on deck. Languages I didn't understand. Lots of noise. The engine kicking over waves to my left. My heart was making lots of noise inside my chest, too. I spoke to the captain on the radio and he asked if I needed medical assistance, which I didn't. In my head I'd imagined I'd climb a rope ladder, sending my bags up first on a rope, but he said that they had the metal gangway ready to use. I trusted that they knew better than me and went along with it.

My fingers fumbled to tie the lines which they threw down. The metal gangway hummed jerkily down towards the water as lines from above pulled *Happy Socks* this way and that. 'Shit, shit, shit!' I throw myself onto the deck as the gangway lurches overhead, and a wave pushes us up into her, breaking aerials like someone breaking biscuits and knocking the light off with a pop. We bounce off each other. Two men are standing on the step at the bottom of the gangway, holding on to the rails and shouting up instructions to the people on deck, as they shout back down. We are pulled apart and move together again. I confirm that they are going to come and tie *Happy Socks* up. Someone shouts 'Jump!' and I leap for the step, landing only with my elbows on it as it rises up away from me. I am left dangling. One of the guys grabs the back of my jacket and pulls it up over my head so I cannot see and the waterproof rubber seal means that I cannot breathe. I don't have enough purchase to pull myself up, nor anything to push against. I can't breathe. The platform is swinging. I slip further down until I am hanging only by my fingertips, legs flailing. I can't hold on. I drop into the water and go under. Black. Panic. My jacket inflates with air, holding me up.

In hindsight I should have climbed onto *Happy Socks* and started again, asking for the rope ladder. Instead, I swam to the line running out to their boat from *Happy Socks* and held on to it, catching my breath. A life ring helicoptered down with a splash. I flipped it over my head and swam towards the platform, which they had now landed in the water, shouting at me to come before the swell took them up again. They rose as I fell and then I wriggled on and was grabbed again as they helped me to my feet. Shouts as a swell came in and we hurried up the gangway. That tiny platform was never going to work. I stumbled up the gangway to the deck. The captain asked for my documents and I explained that they were still on *Happy Socks*, in my bags. I was taken inside to get warm as the crew worked to bring *Happy Socks* up.

I gave instructions as to where the best tie-up points were and eventually, a few hours later as I lay below, corralled in the medical room, I heard that they had her alongside. I asked often to go out and help with instructions again. Finally they said yes. Up on the bridge, I talked to the captain and he relayed my instructions about where best to attach ropes to bring her up as I watched someone down on the boat, feeling hopeful that we hadn't lost her. I went down on deck, wanting to be there when she was brought up and help if I could. My bags had been brought up already. Cheers went up as the guy appeared on deck. I thanked him and he handed me the tracker. Curious, I looked overboard and saw, way below, that *Happy Socks* was not ready to be lifted. The main hatch into my cabin was now wide open. I asked what was happening and someone said that they were not going to lift her up. 'I could go down and tie her up?' No. 'I could tell someone else the exact tie-up points?' No. 'Could I talk to the captain?' No. The captain said they wanted to cut her away. They had to get going.

At first tears slipped down my face and then they cascaded as I watched them cut my little sugar-mouse friend and protector away. I felt helpless, watching after her as long as I could see her, bobbing erratically on her own. Door wide open, side on to the waves. Gone. 'So when is your team going to collect your boat?' I explained that, with the hatch left wide open and the tracker removed, she would likely capsize irrecoverably. She might turn up one day, somewhere, what with storms and currents, but she was for now AWOL. The poor crew, they didn't know what to make of it as I sat against a wall crying my eyes out. In that moment I was bereft. I was frustrated with myself and the situation – if only I had been more assertive and communications were less muddled, she could have been saved. It felt like I had let her down and, until it had run through my system, I was inconsolable as I said my goodbyes.

Day 143: Good Things About Today were:
I'm alive
I'm safe
I've got meds/docs/photos/films

I was grateful to Captain Gupta and his crew for coming to my assistance and for their welcome on board during the week-long run to Montreal. I was happiest sitting out on the deck of the bridge, watching the sea or just being outside and alone, unused to the company of so many after so long alone but craving the company of the sea. I also craved fresh air away from the cigarette smoke inside. 'Freshest air in the world, up here!' said the captain as he stood over me with a cigarette. I loved the perspective of being up high, looking down on the waves and all their different colours and textures. It was also interesting to be amongst the charts and screens on the bridge and to see the request for assistance which had buzzed through from Falmouth and the weather forecasts showing the track of Joaquin.

I enjoyed the smells and routines of the kitchen, the massive vat of spices, which would have been big enough to hold a person, and everything set up for making food in rough conditions. Jason the chef lurched at acute angles as the boat pitched in heavy seas. Joining in with Sunday's communal preparation of dinner while he had a day off was fun but full-on as the whole crew made chapatis, pakoras and curries while listening to loud music. We feasted on delicious curries daily – more flavours than I had ever tasted. I made phone calls home and chatted to the second officer's wife Asha about what it was like being the only woman on board, and a seasick one at that. The cultural differences were interesting: the captain was surprised that my project manager and fiancée were both women. 'So you have abandoned your mother, left her all alone?'

The beaming Labrador-eyed K. K. Roy, chief engineer, proudly showed me around the three floors of the thrumming engine room, hundreds of dials and pistons all chugging and clunking. The ship was driven by a propeller nearly as big as *Happy Socks*. It had an entire room filled with seventy CO_2 cyclinder fire extinguishers, each as tall as me, and its 10,000 horse-power engine used 28 tonnes of oil a day when running at 12 knots. The numbers were as mind boggling as the experience of being there.

The ship pitched and rolled through the northern reaches of Joaquin, and I held on to the bed to keep myself in – waking up hourly still, adrenaline coursing and flashbacks of my third dip in the Atlantic running through my mind. The curtains swished backwards and forwards across their runners. I reckoned floors could be polished by leaving piles of clothes to be thrown about by rough weather. Outside, waves crashed over the deck, rising up from the pitching bow like exploding geysers. The bathroom door slammed open and shut and I had to catch up with my feet as I walked up and down stairs or the narrow corridors. (On that note, a moving ship is a great place to retrain feet and legs again after so long away, a halfway house to the unforgiving nature of land.)

I had first thought I would miss autumn and its rich colours while afloat, so to round Belle Isle in Nova Scotia and head down the St Lawrence felt like a real treat after months away from the colours of land. We sailed past quaint lighthouses, ploughed fields, elfin churches, fishing boats, slinking seals and a few whales diving lazily as I scanned for sightings of belugas. Cormorants flapped about madly overhead. Pilots came on board to navigate as the river narrowed. Pilot apprentice Emily had six months left to go after nearly eight years of maritime school and gave me my first hug since Cape Cod. She had wanted to be a pilot since she was eleven years old. Past Quebec, Becanour, Trois-Rivières and Sorel and then Montreal. I woke before dawn, the day fresh, excited to remember that Lucy was in the same city now, staying with Mylène, who had been helping us arrange everything.

Leaving the boat after photos and laughter with the crew, it was mad to think that just a week before I had been alone with *Happy Socks*, and now there were over a million people within not very many miles. I peered ahead to the lock where Lucy was waiting, crying when I think I spot her, her group shouting and waving. It took what felt like forever for us to be ready to leave. I shook hands with the crew gathered on deck, thanking them for keeping me safe. The gate opened and I ran, laughing and grinning, into Lucy's arms, and we held each other. Emotions that we had both held in could now be released. I hugged Mylène, too, knowing that she knew what I'd been through.

'Look over there,' said Lucy, pointing at the people by the fence. I smiled but didn't know what or who I was looking at. 'In the orange hat.' That should have been a clue. 'Carol,' said Lucy. 'Carol who?' I said, head spinning as to a Carol I knew in Montreal. As she came in for the hug I realised it was Carol Penfield, owner of the health club in Chatham. Not only had she helped us hugely while in town, she had organised a 'Row with Sarah' campaign while I was afloat, raising money for the charities. To get here she had driven for ten hours from the Cape, bringing letters and cards and cupcakes from our friends there.

Some people had asked if I would get another boat and return for another go. Some were sure that I would. Perhaps an earlier me would have done: intent on joining up the dots and of sticking to the original plan. But now it felt right to wrap it up; time to go home and be home. I was proud of all that we had achieved – in having and sharing the adventures. I knew that, although the Atlantic hadn't worked out the way we had hoped, I wanted to finish the final legs of the journey from Falmouth to Tower Bridge as we had planned. With whoever fancied joining in, I would cycle from Falmouth to Oxford and then kayak to Tower Bridge. Between us we chose November 3rd as Tower Bridge day, for its tide times, and for the space in dates from Remembrance Day and Children in Need, which would be taking up time and space at HMS *President* and in the press, respectively. It was also close enough to keep the momentum going before everyone's energy bottomed out. This meant just three weeks of whirlwind action and energy from the team and friends at home to plan and prepare, activating plans, contacting people and pulling in support. From Montreal we would fly home, preparing for a week before heading down to Falmouth to start cycling.

Being with just a few people I knew and having time to be alone with Lucy was a perfect reintroduction to land life ahead of a busy finish. There was a lot of emotion and energy: excitement, gratitude, pride and wistfulness; and nerves and anticipation at being reunited with friends and family. Disbelief that we were nearly there. And so much adrenaline – my head and heart raced and raced at night, making it hard to switch off.

17

The Final Run Home: UK

Falmouth to Tower Bridge | Bike and kayak |
October − November 2015 | 400 miles

Arriving home from Heathrow to banners, balloons and champagne was a gentle and lovely welcome, everything and everyone familiar. My mum came down to visit and I met my not-so-brand-new nephew. My muscles were welcomed home by a very effective (read 'very painful') sports massage therapist called Lizzie, whom we nicknamed Mrs Magic Hands. We arranged for her to come and meet us a couple more times on the final miles of cycling and kayaking. Walking into the local supermarket felt too much, however. Too many people. Too much stuff. Too many choices. Senses overloaded, I walked out and left it for another day.

For the Falmouth to London run we hired a camper van as a sleeping and support vehicle, naming it the Party Bus. The last stretch, in contrast to what came before, was pure fun − for the energy and the togetherness of these final miles, shared with some of my favourite people in the world. Family and close friends joined in as drivers and feeders and cheerleaders, riders and paddlers. Lucy. Claire, my adventure buddy of old. Krissy and Maren, whom I had last seen in New York City. Katy. Siena. Anita and Lars. Justine, my sister of the sea. Others came and went. For legs unused to pedalling and walking, the Cornish and Devonshire hills were a rude but beautiful wake-up. We stayed at the Eden Project, in car parks and campsites and down secret lanes, and at people's homes. At times it was a bit bewildering to be with so many people again, but those closest to me knew that I was still adjusting to company and let it be OK. Lucy and I slept in the cabin over the driver's seat, the curtained cocoon reminding me of *Happy Socks*. Physically, the transitioning and quick miles were brutal and I laughed at my twenty-four-year-old self for dreaming it up, though I thanked her for it, too. Unfortunately, *Hercules'* brakes hadn't been replaced in the way I had asked the bike shop to do so, and they soon failed again. This meant that for a couple of days into Bath the downhills were dangerous as I ground my foot against the floor, burning through the sole of my bike shoe and sending sparks flying as the cleat ground out. My legs were bruised black and blue and I was forced to get a new set of brakes in Bath.

England felt familiar and somehow new, too, as the route took us winding through Cornwall's steep hills and up over Dartmoor's long climbs and expansive emptiness, then up through the lush Quantocks to Bath, across to Swindon and finally to Oxford. Plenty of places I hadn't visited before, reminding me that I wanted to explore more of this country. Blog followers and friends came out to join in, to wave or high five or offer tea and cake, soup and sandwiches. All ages joined in on all sorts of bikes for all sorts of distances – the youngest a toddler on a balance bike who scooted himself to the end of the road.

On the final biking day to Oxford we had our biggest number of riders. Sara and her family came that day, finally joining in with the ride after the very first conversation all those years ago where she had said that she might like to ride across America, which had turned into offering help, which had turned into being project manager. I cried when I spotted the towers of our local power station at Didcot because I was home, and grinned when various members of Lucy's family cheered and waved us on our way through pretty villages and along roads I recognised.

The Thames led us the final miles from Radley to Oxford and I thought I might burst with memories. The church where friends got married. The time we swam from the centre of town out to the pub and arrived in our swimsuits. The stretch where we trained and raced. Arriving at St Hugh's, my old college, I was enveloped in a flood of familiarity as the principal welcomed me back.

Before starting kayaking I joined in with an early morning outing with a St Hugh's women's crew in a rowing shell called the *Sarah Outen*, proud that this was where I had learned to row a decade earlier. Once finally on the move, the kayaking days felt calmer and I was glad of the space and quiet, happy to be afloat again. I paddled *Krissy* and *Nelson* on different days, the Thames worlds apart from where I had last paddled them. I loved that Lucy could paddle, too, and that Justine could be there for most of it, zipping away to an event partway through, leaving me with some of the only miles of the journey where I paddled without her. A couple of other friends joined in and most of Lucy's family came out to wave from lock gates and riverbank, generally with bottles of granny's sloe gin on hand, as we passed through their local realm of Oxfordshire.

I remembered that British wildlife was as good as anything I'd seen on my travels, seeing kingfishers and kites, herons, ducks and coots all out and about on the river. Rowers and paddlers came out to make miles with us. One club gave me a balloon and banner to tie on the front of the kayak. Briony cycled along a stretch in Oxford with me, clocking physical miles after all the mental miles she had helped me through. Through Benson, Wallingford, Pangbourne, Henley, Marlow, Windsor, Egham, Chertsey, Weybridge. Then inside the M25. Then London.

Between stopping to talk to people and the five-day target we had set ourselves, the days stretched long. Sometimes we talked and joked and at others I settled into the quiet inside my head. Everything was building towards Tower Bridge – interviews, details, plans and people. Lee flew in from Minneapolis, the first time that he would meet the rest of the team. George biked out along the river at Kingston and shouted at us – I didn't recognise her until I was up close. It was so wonderful having everyone there to join in after all their support from afar. The night before Tower Bridge felt busy and stressful; lots of people and things to remember, everyone readying for the final push. But though my mind was scrambling, I felt calm, too. Exhausted and wired at once. Part of me didn't want it to be over, and I longed for *Happy Socks* or my tent again, somewhere alone and quiet and known. Instead I retreated to the Party Bus and tapped out the final admin, and quietly sorted my gear. As I packed, I remembered the untold times I had done that over the last four and a half years, way out to sea by myself or on beaches with Justine or alone with *Hercules*, or with Gao in the Gobi or Lucy across North America.

After an early start, the morning was fresh as we boated from the Royal Canoe Club at Teddington, everything feeling better for being on the water and moving. London was just waking up as we slipped through Twickenham and Richmond past moored-up boats and commuters going to and fro along the riverbank. And suddenly it felt like London was all around us, river traffic and road traffic busy with people. Buildings stacked up and squashed in. It had all been a blur for a few weeks now and the day continued as such. A group of paddlers from Chelsea Kayakers and Tower Hamlets Canoe Club joined us in Putney, along with some from Rutland Canoe Club, where I had first paddled as a teenager. Squelching through the mud, we launched and paddled downstream, ticking off bridges on our deck maps against where the schedule said we should be. Seeing a group of children cheering at Chelsea Bridge, I got out and ran up the ladder to talk to them and answer their questions. As my heart rate sprinted, bridges slipped by, some of them with people waving or cheering on them – some of them I knew and others I didn't. It was overwhelming at times. The RNLI, the police and fire services, the Port of London Authority had all come out to escort us in. A press boat appeared with photographers and journalists behind tripods and huge lenses. Seeing Lucy amongst them, I felt connected and more grounded. Photographer James and our favourite BBC journalists Sarah Teale and Ben Jackson, who had followed the journey all the way from the start (and before), were there, too – making the cameras feel less intimidating. Past MI5, Westminster and Big Ben, the London Eye, the Southbank. The final bridges: Waterloo, Blackfriars, Millennium, Southwark, London.

And then, all of a sudden, somehow taking me by surprise, Tower Bridge is just downstream. There it is. The end of a chapter. What does that mean? The end, the end, the end. My swinging between tears and laughter continued. This was the first time in the whole expedition I had been early. Jenny wanted me under the bridge at 12 noon and not before. Suddenly I wanted to be alone. I wanted to turn back and away from it all, daunted by the idea of all those people ahead. I paddled down the side of HMS *Belfast* and breathed deeply, feeling tiny between the huge ship and the exposed banks, the tide almost on the turn now.

We gathered again upstream of the bridge and I found Justine. 'Can I have a hug?' I asked. 'Of course you can!', and I cried into her shoulder. 'If I don't get a chance to say it in there, then thank you, sister. I couldn't have done this without you.' Here we were in the same place as we had been on April Fools Day in 2011, with that same riot of emotions, and that same excitement, not knowing what lay downstream.

I was coming home with so many new things. Treasured memories of the miles beneath my boats and under my wheels. The lessons of the journey and its questions, too. The scars and the energy of the places and people I had met. The memories of those I would never meet again, and those who would never know what difference they made and what part they played. A faith in the goodness of people and a deeper respect for nature. A sense of perspective. A greater sense of justice and inequalities. A greater sense that there is often no black and white in life, but many shades of grey. Satisfaction of having inspired thousands of children around the world and raised £50,000 for our charities. With my invisible peloton in full force, I was paddling towards some of the key people who had helped make it happen, who had believed in the journey and supported me through storms, both metaphorical and physical.

As I paddled under the bridge, horns blared and the fire boat sprayed its water cannons. People cheered and I looked up into faces I recognised, people I loved. I grinned and cried and waved. The press boat took my photo in front of the bridge with the flotilla behind and around me, before I paddled back to wave at all the children who had coached down from Inspire+ and Stamford Schools, just as they had done for the launch. The crowd of my guests cheered from HMS *President* and my tummy surged as I waved and paddled over to them, unable to contain my emotion. I rafted up alongside the pontoon, Sara bringing me in and hugging me. Nervous of the people at the top, I jogged up the ramp, now steep with the outgoing tide. A dense wall of lenses clicked frantically at me as everyone cheered. I squeezed Lucy in a hug and kissed her, feeling quite overwhelmed. 'I love you. Thank you,' I whispered. Next was Mum and my brother Matt, whom I hadn't seen for two years, and Fiona from Accenture. Words couldn't find their way out from my stuttering brain, evaporating into something between giggling and tears as I waited for an instruction, not really knowing what else to do but grin.

A gospel choir, the same who had sung me out on launch day, sang in the background. Someone from G. H. Mumm handed me a bottle of champagne as large as a small child and told me to point it away from the crowd. 'Hold your thumb over the top and go for it,' she said, and as the champagne exploded out so, too, did my laughter, charged with all the emotions of the last few years. It was exhilarating and I tipped it up to fill my mouth. 'Do it again, Sarah, but point it this way and shake harder!' said one of the lenses, though I am not sure their colleagues approved as, on my second and even bigger spray, everyone lurched backwards. There were hugs with Sara and Justine as they came up the ramp, all of us swigging from the magnum. Jenny shepherded me through a blur of interviews, some beaming live into lunchtime news; family, friends and sponsors jumping in for hugs and hellos as I moved from camera to camera, journalist to journalist. 'It's like we've all just stepped out of a time warp,' said a friend, and I agreed. Lots of my friends were now married or engaged. My friend Emma was heavily pregnant, almost due. I walked down the line of the base crew in their formal dress and shook their hands, thanking them for the welcome. Next to them the gospel choir were singing Elbow's 'One Day Like This', one of my favourite songs. Amid the chattering and the champagne and the cameras I stood and watched, beaming and singing along.

18

Downstream: UK

Tower Bridge and Beyond

I am a part of all that I have met
Alfred, Lord Tennyson

Lucy and I left the team meal early that evening to take the train to Manchester for *BBC Breakfast* the next morning, both of us wide-eyed with lack of sleep and adrenaline. Lee stayed with us for a few days and, in between a stream of interviews, I took him to Oxford to see the city and to the farm to see the countryside. Being up on the hill overlooking Oxfordshire and wandering through the cool of Christchurch's ancient cathedral was peaceful and soothing. One journalist described our lounge as a locker room, steaming piles of kit everywhere – and it wasn't far off the truth. It was all awhirl for the first couple of months, busy with media, sorting gear and seeing family and friends again. On the Atlantic I'd agreed a book deal, so now I actually had to write one. At the end of November I gave a talk at the Royal Geographical Society in London for the Transglobe Trust, who had been such loyal and generous supporters throughout my journey. I was proud to be presented with the Ginny Fiennes Memorial Award in front of an audience which included so many of the people who had helped make it happen.

In December Lucy and I snatched four days away in a log cabin amongst the hills and heathers of Pembrokeshire for a much-needed break and some time out together. In February I toured forty-five schools in a week as part of my ambassador role with Inspire+. Alongside that, there was the goal of our wedding, set for the end of June, just before harvest.

In early January I had a text message saying 'wasn't it great that *Happy Socks* was under tow'. What? She had been sighted twice in those three months up to now, once ten days after pick-up and the next time in early December. She had been blown north-east by all the storms that had wreaked havoc in the UK: Abigail, Barney, Charlotte, Desmond, Eva. I followed emails and phone trails to find that *Happy Socks* had been found and towed ashore off the Irish coast. I burst into tears. A walker had spotted her bobbing half a mile offshore and called the coastguard. The RNLI crew from Castletownbere were dispatched and, on finding her, relayed the boat name back to the coastguard, who were able to tell them that I had evacuated in October. Nonetheless, the wonderful RNLI decided to try and bring her under tow. Too rough for anyone to get on board, they used a grappling hook to grab her. On the third attempt they succeeded in attaching a line, by which time she was just 50 metres from the unforgiving cliffs. Amazingly, she was still upright.

In a twenty-four-hour through-the-night driving mission with Lucy and her dad we travelled out to County Cork to thank the crew who had saved her and to bring her home. I thanked *Happy Socks* for keeping me safe and apologised for leaving her out there, wondering at what she had seen and where she had been. If only she could talk. The back cabin was full of water, and there was a couple of inches of gravel in the bottom, making me think that she had come ashore to a beach somewhere and been washed out again. The deck was full of holes where the grapple had cut in and torn bits out and it now sported a growth of green weed and slime. It took some time to empty, clean and dry her out, returning her to at least a cleaner version of her new *Holey Socks* self. But in doing so, I found peace and closure, and it was a special moment when we got *Hercules*, *Nelson*, *Krissy* and *Happy Socks* together for photos. With debts from the expedition to pay off and no way of doing her up myself, I sold her in the spring to someone planning another solo row, which felt painful in some ways but positive, too. Boats are meant for the waves, after all.

When I first got back, pilates, physio and sports massage helped me rebalance physically, once I had truly understood the meaning of 'rest'. Apparently my initial activity choices of rugby and boxercise were not deemed restful and the pilates instructor told me in no uncertain terms that I needed to take more care of my body. 'You're thirty years old, Sarah – that might mean another seventy years – you have to make it last.' I listened carefully to them after that, rehabbing with a phased reintroduction to weight-bearing activity. This meant just twenty minutes a day walking and cycling for the first month before gradually increasing it. From April 2014 to the finish I had only had the odd week here and there off the bike or kayak, meaning that my back was very stiff and muscles tight from overuse. It was amazing just how healing the resting was in letting tired muscles and joints release. In letting go. That was probably the thing I'd learned most about on this journey: the value of letting go. Letting go of control, of the outcome, of yourself, of what you think your goals and plans are, of what other people think. I have always been very goal-oriented, intent on finishing and succeeding just because I had said I would do something, stubborn and determined. I have pushed my body and my mind to ridiculous limits and extremes, and my body and brain have at times totally and completely fallen apart because of it, in pursuit of goals and experiences. I don't regret it, because the journeys have been amazing, but it has taught me to seek more balance now, and more connectedness – time with and for my family and friends.

At the end of May, a month before our wedding, I had a breakdown, and four months on I am still working through it. A delayed reaction to coming home, perhaps, a giant leap of transition. Someone had told me to take my time in coming home and, although I thought I was, I fell into a dark hole of depression and anxiety. A bit like with the physical release of rest, it feels like it is finally time to let my head rest, too. I am healing it with as much time and space outside of my head as possible. Time with Lucy. Laughter and reassurance to combat the demons within and ground again. Time in the garden. Time on the bike. Through movement and mindfulness I am refinding inner stillness, energy and release. In rebalancing and finally coming home, I am reminded that everything is a process, a journey in and of itself. And of the value of listening: to our minds, our bodies and others, rather than just stubbornly pushing on. That in falling apart, there is opportunity to reset and change direction.

Lucy and I got married in June 2016 on top of a hill under thunderous, rainbow-carved skies, surrounded by friends and family. Quite by chance, we had chosen Pride Weekend and the anniversary of same-sex marriage becoming legal in the USA.

So what's next? For now I am focusing on wrapping up the journey. I am giving talks, I would like to write a couple of children's books and plan to make a film using footage we shot during the expedition. I am not sure that I am ready to be inside a classroom full time just yet, but I am keen on sharing the joy and benefits of a life outside with those who don't ordinarily get those opportunities. One day we dream of running an adventure farm – to get youngsters outside and connected with nature, building self-esteem, skills and having fun. I shall always wander and roam and have ideas for journeys I would like to make alone and with others, but for now, I am enjoying being home and together with Lucy, and working on finding balance again.

Physically my immune system is much stronger these days and we are doing some DIY immunology to reintroduce dogs into my life.

By the time this book is printed, we will have had a visit from my Chinese cycling buddy, Gao, too, along with his new wife, Tian Tian. He is doing well and has a new bike, *Stranger II*.

And finally, news of another special wanderer in my life. Just days before this manuscript was due to go to print I received an email from the US Coastguard. My rowing boat *Gulliver*, AWOL since 2011 after Tropical Storm Mawar, was sighted some way north of Hawaii. Fingers crossed he does a *Happy Socks* and finds his way ashore one day.

Who's Who

Being a soloist for much of my time means that my boats and bike are as much of my team as anyone else. We look after each other. To answer 'why is your boat called *Happy Socks*?' and so on, here is the story on their names.

Nelson – kayak

Named after the late, great Mandela and the naval Lord Horatio Nelson for their tenacity, bravery and seafaring brilliance. I used *Nelson* for the London to France leg in April 2011 and the Russia to Japan leg in the autumn of 2011. I paddled him some of the way back to London in 2015.

Hercules – bike

Not wanting to ride 15,000 miles on a girl, I opted for a strong male name. I chose Hercules after the son of Greek god Zeus: Heracles. Apart from murdering his family his strength and effort seem exemplary, hence calling my bike *Hercules*. Herc for short. He has survived the Gobi Desert in China and the North American winter and now I ride him locally or afar if I have the chance.

Gulliver – blue ocean-rowing boat

Sometime before starting on my journey in 2011 I spent a memorable weekend in Oxford with two very dear friends, twins Krissy and Maren Hallenga. Besides gin cocktails and gelato, one of the activities that weekend was a cinema trip to see *Gulliver's Travels*. Krissy has stage IV breast cancer and was facing her own expedition at the time. *Gulliver* was left adrift on the Pacific in 2012 after I was rescued by the Japan Coastguard. We had a sighting of him reported some way north of Hawaii in October 2016. Watch this space.

Happy Socks – white ocean-rowing boat

Following my rescue from the Pacific in 2012 and losing my boat *Gulliver*, I bought the second-hand sister boat to *Gulliver*. She was called *Socks*. Wanting to keep something of her name but make her my own, I named her after the colourful stripy woollen socks that my mum knits. We call these Happy Socks. I rowed from Japan to Alaska and two-thirds of the way across the Atlantic in *Happy Socks*. Cast adrift after I was picked up ahead of Hurricane Joaquin, she was blown north-east by winter storms to be found in south-west Ireland in January 2016.

Krissy – kayak

Named after my dear friend Krissy Hallenga, for her spirit and energy and sparkle, *Krissy* is a three-piece kayak. We had her built for the Aleutians kayaking journey in 2014, so that we could transport her more readily. Additionally, I paddled her under Tower Bridge on 3 November 2015.

Acknowledgements

So many people dared to believe in and support my journey before, during and after. It was, above all else, a team effort. I know that I will have missed people from this list, so forgive me if that is you. To the nameless people of the road who helped or cheered and those who donated to my charities: CoppaFeel!, Jubilee Sailing Trust, WaterAid, MND Association.

To *Hercules, Gulliver, Happy Socks, Nelson* and *Krissy.*

To my favourite person in the world, Lucy.

To my wonderfully supportive mum and my cheeky wee brother Matthew.

To my team who have believed in me and the journey, weathered the storms and shared in the surfing, who have picked me up and carried me through. Through tears, tiffs and smiles – we were in it together and I shall always be grateful and proud: Sara 'Chief D' Davies, George 'of the Gin' Outen, Justine 'the Machine' Curgenven, Dr Briony Nicholls, Jenny Ellery, Dr Caroline Knox, Dr Sean Hudson, Lee Bruce, Tony Humphreys, Rebecca 'FGm' Rees, Jim Shannon, Katy 'Twin K' Allen, Carol and Anthony Allen, Mel Jarrett, Claire Rasell and Tim Moss. And to your families, too, who often lost you to the expedition.

Major sponsors and supporters: Fiona O'Hara, Susan Scott-Ker and Gilly Bryant – Accenture; Reece Pitts and Matt Desch – Iridium; Lucy Cotterell, Sam Iussein, Alison Smith and Chris Rodi – Mars; Peter Englisch and Andrea Baars – EY; Susie and Steve Hewson and Teresa White – Natracare; Anton Bowring, Sir Ranulph Fiennes and the Trustees of the Transglobe Trust.

Satellite team: Jen Barclay, 'Sister Em' Emily Allen, Krissy Hallenga, Maren Hallenga, Coach Barry, Lizzie 'Mrs Magic Hands'

Atkins, James Sebright, Rin Cobb, Crooky, Dave Cornthwaite, John Perrott, Ricardo Diniz, Rob Eustace – Mark3International, Team Cameron, Karel Vissel, Kelly and Caz Morita, Tari Martosudirjo, Mike Sims-Williams, Ant Goddard – ZeroSixZero, Jamie Fabrizio and Emily Adkin, Justin Adkin, Phil Morrisson, Emily Chappell, Andrew Wilson, Digital Explorer, Team Choshi, Karasawa-san, Shin Yoji, Kaz Ebata, Kay Tsubaki, Carol Penfield, Team Ryders Cove, Mylène Paquette, Gao and Stranger, CoppaFeel!, MND Association, Jubilee Sailing Trust, WaterAid.

The Japan Coastguard, Falmouth Coastguard, Irish Coastguard, Canadian Military Surveillance teams, Hubert Pinon and the crews of *Diadem*, *Eraunsia* and *Le P'tit Mousse*, Captain Gupta and crew of the *Federal Oshima*, FedNav, Castletownbere RNLI and Aldburgh RNLI.

The late Mr Ootake-san and Mrs Ootake-san, the team at Kasa Zima Marina, Ed Phillips, Lincoln Taylor, Elaine Smiloff, Family Spitler, Billy and Lizzie Pepper, City of Adak, Homer Bike Club, Half Fast Cycling, Sally and Mike Swetzoff, Crystal and Bill Dushkin, City of Atka, Scott and Agrafina Kerr, Jill Fredston and Doug Fesler, Hector Mackenzie and Miche Genest, Pam and Jim, Dick Fast and Maggie D'Arcy, Bill Burlin, Iohan, Lisa Taylor and Peter Brondz, Sonja Leverkus, Family Keeler, Family Noga-Martin, Darrell Kazcyznski, Family Evans, Currie Gillespie, John and Jane Millar, Brenda and Garth Millar, Byron Suley, Phil O'Brien, Ruth Mays, Judy Bartel, Family Scheurich, Colleen and Jerry Sparrow, Hallo Bay Bear Camp, Shelagh Egar, Katie Spotz, Family Engelhardt, Roz and Bill Coleman, John Dickson, Carol and Dave Penfield, Colleen Murphy, Joyce Hutchings and Amy Latham, Sharon and Alec Bloyd-Peshkin, Bonnie Perry, Marj Burgard, Sandy MacFarlane, Barbara Crellin, Family Engelhardt, Alex and Yulia Yemchenko, Max XX, Sergey Vachugof, Greg Beliakov, Mary Hardwick, Colin Angus, Family Engelhardt, Cinnamon Letters, Patrick Joyce, Delphine Yue Gao, Rob Thompson, Leon Roode, Sherry and Doug Ruberg, Della Trumble, King Cove CC, Nikolski, APICDA lodge Nikolski, Jan Sims, Anita and Lars Phillips.

Sponsors: Vincent Brittain and the team at Inspire+, Ed Burrows of Barnsdale Lodge, Barney and Chris Sturgess of Sturgess of

Leicester, Robert and Dee Hinch of Greetham Valley Golf Hotel and Conference Centre, Tim Turnbull and Yoji Shirani – Aquapac, Giles Bryan – Ipadio, Nick Farrell – YB Tracking, Mike Webb – Rockpool Kayaks, McMurdo, Jane Gilbert and ESJG Limited, Santos, MSG Bikes, Kokatat, Lyon Outdoor, Ortlieb, Tubus, Dr Bietzk, Brooks, Reed Chillcheater, GreenPeople, Munchy Seeds, Stamford Endowed Schools, Greshams, Assos, Peter Kellner, VIP Weather Writer, Marlec, Powertraveller, Rutland Trust, Oakham Memorial Institute, the late David Barre from Saab, Team MacDonald from Mactra, Gill, Berghaus, Royal Navy – HMS *President*, Col. Steve Richards, Termac, Expedition Medicine, Butcombe Brewery, Starlift Enterprises, Rutland Worldwide Freight, Core Cambridge, Flat Earth Sails, Karitek, Rutland Watersports, Rutland Cycling, Sam and Advance Performance, Mitchell Blades, Natural Balance Foods, Lifeventure, Lifesystems, Green Traveller, Sawyer, Sea to Summit, Pro-Negotiations, Nuun, Manfrotto, Expedition Foods, KEEN, Hennessey Hammocks, Goiot, Plastimo, MSR, Icebreaker, Timex, Kinetic, Buff, Roanoake, Act-Q-Patch, Look What We Found, Torq, Concept 2, Blaythorne Equipment, C. S. Ellis group, Schwalbe, Chatham Health Club Rowers, Knog, Spiel Design, Vinnie's Vinyl Signs, Walkers Shortbread, Spare Air, Whitby & Co., Leatherman, Pentax, Patrick MacGlinchy – BackWoods Survival School, Martindale Group, Cewe, Alpkit, Skhoop, Pip&Nut, Healthspan Elite, Kelvin Hughes Chart Co., Holiday Inn, St Hugh's Boat Club, Chatham Health and Swim, Alan Cohen and team at Ryders Cove, Team Choshi – Choshi Marina, Pleasant Bay Community Boating, Ship's Light, Chatham Bars Inn, Sugru, Zatworks and Scott Dickerson, TCR Bike Labs, Richard, Zoe and Maya Fleming, Chad and Laura Nixon, Larry from the Prairie, Wei Fung, Matt and Rowena Gulland, Shaun Weaver, Evgenia Ryabinkova, Sergey Skylarenko, Laura Crowley, Tina Anderson, Sandy and Bill Stevens, Wilbert Hamstra and Ann Maje Raider.

Thanks to Kate Hewson, Louise Richardson, Ben Slight, Nick Brealey and teams at John Murray Press and Nicholas Brealey Publishing for the expedition that has been this swift book-making.

Illustration Credits

Unless otherwise stated all photographs are taken from the author's collection.

Additional sources: 1 above © Jim Shannon; 3 above reproduced courtesy of Ricardo Diniz; 3 below © Reuters; 5 above reproduced courtesy of Justine Curgenven; 5 below photo by Michael Armstrong, used with permission from *Homer News* © 2014; 8 above and below © James Sebright.

Every reasonable effort has been made to trace copyright holders, but if there are any errors or omissions, Nicholas Brealey Publishing will be pleased to insert the appropriate acknowledgement in any subsequent printings or editions.